THE BOSS

THE BOSS

The Life and Times of Horseracing Legend Gordon W. Richards

John Budden

MAINSTREAM
PUBLISHING

EDINBURGH AND LONDON

First published in Great Britain in 2000 by
MAINSTREAM PUBLISHING COMPANY (EDINBURGH) LTD
7 Albany Street
Edinburgh EH1 3UG

ISBN 1 84018 090 0

A catalogue record for this book is available from the British Library

Typeset in Footlight and Garamond
Printed and bound in Great Britain by Butler & Tanner Ltd, Frome and London

Contents

Foreword

I first met Gordon Richards in the horse-box park at Newcastle racecourse in 1966. I was working for Wilfred Crawford and had driven down from East Lothian. Gordon shouted to me to unload his horse from the box. I told him I was busy with my own horses – to which he replied, 'If you don't unload him, son, you won't be riding him this afternoon.' I hadn't been booked for the ride at that stage and didn't know what horse it was. However I unloaded Playlord and rode him that afternoon.

Thus our 32-year friendship began. Both our careers developed from that time. Gordon, Jean and I were a partnership. Jean was a formidable lady and a lovely person, the driving force behind the whole team. We all missed her dreadfully when she died. She left an enormous gap in the Greystoke set-up. My relationship with Gordon was by no means a smooth ride. There were lots of ups and downs, rows and arguments, but we always remained firm friends. He was a hard boss – but a fair one, an excellent judge of a horse and a brilliant trainer of both horses and jockeys.

I feel privileged to have been involved in Gordon's very successful career and I feel sad that he did not live long enough to enjoy retirement. But would he ever have retired?

Ron Barry
Pooley Bridge
February 2000

Introduction

I settled in Cumbria two years before GWR – Gordon W. Richards – arrived in Greystoke. By the time the Richards family moved permanently into Castle Stables, the editor of the *Cumberland News* had seen the light and finally agreed that his readers were as interested in National Hunt racing as they were in the daily soap opera of Carlisle United.

As the scribbler behind the weekly instalments of 'Basil Budden Over the Sticks', I was aware from the start that in GWR Cumbria had attracted a huge talent. The exploits of Playlord and then Titus Oates made exciting copy and the man himself had a charisma unmatched by the majority of the area's top sportsmen. I got to know the family more closely when Joey, Gordon's daughter, arrived at Lime House School, whose pupils had the dubious benefit of my occasional instruction for nearly a decade.

I use the adjective 'occasional' advisedly, as even then more staid members of the staff suggested that my heart lay with the racecourse rather than the classroom – a claim in which there was more than a grain of truth! With Joey at Lime House, and the Greystoke horses playing an increasingly high profile in the *Cumberland News*, the idea of committing Gordon's life story to print was always at the back of my mind.

In addition to his steadily increasing stature as one of the North's top trainers, and the rich fund of colourful incidents associated with that rise to fame, there was a touch of the Catherine Cooksons about Gordon's life story – not exactly a rags-to-riches saga, but in racing terms something akin to that. Perhaps 'saddle-cloth to tweed suit' would be a more appropriate description!

The seed germinated during the 1990s; but The Boss, as he was known, needed a great deal of persuasion and both of us found time to be at a premium. Lack of time very nearly scuppered the scheme. Plans for the book to be written in autobiographical format had already been agreed when The Boss's health began to fail. It was understandable that Gordon should want to devote what energy he retained to the training of his horses. The effort he required for lengthy sessions talking into the tape recorder was to put too great a strain on his lungs, though happily he did find time to reveal the fascinating aspects of his childhood and apprenticeship before more pressing priorities prevailed.

Even with the limited time available, it was apparent to me that 'ghosting' GWR's autobiography would be a fun experience. His memory was razor sharp and his eye for detail equally accurate. He was a natural storyteller and would, without doubt, have revealed a web of compelling personal recollections. To achieve similar magnetism at second hand has been no simple task. Had it not been for the cheerful patience and willing co-operation of family and friends, this biography would never have been completed.

I would in particular like to thank Nicky and Joey for their invaluable contributions and I remain equally grateful to Gordon's owners, jockeys and stable staff for agreeing to disclose such a quantity of relevant but often personal material. On a similar subject it is, I feel, important to explain that the narrative related in the first five chapters of the book is the result of GWR's own reminiscences. Every effort has been made to check the veracity; should there be some discrepancies, perhaps the circumstances will be understood.

While compiling this biography I have also read several relevant books which have provided much food for thought. Ivor Herbert's *Six at the Top* has long been an inspiration; while both *The Sea Pigeon Story* by Bill Curling and *Jonjo, an Autobiography* have confirmed a number of half-forgotten episodes.

The choice of illustrations in a book is always a thorny issue. In his 30 years as a trainer The Boss saw many exciting horses pass though his stable, and my aim has been to provide the pick of each generation. The artistry of our top racing photographers never ceases to surprise and delight. The works of Ken Bright and Ann Grossick, plus the contributions from newspapers and photographic agencies, are much appreciated. Similar sentiments are extended to Ron Barry for supplying the foreword; and to both John Randall and the *Racing Post* for the inclusion of the Gordon Richards Factfile at the end of this book.

Finally I would like to emphasise what a privilege it has been to write the biography of one of the finest steeplechase trainers of the twentieth century. He was, without question, one of the 'greats'. His achievements will never be forgotten.

John Budden
Newbiggin
February 2000

ONE

Leader of the Pack

Gordon W. Richards, long regarded as 'the hard man of the North', might have mellowed with the passing of nearly 40 seasons in the training ranks, but few would deny that even to the last he ran the tightest of ships at his beloved Greystoke. Like many outstanding leaders and all really effective headmasters, Gordon never lost the keen cutting edge that could silence the cockiest miscreant with a single withering lash of the tongue or a sudden hardening of the steely blue eyes. His relentless pursuit of success at the highest level stemmed partially from the competitive instincts of a far from privileged childhood, but arguably had its origins in the character-building example of a powerful maternal figure.

The Boss inherited much of his pugnacious determination from Gladys, his mother. His was a difficult birth and the doctors warned against further children; advice which the intrepid lady chose to ignore. For upwards of ten years the well-meaning GP beat a familiar path to the door of the unpretentious home at Widcombe in Bath where the eldest Richards was born on 7 September 1930. Gordon was fond of explaining: 'I was a ten-pound baby and though I nearly killed my mother and she was told not to have any more babies, she had her own ideas about life and had no problems producing another nine – five boys and four girls!'

The family doctor got his original message badly wrong. Sixty-eight years on Gladys led the mourners at the funeral of her eldest son. She is still going strong today in her late 80s. Gladys spends a lot of her time staying with Sue and Fay, her married daughters who live in the London area. To give them the occasional break she travels north to Cumbria three times a year. Once safely ensconced at Greystoke, she tries to take over the house as if it were her own.

In the summer of 1998 Gordon reflected: 'Her memory is razor sharp. Mother always wants to organise the cooking and is a dab hand at mixing the drinks. It seems that having me wasn't such a disaster after all. She has racing in her blood too. Arthur Thompson, her father, a distant cousin of Neville Crump's stable jockey, rode a number of winners in his time. You mustn't forget Father either. He followed the form every day and when I was a teenager, he took out a permit to train and provided me with my first winner.'

Thomas Herbert Richards has been described as a 'timber merchant'. Nowadays that gives rather a grand impression, suggesting large warehouses stacked full with neatly trimmed piles of planks, skirting board and shelving, together with state-of-the-art power saws, a fleet of timber transporters and an additional DIY business on the premises as a bonus. There was nothing like that at Widcombe in the '30s. Richards senior dealt in wood right enough, but he was a jack of all trades; and as soon as Gordon grew past the toddler stage he was expected to lend a hand with the business. Father kept a team of cobs both to clear the nearby woods of fallen timber and to pull the delivery carts.

By the age of four the youngster was getting the hang of riding the cobs bareback to and from the woods and the grasslands where they were kept during the summer months. At Christmas the Richards wagons were on hire to the local stores for the delivery of their Yuletide orders around the city of Bath. Gordon soon learned how to harness the cobs and back them between the shafts, as well as carrying out the dirtier jobs like feeding and mucking out the stables.

The Richards business flourished. Thomas Herbert would turn his hand to just about everything from sawing up and delivering logs to preparing slats, measuring up wood for coffins and dealing with orders from all the local joiners. Meanwhile another son, Tommy, was born less than two years after Gordon. He was followed by Donald, then the four girls and, to finish off, another three boys – though by the time they came along Gordon was safely away from home.

The house wasn't that big, so there was plenty of doubling up in the beds and lots of handing down of clothes. Being the eldest, Gordon was the luckiest; but he still had to put cardboard in his shoes, to cover up the holes, and one of his clearest memories was the weekend scrub. Each Saturday evening the old steel bath was removed from its hook on the kitchen wall, dumped down in front of the fire and filled with hot water.

Tommy recalls: 'Mother would have three of us in the bath at any one time. She allowed no nonsense. We climbed in at the far end and, one by one, moved along to the front where she scrubbed you all over before rubbing you down on the sheet that had been laid close to the fire to help keep it hot. The last moment was the worst. Mother always left the washing behind the ears until the end and many was the time that I thought she was going to rub all the skin off them!'

Luxuries were scarce but Gordon's childhood days were busy and happy. Neither he nor his brothers and sisters ever wanted for food, though that is not to say that they did not scrounge for the little bit extra. They knew all the best places for blackberries and like most kids of that generation dared each other to nip over the walls of the wealthy and hide a couple of apples under their shirts.

Gordon attended the local school until he was packed off to work at the age of 11 and every Sunday it was his job to lead the family to Sunday School. Gordon and Tommy were specially dressed up in their best grey shorts with strict orders from Mother to 'walk properly and come straight back'. She always expected the shorts to be returned spotless so that they could be hung up again spick and span for the same ceremony the next week.

Gordon was four and a half when his father bought him his first pony. One of his first public appearances was riding the pony in the annual Bath Carnival Parade. He paraded as 'Gordon Richards – the Champion Jockey'. Old photographs show him very much looking the part, but he returned home more than a little sore. He had been riding bareback for nearly two hours!

Gordon and Tommy were very close as children and remained so for the rest of their lives. They shared the same interests and Tommy was to serve his apprenticeship at Keith Piggott's Lambourn yard. He remembers his elder brother's leadership qualities from an early age: 'Gordon commanded our own little gang of friends and one of his most successful ploys was to make us pretend that we were "war-time orphans", all poverty stricken and starving. The Americans were beginning to arrive in the West Country the summer before Gordon was sent away to Poole and the gang used to sit on the wall alongside the railway line into Bath station where the trains had to slow to a walk. On a signal from Gordon we all sang out in chorus, "Oh, Mr Soldier man, we are all poor children. We have no money. We have no food. Take pity on us!"'

Apparently it was an act which never failed to work. Coins and chewing gum would come flying out of the compartment windows and there were some frantic scrambles in the grass searching for the booty.

Gordon – 'GWR' – no doubt got more than his fair share. He was a bit of a scrapper with a reputation for being less than careful with his fists. From his earliest schooldays he had been going to the Percy Boys' Boxing Club in Bath and knew a thing or two about the noble art of self-defence. He was a regular at the club, attending at least twice a week, and he loved it.

When questioned about his boxing prowess, Gordon was fond of saying, 'Yep, I suppose I had a bit of talent for it. I wouldn't have kept it up if I'd been getting a bloodied nose every time I went!' Later on Gordon was to consider turning professional. He had several bouts in the Swindon boxing booths during his apprenticeship with Ivor Anthony and then again on the Town Moor at Newcastle soon after he had moved to Northumberland.

More recently he was in the habit of going through his old shadow boxing routine as he was waiting for first lot to tackle the all-weather gallop at Greystoke. He reckoned that it kept him light on his feet and got the blood circulation moving on a crisp Cumbrian morning.

Shortly after his 11th birthday Gordon's childhood ended without warning. It was a spur-of-the-moment departure. His father came in from work, called him over and said, 'I've got you a job with the "gee gees". You'll be riding on the flat with the best of them before you're much older.'

Gladys saw to it that her boy's small suitcase was neatly packed with a new set of clothes and within a couple of days Gordon was on his way to Dorset. His father had contacted Louie Dingwall at Poole and arranged for him to be enrolled as the stable apprentice.

The family's long-serving Austin Seven was pressed into action for the trip.

Well over 50 years later Gordon retained a vivid picture of that battle-hardened 'box on wheels'. He chortled, 'It was a fair old runner with an enormous gear lever sticking up between the front seats. Austin Sevens were under-powered as well and several times on the journey south I had to get out and watch Father reverse up the steepest of the hills.'

Mrs Dingwall's establishment was on the outskirts of Poole, right down near the sea, surrounded by several companies of marines who were encamped and undergoing training amidst the sand-dunes. Gordon was the only apprentice in the yard and each morning Mrs Dingwall and he would ride work in relays two at a time.

Homesickness was no problem. In contrast to the tales of woe endured by many apprentices of his time, Gordon lived a life of luxury. For starters he had his own bedroom – the first time ever that he had enjoyed such a privilege. Then he was treated very much as a member of the family and Mrs Dingwall even paid for his education. Each afternoon he would have lessons from a private tutor, a retired teacher from Poole: two hourly sessions before returning to the yard for evening stables. This was hardly an arduous task either, because at no time during his nine-month stay did the Dingwalls have more than eight horses on the premises.

Louie also owned Sandbanks, a big rambling hotel right on the beach. This was no longer filled with holiday makers but well patronised nevertheless by a constant supply of Royal Marine officers, living in relative comfort while their men slummed it among the dunes. In addition to the horses and the hotel the family had a fleet of buses garaged behind the stables, so with hindsight there wasn't much time left for trips to the far from frequent wartime race meetings. Gordon remembered a couple of visits and when one hears of the miserable life endured by so many young apprentices of that generation, it has to be said he was given a very gentle beginning by comparison.

Mrs Dingwall had no grass gallops. She worked the horses solely on the sand and each morning the trainer and apprentice had to thread their way carefully between the narrow gaps in the lengths of barbed wire defences. As they went along Louie Dingwall used to pass on a bit of advice and talk a lot about the horses that they were working. As far as Gordon could remember they had all won the Ascot Gold Cup or were related to other big race winners. The memory might be playing a few tricks here but what is definite is the fact that, Ascot winners or not, they used to pound up and down the beach every morning, following the same route so often that the horses themselves would frequently start to pull themselves up through sheer repetition.

There were other excursions as well. The Dingwalls had to keep their hotel residents well fed and there were regular visits to the market at Poole to buy supplies. Louie Dingwall was no back number when it came to bargaining with the stall holders and Gordon used to accompany her to carry off the purchases. For an 11-year-old boy, life at Sandbanks was luxury.

Thomas Herbert was not so pleased. He had been fretting at the lack of apparent progress, impatient that his son had not yet been given a ride on the racecourse. Louie's insistence that Gordon was 'a nice little rider coming on well' didn't cut much ice back in Widcombe and after only nine months at Sandbanks father opted to remove his son and dispatch him to what he described as 'a serious racing stable'.

J.C. 'Jack' Waugh was a top trainer with a countrywide reputation for producing major handicap winners. His was a proper yard, run according to long-established traditions and situated at historic Downs House, Chilton, not far from Didcot and close to the rolling downs of East Ilsley. These stables have sent out a catalogue of winners through the years. Verly Bewicke trained there in the '70s after moving south from Northumberland and won all those handicap chases at Sandown with Roman Holiday and Money Market. He was followed by James Bethell, who in contrast saddled several decent winners on the flat before transferring his string north to Middleham, where he still resides today.

TWO

Off to Jack Waugh

Gordon was almost 12 when he started his official apprenticeship at Downs House, the youngest by at least two years and the only member of the staff who still needed schooling. The guv'nor knew what stage he had reached and arranged for a nun to give him lessons every afternoon.

Did any of today's trainers have one-to-one instruction from a nun while they were serving their apprenticeships? Somehow I doubt it, but there was no escape. Mr Waugh expected his word to be obeyed and for the first six months at Chilton Gordon slaved away at his books.

That wasn't the only place where GWR kept his nose to the grindstone, either. Jack Waugh maintained a major operation at Downs House. The Second World War was to last for another three years but the stable housed some 40 horses and in addition there was a huge acreage of farmland to work.

Despite the war restrictions the yard was organised in the most professional manner. The gallops were among the finest in the country, tended with loving care by experienced gallop-men who took real pride in their work. Mr Waugh employed his own trials jockey and Sam, his head lad, not only ensured that the yard was as clean as a new pin, day and night 365 days a year, but also saw to it that the apprentices were brought up in the old-fashioned routine of hard work, good manners and respect for their elders.

Once morning exercise was finished the lads faced a variety of jobs. They did plenty of work around the farm, particularly at harvest time, and took their turns on the 'domestic rota' – polishing the brass coal scuttles, burnishing up JC's special leather riding boots and cleaning his car. (Mind you, the indoor jobs had their compensations. Much of the time was spent in the kitchen quarters and Cook seemed to have a soft spot for the youngsters.)

The Waughs enjoyed a fine table despite the rationing. Not much corned beef or spam, but the best joints of beef and lamb with the 'left-overs' saved for curry and shepherd's pie. If you were in the right place at the right time you never needed to go hungry.

'There will be some good stuff coming back in a moment, young Gordon,' was one of Cook's favourite sayings. And as Gordon was as thin as a rake for his first two years at Chilton, he was quick to take the hint and put a few extra minutes into producing the best possible sheen on the guv'nor's boots.

The drudgery apart, they were exciting times with Jack Waugh. Riding first lot on classy thoroughbreds high on the downs above East Ilsley was a far cry from trundling along the beach at Poole. While his weight remained under the minimum mark, the prospect of making the grade on the flat remained a reality.

Gordon's recollection of his first ride in public never dimmed. He relived the occasion many times: 'I made my début at Salisbury in an apprentice race on a horse who was being set up for the Cambridgeshire. I had been at Chilton for little more than a year but had ridden work on the horse several times. He was a nice horse and I thought he would go close.

'What I hadn't counted on was the fuss that my name would cause even before I got to the paddock. There had been no "Gordons" in our family and I'd been told at home that my father had been keen to give me the name after the champion jockey he had idolised for so long [Sir Gordon Richards, champion jockey 26 times between 1921 and 1954, who was knighted in 1953 and died in 1986].

'Anyway, there I was standing next to the scales, all dressed up, you see, in my breeches and boots, waiting my turn to be weighed out.

'I jumps on the scales with my saddle, all innocent like. But the Clerk of the Scales gives me a funny look, puts down his pen and says, "Well young Richards, what are we going to do with you?"

'Uncertain what he meant, but remembering my manners, I replied, "What do you mean, sir?"

'"Well, my lad, we can't have two Gordon Richards," explained the official, clearly unsure of his next move.

'Quick as a flash I answered, "You'll just have to put me down as Gordon Richards the Second, sir!"

'"No, we can't have that," he muttered, and the conversation could well have gone on in the same vein for some time longer had a familiar voice not suddenly interrupted from behind me. It was the boss himself. He tended to stutter a bit in public, but on this occasion the words came out sharp as gunfire.

'"Just put in an extra initial. Give him a *W* for Waugh and let's get on with it!"

'There was no arguing with that. The Clerk did as he was told. I got a bonus *W* in my name and the lads back in the yard christened me "Waughy" for the rest of my time there.

'My pre-race instructions were something along the lines of "don't be hard on him". I wasn't sure what that really meant, but was too nervous to ask and finished fourth – probably closer than I should have done, though no one made a fuss.'

Not long afterwards Gordon was back at Salisbury to partner Duke's Jester, a decent staying horse, in a competitive handicap alongside such household names as Charlie Smirke, the Elliott's, Cliff Brown and several other top jocks.

He was taken to the races in Jack Waugh's Rolls Royce, sitting in the back with the man himself. It was a quiet drive but as they reached the racecourse car park, the guv'nor leaned across and repeated the same orders as he had issued before Gordon's first ride: 'Don't be hard on him, Gordon.' In the paddock Gordon was given the leg up by Cliff Brown, the trials jockey, and as he took hold of the reins Cliff said to him, 'Now remember, lad, just do as you have been told. I'm sure the old man will want this one just to have a nice run. Don't be hard on it.'

He might as well have been talking to a brick wall. The teenage Richards had seen all the big name riders and was determined to show them that he was every bit as good as they were. In the race itself Duke's Jester ran far too well. The duo finished a close fourth, having been fighting it out with the big boys all the way up the straight.

Back in the unsaddling enclosure the guv'nor's face was like thunder. He said nothing to his apprentice jockey but turned to Sam, the head lad, and stuttered, 'Y-y-you l-look after him and bring him home.'

It was the one and only time that Gordon travelled to the races in a Rolls and returned in the back of the wagon. Little did he realise it at the time but there was worse still to come. News of the failure of 'Waughy' to obey riding orders had gone before him and on arrival a noisy group of fellow lads made no secret of his impending fate. The unanimous view – and the 'gallows party' wasn't even taking bets about it – was that the clown was going to receive a severe thrashing. And that he deserved it.

Gordon filled in the gaps in vivid detail: '"No one gives me a hiding," I shouted back, but as Sam led me out of the yard and through the gate towards the guv'nor's office my confidence ebbed.

'Once inside that office, my legs turned to jelly. The boss was standing four-square in front of his desk, the dreaded "long tom" tucked with coiled menace under his arm. The head lad was dismissed with a curt "thank you, Sam" and the full glare of the guv'nor's flushed and angry face focused on me. He was a very cross man indeed, though as always still with his emotions under control.

'"Gordon", he growled, "you've been a naughty boy today. You didn't do as you were told and you must learn by your mistakes."

'With that said he unfurled the whip and set to work with a will. The blows rained all across my back, my bottom and the back of my thighs; but I was a cocky sort of lad and I managed to stand there, fighting back the tears, and take my punishment.

'After it was all over he explained that Duke's Jester was being kept for the Cesarewitch with Doug Smith specially engaged to take the mount. He added, "Now, thanks to your stupidity, the blindest of bookmakers knows the score and we've lost the price. Get out and do what you are told next time."

'Through misty eyes I felt like saying, "But Boss, I can ride him better than Doug Smith" – and then decided that silence was golden!'

Gordon never had another ride in public for the Waugh stable, but the incident at Salisbury was not to blame. A combination of factors was responsible. He wasn't exactly flavour of the month after the Duke's Jester affair but the guv'nor forgot about it after a while. Later that summer Gordon had a nasty accident on the roads. He was dragged some distance and tore a lot of skin and tissue off the front of his legs. He had to spend a while in the Radcliffe Infirmary and it was even longer before the damage healed sufficiently to allow him to ride again.

He was starting to put on weight as well and several months of inactivity aggravated the problem. GWR was no longer the skinny slip of a lad who had arrived at Downs House all starry eyed and secure in the belief that he was the next champion jockey. The scales told their own story. If he was going to continue as a professional jockey it would have to be 'over the fences' – but there again he was not yet 15 and not half-way through his apprenticeship.

For all his boyish pranks he had made a good impression with the guv'nor and was on very friendly terms with both Ann, his daughter, and Tom, his son (who of course was later to take out his own licence and train with consistent success). Most afternoons Gordon was put in charge of the more inexperienced lads, the ones who had come to the stable without properly knowing how to ride. Ann and Tom used to join the party on their ponies and it was Gordon's job to pass on a few tips and build up their confidence in the saddle.

More often than not the party would see a group of young horses grazing unattended in a nearby paddock, leap the gate and organise their own unofficial races. On one such occasion they had reached the bottom of a long, beautifully maintained uphill gallop with a line of the most tempting schooling fences, perfectly positioned and evenly spaced half-way up the incline.

Gordon relived the story with some relish. 'I knew they belonged to George Beeby, the famous National Hunt trainer and father of Harry (from whom I was later to buy so many good horses at Doncaster, including the peerless One Man). George Beeby had saddled Brendan's Cottage to win the Cheltenham Gold Cup in 1939 and was shortly to win a series of top steeplechases for Lord Bicester with such household names as Roimond, Silver Fame and Finnure.

'I knew Mr Beeby by sight. He was a tall, broadly built man with a loud voice and dominating manner. I also had learnt from stable gossip that his schooling fences were the apple of his eye and that he had forbidden everyone save his chosen work-riders to go anywhere near them.

'It was the sort of challenge that I found irresistible and those fences did look so tempting. I was a bit of a show-off, too, and no doubt wanted to impress "my pupils" with my skill and daring as a potential jumps jockey.

'"You wouldn't dare. Mr Beeby will kill you if he finds out," was the general reaction to my plan. It only served to goad me on and in any case no one would be about in the middle of the afternoon. Wheeling my willing mount on to the smooth channel of soft green turf, I dug him in the ribs and sailed over the first two fences without touching a twig.

'Suddenly I heard desperate shouts from my admiring audience and glancing up I saw a whirling cloud of dust and the sound of a powerful engine accelerating fast down the adjacent track towards me.

'There was no escape. Caught red-handed, I could only rein back and wait for the assault. There were two figures: one small and cloth-capped; the other twice his companion's size and clearly not a happy man. I recognised the smaller of the pair as Charlie Smithers, Mr Beeby's work-rider and head lad, a friend of Sam's and an occasional visitor to our yard.

'If I had any doubts about the identity of the other pursuer, they were only to last a few seconds. It was the trainer himself, out of breath and beside himself with rage at the sight of his beloved gallops being vandalised by a wretched stable lad on little more than a grubby pony.

'The interview was short and sharp and contained a string of expletives, delivered at full volume with frightening speed and force. The gist of Mr Beeby's argument was that I was trespassing and that he insisted on knowing whom I was and to which stable I was attached.

'If the enraged trainer was trembling with undisguised fury when asking the question, he all but exploded at the answer. In my politest tones I piped up, "My name is Gordon Richards, sir."

'The cheek of this cocky youngster apparently trying to pass himself off as the champion jockey was all too much for my accuser. He spluttered incoherently at my innocent remark before demanding the name of my employer.

'"Mr Waugh, Sir", I replied.

'"Well, my lad, Mr Waugh is going to hear of this outrage as soon as I get to the telephone and I wouldn't be in your shoes when you arrive back home!"'

With a triumphant snort he turned on his heel and strode back to his car, leaving the now solitary Richards to make his way back to Downs House with heavy heart. JC was waiting at the gate, but Gordon noticed there was something about his demeanour that suggested the whole incident had tickled his sense of humour. True, he stuttered fiercely about the irresponsibility of trespassing when he had been put in charge of teaching the lads to ride. And he sounded off about 'little boys' pranks', and Mr Beeby threatening to give the boy a thrashing. But as he turned away Gordon thought there was the suspicion of a twinkle in JC's eye.

Indeed no more was heard of the matter until a fortnight later. The guv'nor called him over at evening stables. 'Ah, Gordon,' he drawled, 'we'll be shooting tomorrow and I've arranged for you to carry Mr Beeby's gun!'

Gordon continued, 'It was too much for me. I hated to think what might happen if "the big man" arrived for his day's shooting and found "Gordon Richards" waiting at his mark. For the very first time I hesitated to reply.

'"Y-y-you'll d-d-do as you're told", stuttered the boss. But he must have appreciated the situation and the next morning I found myself at the far end of the line, well away from the menacing gaze of George Beeby.'

Come the end of the 1945 season the decision was made. Gordon was growing far too heavy to continue riding on the flat and it was arranged that he should transfer to the National Hunt stable of Ivor Anthony at Wroughton.

Jack Waugh, to give him his due, never wanted him to leave and there was never any question of them falling out. He was keen for Gordon to stay at Chilton to train up as a future head lad.

Gordon always regarded him with respect and affection. Years afterwards he admitted, 'We'd had our ups and downs, but I was very young and the downs had only been caused by my boyish tricks. I think he valued the way I handled things in that I was a hard worker who got to know the horses; could ride out whatever he asked me; and was quite capable, by the time I was moving on, of organising the feeding and the like. Later I gathered that he thought the world of me and was proud of what I went on to achieve. He used to write to me every Christmas and for my part I was sad to leave. But then I was just 15 and still wanted to be a jockey.'

THREE

Jumping – A Different Game

Back home in Bath Gordon's father accepted the advice from Jack Waugh and transferred his son's indentures to Ivor Anthony. It was a bit of a wrench leaving Downs House, but Gordon settled in quickly at Wroughton. And though he didn't realise it at the time, the move provided a crucial boost to his future career.

Ivor Anthony was one of the great jumping trainers of all time. He was a good man too, who loved his horses, knew his job and was always prepared to pass on his knowledge to those that wanted to learn. Gordon rated him highly: 'When I have a problem with one of my horses at Greystoke, I still find myself going back in time and thinking, "Now Gordon, what would Mr Anthony have done in this situation?"'

Ivor Anthony's views on how best to train horses were set in stone and it took a while to get used to his mannerisms. He was a bit cross-eyed and he spoke in a slow deep voice – unless he was agitated, when he let out a high pitched yell which it was folly to ignore.

The trainer spent much of the day dressed in breeches and gaiters and expected his lads to ride out in similar traditional fashion. Gordon learned later that he was a confirmed bachelor and something of a woman hater – he reckoned they were the source of much of the trouble in this world and best left well alone! He was a character right enough, but he had been a fine rider over fences and never missed a morning's work.

Morning work did not start without Ivor Anthony's familiar figure sitting alongside the gallops, very upright and straight on his old dock-tailed hack. Gordon recalled, 'He watched all the schooling sessions and if you didn't do exactly as he had ordered then he would let out that ear-splitting yell, brandish his stick fiercely in your direction and it was back down the hill to start all over again, or you really would be for the high jump! On my first day out with the horses I remember him coming up beside me and asking, "Can you ride, young man?"

"'I hope so, Guv'nor", I replied, a little surprised at the question.

"'This jumping game is very different from what you have been used to," he continued. Without another word, out came the stick as we rode down the village street and he hit me on the knees, hit me on the arms and hit me up the bottom, repeating as he did so, "Bottom forward, hands down, a different game these horses. Good boy. Just keep practising and you'll be all right."'

Gordon's first reaction was to say something cheeky under his breath. Then he remembered that this was Ivor Anthony talking, the man who had been Leading Amateur at the age of 21 and Champion National Hunt Jockey in 1912. The same Anthony who had trained Kellsboro' Jack and Royal Mail to win the Grand National. The one who had sent out Morse Code to beat the famous Golden Miller in the 1938 Cheltenham Gold Cup. The man in whose stable the invincible Brown Jack – Champion Hurdle hero in 1928 and winner of Ascot's Queen Alexandra Stakes no less than six times off the reel in the '30s – had learnt to love his racing. If Ivor Anthony wanted his jockeys to ride in this way it was not for them to argue.

Like Downs House, Wroughton was a top stable. The daily routine in the yard was much as it had been with Jack Waugh. Apart from the fact that Ivor Anthony concentrated all his energies on training jumpers, there were only a couple of real changes. Gordon lived in digs in the village and each morning he was able to pick up hints from a couple of the most experienced jump jockeys in the business.

Danny Morgan was approaching the end of his stint as stable jockey, but he was a tremendous role model for any aspiring young rider. His record speaks for itself.

Danny had won the Gold Cup on Morse Code, the Scottish National three times and the Champion Chase three times and he was to retire from the saddle on the highest possible note by partnering National Spirit to victory in the 1947 Champion Hurdle – a race he had also won in 1934 on Chenango for the Anthony stable. He was later to train with consistent success in Co. Kildare, from where he sent out Roddy Owen to land the Gold Cup in 1959. He was a superb horseman and Gordon watched him close-up with both awe and admiration.

Roger Burford was the other established name at Wroughton. His father had won the 1921 Welsh National on the stable's Mythical and Roger was second jockey to Danny Morgan. His biggest win had been on Poet Prince in the 1941 wartime Gold Cup. Nothing was ever too much trouble for him and his advice was invaluable.

Gordon had joined the yard shortly after Jack Maguire and one of his clearest memories of the first few months at Wroughton was travelling to Cheltenham with Jack in the guv'nor's large black car: 'He sat in the front next to his chauffeur and we shared the back seat. At the beginning of the journey he gave us each an enormous dark boiled peppermint. It was called a "black bullet" and many years later I could still hear him saying in that slow drawl of his, "Now boys – let me hear you chew it, suck it and make it last!"

'On reaching the racecourse car park the lads were given their instructions: "Go and get yourselves a cup of tea and a biscuit. Then take yourselves down to the last jump. Watch those jockeys come over the final fence. Watch them and see how they do it. By the fifth race come back and get another cup of tea and then we'll wander away home."

'Later on the return journey he remarked with a knowing look, "I saw you down there. Did you keep your eyes wide open? Always do as I tell you and it will make my life and yours a lot easier."'

That afternoon by the last fence at Cheltenham might not have taught the pair a lot at the time, but the experience was not forgotten and some 30 years later GWR found himself doing the same thing at Warwick. He was on the lookout for a possible successor to Ron Barry and had been advised that a young fellow called Doughty might fit the bill. To discover if the lad really lived up to his reputation, Gordon followed the Anthony method. He took himself down to the last flight and with his eyes wide open watched young Doughty going about his business at close quarters. What he saw convinced him that the advice was sound and Doughty was offered the job at Greystoke.

It was all down to Ivor Anthony. He was a fine tutor and Gordon grew to like him very much. He reflected: 'Mr Anthony used to try and put me right, y'know in all sorts of other ways too. I lived up the road in digs and had got to know one or two of the girls in the village.

'The guv'nor must have been listening to some idle tack-room gossip because not long afterwards as we were riding down the street, he caught me calling out to one of my new found acquaintances and rode up beside me exclaiming, "Hallo, no, no, no! They're no good to you. They're no good to you! Don't you be even thinking about them!"'

Perhaps because he thought that Gordon's soul was in serious need of being saved from the temptations of the opposite sex, Ivor Anthony was keen to convert him into a regular worshipper. He went to church every Sunday and he kept dropping the hint that Gordon should get into the habit of doing the same.

'He kept on saying, "I want to see you in church next week, Gordon. A little vision on a Sunday won't do you any harm."

'When I hadn't taken the hint by the end of the month, he muttered, "Naughty, naughty, Gordon, you haven't been to church yet."'

Eventually the chauffeur was sent round to Gordon's digs especially to take him to morning service. At evening stables the guv'nor looked him straight in the eye and growled, 'Now you know where the church is – just attend next Sunday!'

Gordon added, 'People have been kind enough to say that I have an "eye for a horse". If that is true then I have Ivor Anthony to thank for helping me to develop the art. He was a past master at this skill. He was pretty good at picking out jockeys too and his number one hate in this department was the unnecessary use of the stick.

'I learned the lesson on the very first occasion that I was asked to take part in a schooling session. Before I had reached the starting point Mr Anthony called me over.

'"Let me get on that horse," he said.

'"You're going to school him then, Boss?" I asked with a puzzled expression.

'"No," he answered sharply. "You get up on this and you can school him."

'"This" was his old hack. I thought to myself, I've come here to ride proper racehorses, not this bloody old cob. Anyway I jumped off and gave the guv'nor the leg up on to the one that I was riding and we swapped horses. My next orders were, "You go down there and you bring him back up over the hurdles."

'The lads below had been listening to this exchange with much suppressed laughter and once out of earshot of the boss Roger Burford muttered, "Squeeze him on, now, kid. Make sure you push him on or he'll prop with you."

'That said, the hack and I lumbered up the slope towards the first flight. A stride before the hurdle, I gave him a shout of encouragement and he immediately put on the brakes and went to jump it like an old showjumper. At the same moment I gave him a backhander.

'It was the last time I tried that ploy. The second I touched his beloved hack with my stick the guv'nor saw red. Shouting wildly, and gesturing at me with his stick to stop at once and come back, he yelled, "What the heck were you doing boy?"

'"He was going to stop, Guv'nor," I replied with as much conviction as I could muster.

'"No, he wasn't going to stop," thundered Mr Anthony, still flushed and indignant at my action. "You go down again and do as I said. You sit quiet as a mouse and squeeze him up over those hurdles. Squeeze him with your knees and legs and he'll jump them, you'll see."

'Well, I obeyed orders this time and duly squeezed him into the first flight. He was just as slow, but he jumped the hurdle as though it was a five-foot pole and rails and the whole process was repeated at both the next two flights with me squeezing for all I was worth.

'The guv'nor had calmed down by the time I trotted his hack back towards his position halfway up the hill.

'"That's more like it, boy," he grunted. "Now get back up on this one and do the same with him."

'It was like swapping an ageing Land Rover for a Porsche. He gave me a lovely feel and as I squeezed him into the hurdles he saw a perfect stride and flew each one like a bird.'

It was the same with all the horses trained by Ivor Anthony. They were properly educated long before they ever reached the racecourse and they could all be ridden with confidence, whatever the conditions.

Richards had his first ride in public for the Wroughton stable at Hereford in the 1946–47 season. Looking back, he couldn't remember the name of the horse, but he recalled, 'I do know that we got round safely as one would expect. All in all I must have had about a dozen or so rides for Ivor Anthony without a win – but then you must remember that there wasn't anything like the amount of racing we have in the '90s and that I was still under the age of 18.'

The guv'nor was very good about letting Gordon off to take any outside rides that were offered and it was around this time that his father was sending out a regular number of runners at the West Country jump meetings. He had rented a small yard in the hills a few miles out of Bath and had taken out a permit for the first full season after the War.

Richards senior had six horses in training and whenever Gordon had a few days' holiday at home, he helped ride them out. Despite the doctor's warning words the family had continued to grow. Reminiscing during his last summer, Gordon explained: 'Apart from Tom and myself, who were sent away to racing stables early on, the rest of my brothers turned out to be strapping great lads. None of them wanted to leave home and to this day they still live in the Bath area.

'Paul, my youngest brother, runs a successful building and double-glazing firm. He was Chairman of Bath City for a long while and employs two of his elder brothers, Max and Archie – sometimes described as "the best woodman in the county" – in the business with him. Donald, better known as "Curly" and the next one down from Tom, is the only one of my brothers to have died. He was an inveterate practical joker and on one of my short trips home from Wroughton he nearly caused me lifelong damage.

'We were putting up a new paddock fence. It was my job to bang in the posts. To give myself enough height, I was standing on the ample rump of the same pony which I had ridden in that carnival procession round the streets of Bath. The first few posts had been driven into place, and I had just raised the sledgehammer to continue the good work, when Curly whacked the pony on the backside and I narrowly avoided landing legs astride on the top of the post! Poor Curly had to run for his life and if he hadn't grabbed the pony and scarpered, he would certainly have felt the force of my short arm jab into his ribs!'

It was Thomas Herbert who provided his eldest son with that elusive first winner. Gay Dancer didn't have much turn of foot but he was a trier and he liked the tightish bends round Taunton. For a 17-year-old with limited race-riding experience, Gay Dancer was the ideal mount. He was best ridden near the pace and, turning for home, he was tracking Arthur Mullins's mount. Once the field straightened up for home, Gordon took on the leader and kept poking and poking on the inner to wear him down after the last, going on to win in determined fashion.

Martin Pipe also had his first winner at Taunton but to the best of his knowledge GWR has never saddled a runner at the Somerset course since he took out a licence nearly 40 years ago!

Gordon had to wait his turn on his father's horses. The shrewd permit-holder used the top names when they were available and leading jockeys like Tim Molony, Johnny Gilbert and Ken Mullins all rode him winners. Fairy Mesh, as game as a pebble but a little short of finishing speed, was the stable money-spinner. That mare was hardly ever out of the first three and young Gordon had Tim Molony to thank for persuading Thomas Herbert to let him ride her a winner: 'Fairy Mesh had run up a sequence of seconds for the leading jockey and after one of these near misses I heard him say to Father, "Tom, you want to let the boy have a go on her next time. He rides her well and the mare could do with another few pounds off her back."'

Thanks to that timely word from Tim Molony, Gordon was given the chance and Fairy Mesh was another winner for the Richards family combination. It seemed that father was beginning to trust son's judgement because in the 1948 Champion Hurdle he had enough confidence to put him up on Mask And Brush – the best horse in his stable. The pair finished fifth behind National Spirit and just taking part made the blood tingle. It was quite a change from small races round Taunton and Hereford.

Gordon's 18th birthday the following September sparked off some heated debate. National Service loomed and his father hatched a plan to keep him out of the forces and leave him available to ride for the stable in the 1948–49 season. If you signed up to go down the mines for the duration then you escaped the military call-up. There was a coal mine near Wells in Somerset, but despite the wishes of Richards senior, Gordon didn't relish the prospect of two years underground for the sake of a few extra winners. Much to his father's disappointment he opted for life in the Army.

A lot of youngsters found the discipline of army life a sudden shock to the system, but for a lad who had been sent away from home at 11 and was used to fighting his corner from an early age, it was a doddle. In fact after the six weeks' initial basic training, the routine was boring rather than stress-making. Gordon joined the Glorious Gloucesters, the local regiment with their headquarters in Bristol. His battalion was never sent abroad and the frustrated recruit spent most of his National Service stationed in Devizes, determined to keep himself as fit as possible. He did plenty of running and his experience in the boxing ring paid off handsomely.

Those childhood sessions at the Percy Boys' Boxing Club in Bath had given him a taste for the sport which he never lost. Though modest about his boxing ability, he was pretty good. His mother didn't like him fighting, but she has still got a drawer full of medals and cups which Gordon won as an amateur. When he went north, he had several fights for money on the old Town Moor at Newcastle. Len Barry, GWR's trainer and a professional fighter himself, was keen that he should take the boxing further but by then Gordon was working full-time as a jump jockey and the idea didn't appeal.

Mind you, the ability to use his fists to gainful effect saved many a hungry night at Wroughton. A lad's pay didn't buy many portions of fish and chips just after the Second World War, particularly if the odd shilling bet had gone astray at the races. More often than not it was up to 'young GWR' to earn the crust – literally. Funfairs and circuses abounded in Swindon and the boxing booth was a popular centre of attraction, with a resident 'hard man' only too happy to tear a strip off any ambitious local bold enough to take him on. To Gordon trading punches and keeping on one's feet for the required time was money for old rope, and more often than not Messrs Richards and Maguire travelled home to Wroughton with full stomachs and a little cash left over for the following morning.

Keen boxers were especially welcome in the Army. They were also allowed generous time off to train for inter-regimental competitions. With his unit based at Devizes, not far from Wroughton, Gordon was able to continue riding out with the Anthony string throughout his stint in uniform.

Shortly before he was discharged from the Gloucesters, Gordon received the invitation that would alter his life and mould his career as a leading jumps trainer. The guv'nor called him into the office with news that there was a job coming up in the North, which he thought Gordon should consider taking. He explained: 'Major Gus Renwick, who has his horses trained up in Northumberland, is looking to retain his own jockey. There will be the chance to ride the other horses in the yard and the opportunity for outside rides as well. I will give you a good reference and I think you would be foolish not to go.' Gordon took him at his word and never regretted the decision.

FOUR

Culture Shock Up North

They say that you don't feel the cold when you are young and fit. Well, the muscular Richards satisfied both these categories at the time he moved north to take up his post as stable jockey to Johnny Marshall at Chatton, near Alnwick, but that first winter in Northumberland was the coldest he'd ever experienced.

The wind gnawed into the bones. He'd never seen snow like it and quite apart from the weather, life in this remote rural outpost back in 1950 was primitive compared with the cushy existence to which he had been accustomed in the softer climes of the South West.

Chatton Park was one of several large estates owned by the Duke of Northumberland and let out to well-heeled tenant farmers. The Marshalls lived in the big house, surrounded by the stables and the main farm buildings. The lads lived 'out' in Chatton village. Gordon was found digs with an elderly lady and her two sons (quickly labelled by the new arrival as 'lazy beggars'!). From the start landlady and lodger got on well. Gordon recounted: 'She took to me and I took to her. I used to help bring in the logs and fill the coal scuttles. Mind, they needed plenty of filling because the roaring fire in the hearth was the sole source of heat in the house. There wasn't even an outside toilet either and my first job every morning was to ferry the slops across the back garden and tip them into the home made septic tank.

Gordon wasn't yet 21, a non-smoker and not much of a drinker, so his first visit to the Chatton Arms was something of a culture shock: a haze of smoke, half tobacco, half fumes from the log fire; bare cement floor; and round oak tables. Just visible through the smoke was a bulky figure in old shepherd's boots, the type with turned-up toes and huge hobnails on the soles. He proved to be the landlord. The sons introduced Gordon as 'the new lad from Chatton Park' and he was offered a pint of draught beer on the house as a welcoming gesture, provided that he walked round the bar and helped himself. It was beautiful beer – some of the best that he had ever tasted.

There weren't many locals in the pub that night, but he remembered sitting next to an old fellow sipping his beer in the far corner. He reminded Gordon a bit of Ivor Anthony, chewing over a black bullet, taking the occasional swig from his pint pot and drawing noisily on his half-lit pipe. To make casual conversation GWR asked him what he did.

'Not a lot,' he said between gulps. 'But when them's wanted, I dig the graves in the churchyard!' All in all it was a cheerful beginning at Chatton.

Fifty years ago the pace of life was much slower than today. Gordon had come north to ride as Major Gus Renwick's retained jockey, but there wasn't much racing and Chatton Park already had the assistance of the ultra-capable Barney Cross. If you went racing three times in a week it was a real treat. 'Anyway, there I was and I wasn't just a jockey,' added Gordon. 'I was working for my living as well. I'd always been a worker and what with the jobs around the farm and the travelling there weren't many spare moments left over.'

The travelling itself was time consuming. Chatton was some 40 miles north of Newcastle and motorways were a dream of the future. Getting to courses like Wetherby or Ayr was a major hike and even going to visit Johnny Marshall's father, old Major Marshall, at his house near Kelso was a lengthy trip.

The Major lived in a lovely big place called Cherrytrees. It was one of those grand country houses built on a terrace overlooking its grounds, and to reach the front door you had to climb a steep flight of stone steps. Gordon was taken there soon after he had arrived and met the family. Major Marshall's appearance proved something of a shock to Gordon. He was wearing the taggiest, dirtiest, most bloodstained old coat you'd ever seen. The visitor thought, 'This man is meant to be a near millionaire and he is wearing a coat like this!'

Johnny Marshall was very amused at his reaction: 'I saw you staring at Father's jacket, Gordon,' he said on the return journey. 'It's all right, you know. He has got a few smarter than that one, but it's just that he loves wearing it to shock visitors!'

In time Gordon got to know the Major well. Like his son, he was one big gentleman and he loved his racing. With the benefit of hindsight Gordon had Ivor Anthony to thank for persuading him to take the job at Chatton. It wasn't a big stable, but Anthony had convinced the doubting Richards that opportunities would open up. How right he was to prove.

Major Renwick and Johnny Marshall, GWR's two immediate guv'nors, were on first-name terms with many of the leading figures on the northern jumping circuit. What's more, they took the trouble to introduce Gordon to their circle of friends and made sure that he enjoyed his time in Northumberland so much that he never even thought of returning south.

Major Renwick lived at Rothbury, close to the land on which the annual race meeting was held, and in 1958 he handed over £8,000 for the building of the new stand and saddling stalls there. He was a substantial owner in the early '50s. Almost all his horses carried the prefix 'Holystone' and they were all trained at Chatton Park.

Johnny Marshall bred and trained his own horses as well, with some success between 1947 and 1955. Subsequently he had a few jumpers in training with Raymond 'Barney' Cross, while he concentrated on his farming and acted as a steward at a number of northern courses. He was also a member of the old National Hunt Committee and then the Jockey Club. He remained a great friend and supporter of Gordon's (until he died a couple of years before Gordon).

Johnny was well known in the area. One of his contemporaries was Dick Jeffreys, who lived at nearby Chillingham Newtown. Dick and Johnny were both mainstays of the Chatton cricket team and, being young and fit, it wasn't long before Gordon became a regular in that side. The village team played all over, from Coldstream in the north right down to villages like Longhorsley in the south. Johnny Marshall and GWR were the side's all-rounders. Dick Jeffreys was one of their best batsmen. He was also the skipper and an artful fellow at the best of times as Gordon recalled: 'When we were playing at home he used to ring up to see what was going on and if he heard that Johnny had tossed up in his absence and that we were in the field then he wouldn't hurry to get to the ground. He liked his batting but reckoned that fielding was a bit of a chore!'

Dick Jeffreys was a well-to-do farmer and bred his own jumpers. His best known horses were Sham Fight and Sebastian V. Both of them were home-bred and both won the Scottish National (Sham Fight at Bogside in 1961, Sebastian V at Ayr in 1977). Tommy Robson, whom Gordon was later to succeed at Greystoke, both trained and rode Sham Fight while Ridley Lamb was on board Sebastian V. The following year the pair of them were pipped in the 'big one' by Lucius, Gordon's first Grand National winner. More of that later on.

Dick died during the summer of 1999, in his late 80s. He and John, his son, had Rule of The Sea and Hockley in training at Greystoke some ten years previously. Rule of The Sea was a good sort. He'd won four times over hurdles for Andy Scott before he came to Greystoke. Put over fences as soon as he joined the Richards string, he won first time out at Ayr. Gordon thought he'd go on to set up a sequence but he fell next time at Kelso and had to be destroyed. Hockley didn't have a lot of luck either. Gordon bought him for 6,000 guineas out of Richard Hannon's stable at the Newmarket Sales. He won a small hurdle at Edinburgh, but he didn't have the best of legs and never got his head in front again.

Gordon revealed that he used to help out on the Jeffreys' farm in the summer doing odd jobs and bringing in the hay. Back in the early '50s the jumping season tailed off at the end of April and didn't restart properly until September. There was a lot of time to get stuck in with the harvest and GWR learned much of what he knew about the veterinary job from a man called A.B. Tullie, who was a top class vet as well as being an amazing fellow.

Gordon explained: 'I'd spend a couple of months each summer driving him around Northumberland. He specialised in horses and it was a fascinating experience seeing him work at the various stables we visited. Often he'd ask me to give him a hand and sometimes he'd say, "Now you do that, Gordon. I'm busy over here."

'It was all grist to the mill. I was learning the training craft on the shop floor without even realising that I was doing it. They were long days out in the sun with AB.'

Activity began around breakfast time with an early morning inspection of AB's aviary. He had an extraordinary collection of exotic birds, every imaginable type, kept in vast cages on the lawn in front of the house. His 'chauffeur' would arrive deliberately early to get a good look at them. Then AB would emerge from the house, usually with odd bits of plaster dotted about his face to cover up the results of his erratic shaving. Whatever the urgency, his first job would be to inspect and say good morning to each bird on parade; only then would he agree to consider the daily routine.

After the birds, it was into his surgery to make up the medicines. He seemed to mix the potions by eye – never bothering to make accurate measurements – and chucking in this and that with gay abandon. 'Mind you,' said Gordon, 'he had a terrific reputation as a vet. He was a top man, was A.B. Tullie.'

It was always said that Barnes Park would never have won the Lincoln in 1951 if AB hadn't allowed him to be worked across his land. George Boyd, his trainer, had incurred the wrath of the Jockey Club and though his licence was restored shortly before the race, there would have been insufficient time to put the vital edge on his preparation without Mr Tullie's co-operation.

If Gordon wasn't quite sure about the ingredients, he never doubted the effectiveness of his tonics and he was to gain first hand experience of AB's skill after he had visited Chatton to check over a horse who had suffered a heavy fall. At the time Johnny Marshall trained this chaser, which Gordon had ridden on a number of occasions without success. He showed ability on the gallops but on the racecourse he would stop to nothing as soon as you asked him to go and win his race between the last two fences.

Nowadays it would be fashionable to blame 'the virus' but back in the '50s the idea was unheard of (and anyway it couldn't have been a virus because none of the other horses in the yard were infected). Gordon reckoned that he must have had a funny heart, this horse. But he was certain that the gelding had what it took to win a race and was determined that AB should have a look at him. 'This horse has got a lot of ability,' insisted Gordon, 'but after travelling on the bit throughout his race he just goes from running to nothing within a couple of strides. Whether he's breaking blood vessels, or whatever, I don't know – but if he is, nothing is showing up for certain.'

AB looked the horse directly in the eyes. He then gave him the once-over before asking GWR again if he thought that the animal was any good.

'Pretty good, Boss,' continued the anxious jockey. 'He's got a turn of foot all right, but he won't last home.'

Without more ado, AB rummaged in his black bag and produced a small bottle of nameless liquid. 'Here,' he went on, 'the next time he runs, give this to your head man and tell him to put it in the morning feed.'

Gordon passed the mixture on to Davy Moffatt with the comment that Tullie had made it up special, like.

'Oh, that won't work. That won't work,' repeated Davy in his usual manner, but he wasn't allowed to let the matter rest.

'Give it to him, man, before he runs next,' insisted Gordon. 'The vet says that it is all right and it can't do him any harm.'

A week later, and without another word being exchanged between head lad and jockey, the horse in question won without Gordon even having to put him under pressure.

'Ouch, that must be marvellous stuff,' muttered Davy, as he met them in the winner's circle. 'We must try it again.' The dosage was repeated on a couple more occasions and it worked a treat! The contents of the bottle remained a mystery. Like all AB's bottles, it had his label stuck to the outside, but that was all. He used to be called 'Mr Magic Bottle' all round the yards in Northumberland, not without good reason.

Gordon worked with numerous head lads during his 57 years in racing, but none of them were more 'way out' than Davy Moffatt at Chatton Park. 'I got more laughter out of him than any other,' he reflected; 'Davy was always experimenting, providing he thought of the idea himself. That's why he was slow to use AB's tonic, because it wasn't one of his ones. As a rule, he liked nothing better than to dabble with his own medicinal remedies and herbal additives to the feed.'

Davy liked his Saturday nights. His routine never altered. It was down to Wooler for his evening drink, back home for his fish supper, then on to wherever the weekly dance was being staged. He expected to be given a lift and it was usually down to GWR to provide the transport.

One Saturday in December Gordon had been delayed coming back from the races and on a country road, not far from Wooler, he came across this strange figure weaving his way along the verge. Normally he would have recognised Davy straight away, but this fellow had snowy white hair. The head lad's crop was a grizzly, greyish-black.

Gordon continued, 'I pulled over and seconds later I had no doubts about the identity of the shape. In the high-pitched squeal which Davy invariably employed when upset, it shrieked, "Where you been? Where you been? You're late. Very late. My fish supper will be getting cold!"

'Eventually I managed to calm him down and once we were in the car I asked him what he had done to his hair.

'"What d'ye mean? What d'ye mean?" he cried.

'When I told him that his hair had turned white, he refused point blank to believe me.

'In fact he went on calling me "damned daft" until he reached his house and looked in the mirror. It transpired that he had sprayed his hair with "White Christmas" instead of Brylcreem and he had to spend most of the night washing it out.'

The same Davy Moffatt once persuaded Gordon to come with him to the doctor. 'I want you to be there,' he insisted. 'He might do something to me!'

The doctor diagnosed piles and gave Davy a packet of capsules, telling him to apply them and come back in a week's time for a check up. Gordon said the following Friday he asked the head lad how the treatment was working: 'He replied, "Just the bloody same, just the bloody same. You'll have to take me back."

'So that evening we returned to the surgery and before the doctor could even open his mouth, Davy blurts out, "Those pills you gave me last week are no ruddy good. I might as well have stuck them up my arse for all the damned good they've done me!"

'Poor Davy, he was a simple soul but a rattling good head man all the same.'

Major Renwick had two ambitions in life. One was to win the Waterloo Cup and the other to own the winner of the Scottish National. He landed the Cup, right enough, but never carried off the prize at Bogside. After Gordon had been at Chatton for a couple of seasons Major Renwick told him that he was entering his promising young chaser Holystone Beacon in the Scottish National. Now this was a useful prospect. GWR had won on him three or four times, but he'd also given the stable jockey a crashing fall and caved-in ribs going down the hill at Carlisle.

Holystone Beacon was still only five and Gordon said to the Major, 'Give him another year, Guv'nor. He's too young and too weak just now.'

'No, Gordon,' he replied. 'He's got to run. I might not be around in another year's time!'

So Holystone Beacon went to Bogside and finished a gallant fifth. Come next season it was the horse rather than the Major who was no more. He had started odds on for a race at Hexham in the autumn but fell at the final open ditch when leading the field and broke his back. If he had survived he was going to be aimed at the Aintree Grand National.

Gordon valued his time at Chatton Park. The partnership with Johnny Marshall was a happy one. Trainer and jockey invariably shared the same car to the races. Verly Bewicke came with them as a passenger if he had a runner at the same meeting. On one occasion at Rothbury races, while Gordon was working for Johnny Marshall, Major Bewicke had asked him to come and join the staff at Alnwick to ride as second jockey while Stan Hayhurst was away doing his national service. The conversation took place in the Gents and Gordon recalled later: 'I was flattered to be asked, but Major Renwick was paying me a bit of a retainer and he was looking after me, so I turned down the offer and stuck with Johnny Marshall.

'It was the right thing to do, though career-wise I would have been better off with Bewicke because he had a lot more power with the horses y'know. It was around the time of Kerstin and Gentle Moya and the stable had a big reputation.'

Verly Bewicke liked to run his horses at Wetherby, which was also one of Major Renwick's favourite courses. The two stables were within ten miles of each other and Gordon used to drive them both down to Yorkshire in

Renwick's car. At Catterick the trio were in the habit of stopping at the Bridge Hotel for a drink. Owner and trainer both had pink gins while the driver made do with a juice. Once, Major Renwick paid for them with one of those old white fivers, but didn't bother to pick up his change. It was all too much for GWR: as they were going out of the door he remarked, 'Wait a bit, Guv'nor, you've left your money on the bar.'

'Don't worry about that, Gordon. Just leave it there,' replied the Major, heading to the car.

On the excuse of 'spending a penny', the opportunist jockey nipped back to the bar and whisked up the cash, saying to the staff, 'The Guv'nor's sent me for his change!' Three quid might not have been much to wealthy owners but it was a lot of money in those days, particularly to a young jump jockey still trying to make his name on the circuit.

Not long after the incident at the Bridge, a chance stop-off in Newcastle led to the most important decision of Gordon's life. His eyes moistened as he told the story. 'Johnny Marshall and I were on our way back from Doncaster races in his Humber Super Snipe, a great big battleship of a car – like a Rolls Royce to me when I was allowed behind the wheel.

'I must have been burning up the A1 that evening because Mr Marshall said, "Steady now, Gordon. I think we'll call in at the Station Hotel for a snack and then I'll drive back to Chatton."

'The Station was a fashionable place in the '50s. The racing set often used it as a rendezvous. It was a convenient point to break the journey back to Northumberland from the Yorkshire tracks and frequently used by the likes of Johnny Marshall and Danny Moralee [the well known amateur rider, who lived at Chathill].

'That evening the bar wasn't crowded. A few guests were ordering their pre-dinner drinks and sitting in an armchair next to the fire was a strikingly attractive young lady reading a book. Johnny must have seen me taking an interest because as soon as we had got our drinks he motioned me to follow him and headed for the fireplace.

'"Hallo, Jean," he called out. "I don't think you've met Gordon, my jockey. We've been down at Doncaster. Gordon, this is Jean Charlton."

'Well y'know, I must have made some sort of impression on her then and there. I was certainly struck. I can see her now: having a drink, putting down her book and chatting happily away as though she had known me all her life.

'She was a "county girl" and Johnny Marshall was friendly with the family. Later I found out that Gordon Charlton, her father, was a biggish landowner who also owned a number of pubs in Newcastle. He liked his hunting, too, and still rode to hounds, even though he'd had half his leg shot off in the War.

'Though we hadn't come across each other before this meeting in Newcastle, Jean was a regular racegoer during the jumps season. Her sister was married to Andrew Robinson, who farmed near Seahouses and had a couple of chasers in training. She had her own hunter and it was obvious from this first introduction at the Station Hotel that horses played a large part in her life.

'Jean was to play a much more important role in the way my future was to develop. I was determined to see her again and from that moment onwards would be looking for her in the stands whenever I was riding.'

Gordon and Jean met up again at the races and after that they started dating. Gordon added with justifiable pride: 'We were married at Berwick-on-Tweed in 1954. I was 24 and Tommy Mallory was my best man – he wasn't a bad old pilot in his time. Neither my mother nor my father came to the service, but this was to be expected. Mother still had her hands full with all my younger brothers and sisters, while Dad behaved very oddly about family weddings. He didn't like any of his kids to get hitched, y'know. It was the same with my sisters. He didn't go to any of their weddings, man! I had to give away two of them myself.

'Jean and I settled into a cottage near Seahouses, on land owned by Andrew Robinson. He'd been a fighter pilot in the War and loved his National Hunt racing. He had plenty of fun and success with those two good chasers Lively Lord and Master Toskin. Danny Moralee used to ride for him. Danny was renowned throughout the Borders as a great horseman. He had been top amateur during the mid-'50s and still had the odd jumper with Arthur Stephenson [known as WA], from whom I was beginning to get several good rides.'

Gordon never worked for WA, but Stephenson had been a friend of Jean's father for a long while and of course the great man had actually both trained and ridden his first winner under rules at Rothbury with T.O.D., who had landed the Nomination Chase back in April 1946.

Gordon used to drive down to Crawleas to ride out for Arthur and at the same time would cross the Pennines to take the odd ride for Jack Pearson, then training from Greystoke's Rectory Farm.

The years immediately after Gordon's marriage to Jean proved fruitful. In addition to his job at Chatton, he was getting a fair number of outside rides and becoming an established member of the weighing room.

They say that you should always go carefully when things are going extra well, and so it turned out. Robert Manners, who trained under permit nearby, liked to have a runner at Perth for the early autumn meeting and he had booked Gordon to partner the ex-WA-trained Sea View in the three-and-a-half-mile chase. It was to be GWR's final ride in public. Not surprisingly he retained clear memories of the occasion: 'We travelled up front throughout the race. Turning for home, I was confident that we were going the best. But Sea View began to tire half-way up the final straight and we fell upsides the leader at the second last. He came over on top of me and I knew I was hurt the moment I hit the ground.'

FIVE

Livery at Beadnell

It is sometimes said that when the police collect eyewitness accounts of road accidents they end up with at least half a dozen different versions of the same incident. Similar confusion would appear to be the outcome of the spill at Perth which ended Gordon Richards's career in the saddle. The rider himself always maintained that Sea View made a hash of the second last because of tiredness. Robert Manners, the owner, won't have any of that. He reckons that it was Gordon, rather than his horse, who began to tire up.

Some might say that Robert was naturally biased in the matter, as Sea View was his horse and he was confident that he had produced him 100 per cent fit for his seasonal début. A third witness is George Milburn, the highly respected former northern jump jockey, who enjoyed a lot of success for Verly Bewicke in the mid-'50s – partnering Gentle Moya, to finish second to E.S.B. in the 1956 Grand National, and Kerstin to chase home Linwell the following season. He later joined forces with Ken Oliver at Denholm.

George's independent opinion is that neither horse nor Gordon were exhausted, but quite simply that Sea View landed clumsily and fired his jockey out of the side door. He continues, 'Gordon was always an odd shape for a jockey. He was very strong about the shoulders and rather short in the leg. In my view he was too top-heavy and prone to be easily unbalanced. What I do remember about the business is that Gordon was furious with himself for coming off, as he had been confident that Sea View would provide him with a much-needed winner. I recall him saying to me, as he was brought back to the weighing room, "George, that's it, I shall never ride again!"'

Gordon had never spoken truer words. Sea View was without doubt his final mount on the racecourse and his frustration at the outcome can be easily understood. He had been angling for the ride all summer, knowing full well that Robert Manners had been getting Sea View cherry ripe for a first time out win at Perth. His persistence had been rewarded with the booking and although he was sent off at 100–6, connections had gone for a touch in the market. They were not amused with events at the penultimate fence!

Memories also seem to be playing the odd trick about the subsequent performances of Sea View. Manners asserts that he went on to win five consecutive chases under the guidance of Jimmy FitzGerald. Jimmy, though, wasn't so sure when questioned at Hexham earlier in the autumn.

He recalls: 'I certainly won the odd race on him but I don't think that I ran up a sequence. What I do remember is riding him once at Cheltenham. He was a bit of a difficult ride as he suffered from a defect to the knee in the near fore, if I've got it right. He wasn't able to flex the leg properly and if he didn't meet a fence on exactly the right stride then he would run left-handed along the fence to compensate and jump the obstacle straight-legged. You had to be waiting for this, particularly when he got tired.'

FitzGerald has vivid memories of partnering Sea View at Cheltenham. He continues, 'I drove all the way down from Yorkshire in dense fog. You couldn't see more than a length of a cricket pitch and I was certain that racing would be abandoned. Amazingly the fog thinned as I came down Cleeve Hill and everything went ahead. I knew that Sea View was a tricky ride, but nothing compared to that drive down to Cheltenham. In the race itself I was up there most of the way, but he got tired turning for home and jumped badly left at the last and forfeited any winning chance that he might have held.'

Just for the record, Sea View did win three times during the 1959–60 season. Jimmy FitzGerald was in the saddle when he won at Kelso's October meeting. Chris Stobbs, then a five-pound claimer with Arthur Stephenson, had the mount at both Carlisle and Hexham. The formbook also reveals that the horse had returned to Crawleas after his spill at Perth and was trained by Arthur Stephenson for the rest of his career.

The Boss had no illusions about his record as a jockey. He always regarded himself as a horseman rather than a top-flight race-rider, though he liked to add the proviso that his limited success in the saddle was not helped by the comparative shortage of fixtures in the north and lack of opportunities to partner class horses.

At the time of his enforced retirement Gordon was still claiming the three-pound allowance and his most memorable 'near miss' had come in 1957. He had finished runner-up to Bremontier in the Scottish National at Bogside on board Merry Windsor, prepared by Jack Pearson – then training at Home Farm, Greystoke and living in the Old Rectory, which was later to become the base for Gordon's most illustrious achievements as a licence holder. George Milburn later described GWR as 'the perfect example of a bad jockey becoming one of the finest trainers in the land'! His words oversimplify the matter, but Gordon certainly gained plenty of practice attempting to extract the very best out of modest performers, an experience that often led him to castigate his own jockeys for what he considered their shortcomings on much classier material.

The immediate prospect for the 29-year-old Richards that sunny afternoon at Perth was bleak. Facing a lengthy period of inactivity through injury with no regular income accruing, he had to provide for Jean together with three-year-old Nicky and Joey, his baby daughter. Only a few months earlier Jean asked him what he intended to do after his riding days were over. He had answered at once, 'I would like to train.' What at the time had seemed but a distant pipe dream had now become an urgent but seemingly impossible goal to attain.

The fall from Sea View had left Gordon with serious back damage. The vertebrae at the base of his spine were crushed. Paralysis had been narrowly avoided, but apart from trying to alleviate the acute and nagging discomfort, the doctors prescribed four months' complete rest.

The Richards family was able to rely on the support of Andrew Robinson. 'Uncle Andrew' was married to Isobel, the eldest of Jean's two sisters. Their mother had died when Jean was only 12 and Isobel had taken over the responsibility of bringing up the youngest member of the Charlton trio. They had become very close and on Jean's marriage to Gordon, the Robinsons had put one of their farm properties at the disposal of the newly-weds.

The cottage near Seahouses remained a secure home for the Richards while they planned for the future. In practice there was just one option. As soon as Gordon was mobile, he and Jean had to turn their combined experience to profitable use and establish a horse livery business.

Gordon had now been resident in Northumberland for close to ten years while Jean's own family had deep roots within the area. The search for suitable premises did not take long. Town Farm, a smallholding complete with stables and paddocks, was on the market in the centre of the village of Beadnell. The rent was negotiated and by the spring of 1960 the yard was up and running. Beadnell, an unspoilt seaside hamlet midway between Seahouses to the north and Embleton to the south, might seem a remote (even isolated) spot to organise a successful livery and horse-dealing business, but a glance at the map proves its proximity to the A1. The village is within comfortable reach of the rich Border estates and lies in the heart of the country regularly hunted by The Percy.

Right from the start Gordon had ambitions to use Town Farm as the springboard back into the racing world – the means to raise the capital that would one day lead to his ultimate aim, the possession of a professional trainer's licence. In Jean he had the ideal partner. Already on first name terms with the local racing and hunting fraternity, she had been working among horses since early childhood. The news that she was opening a riding school at Beadnell was music to the ears of a broad cross-section of the rural population, from prospective members of the Pony Club to Tyneside commuters desperate to learn country skills at the weekend.

Northumberland and the Borders have long enjoyed a rich heritage in both the hunting field and the point-to-point scene. Gordon's racing background was the additional attraction in this sphere. It wasn't long before he was preparing pointers as well as standing hunters at livery. To the north of Seahouses the wide flat expanse of the Bamburgh Sands provided the perfect setting for fast work, while the surrounding fields and hills of Uncle Andrew's substantial farm helped strengthen the horses' legs and build up their stamina.

The autumn and winter months were spent in catering for the hunters and preparing the pointers – by no means a leisurely task. As Gordon told Ivor Herbert in his fascinating book, *Six at the Top*: 'We were in the middle of great hunting country. The Percy was the Duke of Northumberland's private pack. We'd hunt four days a week throughout the season.'

The Boss had more important objectives in mind, but he was happy to cut his teeth on 'fettling up' a small posse of pointers for local enthusiasts who one day in the not too distant future might progress to ownership under rules. Nicky Richards recalls that his father always preferred to travel to Newcastle along the old Military Road, high in the hills between Greenhead and Chollerford. Not long after passing the Roman Fort of Housesteads – set in the centre of Hadrian's Wall and close to the stables of George Reed, the well known National Hunt trainer – Gordon invariably pointed to open moorland on the left of the road and announced, 'That's where I trained my first winner!'

Nicky was never exactly sure which hunt staged the meeting, but the spot mentioned suggests that it might well have been The Haydon. Had the course indicated been a shade further towards Newcastle, however, it could well have been the long-established point-to-point course on the land owned by the Straker family above Corbridge.

Nicky continues: 'The livery business provided the bread and butter, but all the time Father was dealing in cobs and ponies as well as keeping his eyes skinned for a decent thoroughbred which he could buy at a bargain price and make a quick profit. The turnover was quick. Nothing stayed at Town Farm for long and there was no point in me getting fond of a pony, because it was likely not to be there in the morning!

'On the other hand it taught me to get a leg up on every sort of horse and to cope. The paddocks round the stables were never empty. In the morning I could be riding a wiry little pony and then back home after school I might be riding roadwork on a burly hunter.'

Throughout the summer Gordon was kept busy with the Common Riding enthusiasts. Every Border town of any standing would (and still does) stage an annual holiday, on which as many inhabitants as possible take part in the traditional 'beating of the bounds'. Led by the Cornet and his Lass they engage in a series of cross-country rides from one boundary point to the next, displaying their dashing horsemanship to all and sundry before carousing long and loud into the small hours of the night.

A substantial proportion of the assembled throng are mounted on their own horses but there is always a demand for 'spare rides'. Gordon used to travel the circuit with a cosmopolitan boxload of ponies and cobs for daily hire. It was a hectic merry-go-round and The Boss related an amusing story against himself. He was heading for Hawick, with a dozen or so ponies in the wagon, when one of the rear tyres sprung a puncture.

He explained: 'There I was grappling with the spare tyre and trying to keep the jack from slipping when this shepherd fellow drew up alongside and offered to help – which I was greatly obliged for. Between us we completed the job and as he was standing chatting, he looked at the name on the door of the cab and said slowly, "Ah, Richards. You drive for him? They say he's a mean bugger to work for!"'

It seemed a moment for a hurried getaway. Jumping into the driver's seat

Gordon shouted back, 'You're right. He's a real so-and-so, the sort who'd sell his own grandmother for a quick tenner. I'd keep well out of his way if I was you!'

On another trip to the Borders, Nicky recalled, there was a nasty moment when the cargo grew restive and broke out of the side of the box: 'Father used to pack them in all right and they were just loose in the back of the wagon. We went round a sharp bend a shade too quickly. There was a sudden crashing sound of splintering wood and the next moment there they were, leaping out of the side of the box and galloping free all over the moor side. It took us hours to gather them up and Father ended up badly out of pocket. He had to hire a substitute wagon and also pay for the repairs. On top of that, by the time we arrived at our destination the Common Riding was nearly over and nobody wanted a spare mount!'

Later on Nicky remembers working his father's horses at Beadnell: 'Father liked to exercise them on the beach first and then walk them over to Uncle Andrew's farm, where the two of them would discuss how fit they looked, and plan their schedule. Father was always known as an excellent feeder and I'm sure he picked up plenty of tips from the way Uncle Andrew fed his own stock.'

Mention of the beach focuses the mind on *Becket*, the epic historical drama starring Richard Burton. The emotional scene where Henry II swallows his pride and welcomes Becket back into the fold was filmed on the sands at Bamburgh and Gordon was responsible for producing the horses for both sides of this classic encounter. The money from the filming financed Gordon's move to Greystoke; but without Playlord the money would have been worth nothing.

SIX

The Horse that Made the Man

Adam Pringle farmed over the hill from Gordon's Beadnell stables. He followed the tradition of many sporting Northumbrian landowners in that he combined rearing his own beef stock with breeding a few potential National Hunt stores as a sideline.

In Adam's case he had rather more horses than was economically viable. After keeping a careful watching brief on the activities at Town Farm, he decided that Gordon and Jean had the answer to his problems. Without prior warning he arrived in the yard and outlined his proposal. He told Gordon that he had been impressed with his hard work and horsemanship and that he would like him to apply for a trainer's licence, primarily with a view to training the Pringle jumpers.

Always one to call a spade by its proper name, GWR thanked his neighbour for both the offer and the compliment it implied, but admitted that he had been keeping his own eyes open and considered that the task would be a waste of time – the farmer's horses were a motley collection, not good enough to make the grade on the professional circuit. Unabashed by such a blunt assessment of his home-bred beauties, Pringle added in quiet but persuasive tones that perhaps Gordon had not yet had the chance to inspect his pride and joy, the unbroken gelding by Lord of Verona out of his own mare, Playwell.

More out of respect for the determination of his neighbour than out of any belief that the youngster would prove any different to his compatriots, Gordon agreed to cast an eye over Playlord and give his opinion. Later he admitted that he imagined the trip would be a fruitless journey. But the moment the two met, it was love at first sight.

Not that Gordon let his feelings be too well known. He had been dealing with men who drove a hard bargain and he had learnt to keep his powder dry until the crucial push. He contented himself with the advice that his neighbour would be best served by selling all the rest of his horses and keeping Playlord under wraps at least for a further year. 'Do that and I will be delighted to train him,' added Gordon.

Compared with today's devotion to market forces and the paramount desire to acquire untold riches, even at the expense of once-close friends and associates, Adam Pringle behaved with unsullied decency. He swallowed any pride that he might have had and accepted the guidance of a man whom he knew more by reputation than personal experience.

Adam agreed that Playlord should be transferred to Beadnell under Richards's care and be trained by him for a career under rules. As soon as Gordon began to work the new arrival he realised two truths: that this was the sort of horse which would have excited even such a master as Ivor Anthony, his old boss; and that given just reasonable luck, this horse could provide him with the means to attain his dream of controlling his own destiny as an established trainer of successful steeplechasers.

Despite his impatience to grasp the nettle Gordon kept his enthusiasm under restraint. He worked Playlord with unhurried regularity on the beach and across the wide acreage of Andrew Robinson's farm. His first impression of the horse had been spot on. Here was a traditionally bred chaser with more than a touch of potential. He moved like one of Jack Waugh's prized handicappers, yet he had the natural spring of a born jumper.

From their first piece of work together the pair were inseparable. 'Adam Pringle had been right all along,' Gordon was to repeat many times. 'Playlord was a "real" horse – something quite out of the ordinary, something really special. He made me as a trainer. Ron Barry reckoned he was about the best that he ever rode and in my list of favourite horses he has to come out right at the top of the pile.'

Adam Pringle never lived to see Playlord race over hurdles. Only days before the gelding was set to make his début his owner died. Immediate plans were shelved, but in the long term his widow had to face the dilemma of how best to deal with the horse who was a valuable asset to the estate.

She was advised to send Playlord to be sold at public auction. At the same time, stories of his latent ability had gone the rounds and several local parties had expressed their interest in the possibility of a private sale. Mrs Pringle told Gordon that he had first offer as she was certain her husband would have wished the horse to stay with him.

The asking price was £1,400 but money was in short supply at Beadnell and the Richards's steely bank manager refused point blank to extend their overdraft. Gordon, livid at the manager's staid attitude, was all for a more forceful approach; but Jean's saner counsels and persuasive talents prevailed. She explained the importance of the deal to her aunt, who sportingly advanced the loan. The money was handed over and when Playlord travelled to Bogside on 10 April 1965, he was carrying the navy-blue and white epaulets of his proud owner-trainer.

Bogside was the course where Gordon had ridden Merry Windsor into second place in the Scottish National. That April meeting marked the final Scottish National ever to be staged at the Irvine venue. By coincidence the 1965 race went to Brasher – ridden by Jimmy FitzGerald and trained by Tommy Robson, whom Richards was to succeed as Master of Greystoke within a couple of seasons. The National itself was to be transferred to Ayr, a course where GWR would become leading trainer by a huge margin.

The Garnock Four-Year-Old Hurdle was worth a modest £344 to the winner, though with inflation this would work out at around £3,000 in modern day parlance. Such a total would put the prize money on offer for a corresponding race at many of today's northern courses to shame! 'Jumbo' Wilkinson, an old friend of Gordon's and a fine judge of a young horse, had the ride and Playlord went off at 100–6. Jumbo recalls that Gordon had been optimistic in the paddock, instructing him to give the horse plenty of time to settle in mid-division before bringing him from off the pace to challenge between the last two flights.

He adds, 'I was impressed by his confidence and he proved to be fully justified. Playlord gave me a nice feel all the way and quickened like a good thing to take up the running after jumping the last. If I remember right we beat the favourite with Jimmy Fitz on board!'

Jumbo's memory is not playing tricks. The formbook shows that Playlord got up on the flat to beat Originator, the 15–8 favourite, trained by Tommy Robson and partnered by Jimmy FitzGerald, by a comfortable two lengths. Primrose League was a further length away, third. One of the fascinations of National Hunt racing is the longevity of the performers. The same old favourites reappear year after year and in similar fashion the human personalities also remain in the spotlight. Jimmy FitzGerald still brings colour and charisma to the scene as one of Malton's finest trainers and on that spring afternoon at Bogside, 34 years ago, Primrose League was booted home by Johnny Leech – then one of the top northern jump jockeys and today a senior Jockey Club starter.

Jumbo Wilkinson, who himself went on to become a successful trainer at Middleham, remembers Playlord as 'a lovely young horse who was sure to pick up races over hurdles before going on to do his proper job over fences'. He was back in the saddle for Playlord's next outing at Newcastle. The style of his initial win at Bogside had not gone unnoticed and the Geordie punters piled in. Playlord started 5–2 market leader for the second division of the Cohort Novices' Hurdle and once again led at the last flight to outpace the Brian Fletcher-partnered Choice Archesse by a length and a half.

By now tongues were wagging nineteen to the dozen. Scouts for the major northern yards had been touting his name for some while. After two consecutive victories the message was reaching further afield. His price was shaved to 11–10 favourite for his hat-trick attempt in the Bowmont Hurdle at Kelso. He was upped in distance to two miles, four furlongs, but the extra half mile made no difference. Wilkinson eased him home by a length from Prince Blarney with Red Alligator, the 1968 Grand National hero six lengths back in third place. Stan Hayhurst, who rode Red Alligator that afternoon, was impressed with Playlord. Now a steward at Newcastle, Hexham and Sedgefield, Stan echoes the popular view that this one horse was the inspiration behind Gordon's rise to fame. He reflected at a recent Newcastle fixture: 'Some people say that Playlord was unlucky not to have won more races than he did, but I can tell you Playlord was good to Gordon. Those early wins over hurdles got him talked about in the right places and by the time he won the Great Yorkshire he had already proved a terrific ambassador for the stable.'

His three straight wins as a four-year-old had aroused a flurry of interest from potential buyers but Gordon was not going to allow the 'golden goose' to prosper in foreign coops. He made it clear to all bidders that they had no chance of purchasing the horse outright. The most that was on the market was a 50 per cent share and even then there was to be an additional sanction.

People close to him were now calling Gordon 'The Boss'. During the summer of 1965 he made his move. He accepted an offer of £1,500 for a half-share in Playlord from the notorious but charismatic Joe Lisle. This flamboyant Newcastle-based businessman had already gained a colourful reputation in his home city through a close association with the 'entertainment industry' – most notably through his swinging night club, the 'Sixty-Nine', after which he was to name a popular chaser whom Denys Smith would train with conspicuous success.

At the time of his approach to invest in Playlord, Joe Lisle's powerful string of jumpers was still in its infancy but his penchant for a tilt at the ring was no secret and he already owned a useful hurdler called Autobiography. Lisle paid The Boss £1,500 for his half-share but the shrewd trainer, recognising his own facility for losing his temper and falling out with even his closest circle, insisted on one written condition of sale. He was to retain the right to end the partnership without warning if he so wished by regaining Lisle's half-share at cost price. Temper might not have been the sole motive behind this one-sided restraint.

Joe Lisle was to emerge as a 'high roller' in the betting market. Later in the '60s his black-leather-coated henchmen were to send waves of disquiet around the ring when with a simultaneous swoop they would wager thick wads of notes on their guv'nor's carefully chosen selection. Wise to the possibilities, Gordon was taking no risks with Playlord.

Despite Gordon's draconian share agreement the deal went ahead. As an added bonus Joe Lisle sent Autobiography to be trained at Beadnell along with the more modest All On. The 1965–66 season saw the Richards training tally rise to seven wins, the chief contributor to this total being Autobiography. The Joe Lisle hurdler did well in the hands of Nimrod Wilkinson, younger brother of Jumbo, whose retainer to Bobby Renton and additional commitment to the Jack Fawcus stable made him unavailable to continue his association with Playlord.

Right from the start Gordon had disciplined himself not to be greedy with the stable star. Later in his training career at Greystoke, he did on occasions appear to flout this rule, particularly when chasing a sequence of wins with a precocious novice chaser. But he never did so with Playlord. From a handful of runs he scored once in a handicap hurdle at Newcastle, a win which pleased his part-owner who liked nothing better than to record a success on his home course.

The following season – Gordon's last at Town Farm – saw Playlord still in action over hurdles, but under a change of ownership. Joe Lisle was hungry for success and wanted Terry Biddlecombe, the reigning Champion Jockey to partner his horses. The Boss was less enthusiastic. When Lisle allegedly booked Biddlecombe without first consulting his trainer the partnership came to a swift end. Gordon exercised his option, paid over his cheque for £1,500 and once more became the sole owner of his 'meal ticket'.

The search for a replacement partner was short-lived: if Playlord was the horse which kick-started Richards's training career then the arrival of Phillip Cussins as a patron of his yard injected both the capital to expand and the catalyst to attract owners of similar standing. Cussins, the founder and chairman of the Newcastle-based building and property-developing conglomerate which still bears his name, was not a newcomer to National Hunt ownership. At the time he had horses in training with Peter Cazalet at Fairlawne outside Tonbridge in leafy Kent. He yearned, though, for big-time success in his native North East and did not require much persuasion to succeed Joe Lisle. The conditions of the partnership agreement were unchanged. Phillip Cussins bought his half-share for £1,500 and GWR had the right to buy back the share for the same amount if he felt that the two parties were no longer thinking along the same lines.

In the late '90s horses are put over fences at the earliest opportunity. The Irish are happy to send potential jumpers over point-to-point obstacles at the age of four. The French adopt similar tactics with their home-bred chasers. In Britain trainers are loath to change 'tried and trusted' procedures. Most wait until their prospective chasers have turned six and in Gordon Richards's case there were only rare exceptions to this unwritten law.

Playlord would have been schooled over fences as a five-year-old, but it wasn't until the autumn of 1967 that he made his official transition to fences. By that time the Richards team were safely housed at Greystoke and Playlord's real job was about to begin.

SEVEN

Playlord Meets Ron Barry

The progress of Playlord's career over fences is inextricably linked not just with the success story of his upwardly mobile trainer, but also with that of Ron Barry, his partner in all eight of his victories over the major obstacles. Ron had served five years' apprenticeship with Tommy Shaw in Ireland and ridden his first winner on the flat at Gowran Park. Christened 'Big Ron' from a long while back, his first job this side of the water had been with Wilfred Crawford, the former Scottish Rugby Union International, who trained a small but most successful string of jumpers at Haddington in East Lothian. Horses like Lothian Countess, Mirval and Final Approach come quickly to mind. Ron had opened his account for the Crawfords at Ayr in 1964. A year later he was a vital cog in the smooth running of the stable, combining riding with acting as head lad and driving the box to the races.

Though Wilf Crawford had an admirable strike rate, he did not have more than a dozen horses in training at any one time, and Ron was still claiming the five-pound allowance when he had his first introduction to Playlord. He had driven south to Newcastle with a member of the Crawford team and had just returned to the box lines after settling his horse in the stables area when Gordon drew up alongside.

Ron explains, 'I'd never met the man before but he seemed to know me. He was lowering the ramp when he turned and said to me, "Come on son, give me a hand." I thought to myself, *cheeky beggar*, and called out, "Sorry Boss – I haven't got time for that, no time."

'Quick as a flash Gordon replied, "Oh! If you haven't got time then you haven't got time to ride him, have you?"'

The offer of the ride on Playlord led to a hasty rethink on Ron's part. Not only did he help Gordon with the unloading, but he saw to it that Playlord was comfortably settled in the racecourse stables while GWR stalked off to the weighing room to make the declaration.

Alas there was to be no fairy-tale ending to that first encounter. Playlord finished second. Ron continues: 'I got beat and the reason I got beat was because I was given the wrong orders. Playlord had top weight and I was told to hold him up until the last moment. I had him right there at the final flight but was outpaced by a horse ridden by Tommy Stack off 9st 7lb. The Boss was none too pleased that we were beat. In fact he jocked me off next time and I wasn't too happy, though I think the weight beat him then as well!'

During the coming months Ron Barry had another four or five rides for Richards. Although none of these produced winners, The Boss must have been impressed because once the move to Greystoke had been completed, Ron was booked to partner McRob on a couple of occasions and then invited down to school. He was offered the job of stable jockey shortly before the start of the 1967–68 season.

'To be honest I didn't know what to do,' remembers Ron. 'The Crawfords had been very good to me and they were having a great run with their horses. In the end the old man said to me, "Go on, give it a try. If it doesn't work out there will always be a job for you back here."' It was the beginning of a great partnership and a lasting friendship which was to end with Ron Barry mounted on Better Times Ahead leading Gordon's funeral cortège to Greystoke church on that saddest of days in September 1998.

Meanwhile Playlord had thrived since his move from Northumberland to Cumbria. He revelled in the change of scenery and his legs had strengthened up with plenty of work on the ancient turf gallops set uphill above the village of Greystoke, long embedded into the salubrious limestone of the region. By coincidence he had been entrusted to the care of Dick Allan. Then a 20-year-old stable lad, Dick's previous experience had been gained with Bobby Fairbairn at Selkirk and more recently with Wilf Crawford at Haddington, where he had been a colleague of Ron Barry.

Playlord won twice in his first season over fences, but it should be remembered that the campaign was interrupted by foot-and-mouth restrictions. He scored in handsome style at Newcastle in November, handing out a decisive eight-length thrashing to Arcturus, one of Neville Crump's star novice chasers. Then at Ayr, in February, Ron rode him with admirable patience to close on Kilmoray approaching the last, and pushed him out to win by a length and a half.

The season 1968–69 was Playlord's vintage one. Dick Allan reckoned that he was at the peak of his form early in the new year and remains convinced that he would have won the Gold Cup if the ground had not turned into a morass on the morning of the race. He describes Playlord as 'an athletic horse but big and classy, like an Ebor type'.

Much of Dick's time was spent either admiring Playlord from the saddle of another horse or grooming him after exercise. The Boss partnered him in all his work, whether it was a sharp spin up the gallop, a long stretch of hill exercise or merely a ramble through the woodland paths that criss-crossed the Greystoke estate. Even during the day Gordon was known to lead him out of his box and give him an extra roll in the sandpit – a habit that poor Dick found hard to understand.

Ron breaks into a broad smile, recalling the expression of resignation on Dick Allan's face as he watched Playlord being led into paddock to indulge in his favourite pastime: 'Yes, he loved his rolls in the sandpit, did Playlord. And the awful thing was that The Boss would almost always choose the very moment that Dick had got his coat shining like polished mahogany. Half an hour later he would be returned plastered head to foot in a mixture of mud and wet sand!'

The autumn of 1968 saw Playlord kick-start his campaign with a bloodless victory at Doncaster. The Mackeson was next on the agenda. The ground was officially 'yielding' and the distance shorter than ideal. Ron had him well placed on the heels of the leaders jumping the third last, but he could only stay on at one pace to finish fourth behind Jupiter Boy who got the better of a driving finish with Specify to score by a short head.

Back over an extended three miles at Catterick in December, Playlord showed his class by giving away over two stone to all his rivals and running out an effortless four-length winner from Auckland Girl. Weight was no problem to Playlord. As Ron pointed out, 'He was a marvellous horse to ride. You could settle him in behind and he would lob along on the bridle until you asked him to quicken and then he could produce the kind of acceleration that would put paid to all but the very best three-mile chasers in training.'

Playlord was sent off at the generous price of 100–8 for the Great Yorkshire Chase in January. It was to prove a day to forget for the Penrith bookmakers. There was infectious optimism in the Greystoke camp. Playlord looked a picture. He had been working better than ever and the prospect of good fast ground at the Town Moor was the icing on the cake. As Dick Allan remarked, 'Playlord was by Lord of Verona and all his progeny hated the soft. Playlord was a stone better horse on good going.'

Realising that he had the opposition at full stretch, Ron took Playlord to the front jumping four out, and from then on in the chasing group were always fighting a forlorn battle. Playlord won easing down by seven lengths from Domacorn and the latter stages of the race were accurately described by the jockey's uncle as 'a re-run of those old cowboy films with the baddie in front always going well and the posse behind flat to the boards and going nowhere'!

What is more, that posse contained a leading Gold Cup contender in the runner-up Domacorn, plus proven performers like Indamelia and Arcturus. Victory was doubly sweet. Not only did it provide Gordon Richards with the biggest success of his short training career, but it also underlined Playlord's claims to be considered worthy Cheltenham material.

GWR resisted the temptation to run Playlord again before the Festival. Instead he kept him jogging happily amidst the Lakeland Hills and nearer the time stimulated his interest with a racecourse gallop at nearby Carlisle. A day before the Gold Cup Playlord was sent down to Cheltenham. He was a good traveller, but the motorway network was primitive in the late '60s and the journey from Cumbria to the Cotswolds could often take upwards of eight hours.

Dick Allan set out full of confidence. However his hopes sank as soon as he reached Prestbury Park. The ground was already heavy and further downpours were forecast for the following 24 hours. Playlord slept and ate up well in the racecourse stables, but a chance meeting with Ryan Price at early morning exercise summed up the situation to a nicety. Admiring Playlord's gleaming coat and rippling muscles, the streetwise captain barked, 'You've got the racehorse, but I've got the plodder, and that's what will be needed this afternoon!'

Wise words indeed! What A Myth may only have been a jumped-up hunter chaser, but his jumping was beyond reproach and he was a proven mud-lover, sure to stay every yard of the trip.

Dick Allan wasn't the only Playlord supporter to view the rains with misgiving. Back in Cumbria a certain John Budden had returned from supervising the senior's cross-country run in hock-deep mud. Before immersing himself in a hot bath he had taken the disloyal precaution of investing his fiver on What A Myth. Never has an 8–1 winner been received with a stonier silence!

Ron Barry, donning his Jockey Club Inspector of Courses hat, stresses that under today's guidelines the race would never have been run. 'There's no way a Gold Cup would be staged in conditions like that nowadays, but 30 years ago it was a different world and no excuses were made. We just accepted that our hopes had been dashed by the weather.'

In the event Playlord ran a courageous race. He came with every chance but could not quicken in the cloying mud and weakened into third place approaching the last. Domacorn, whom Playlord had thrashed by a long-looking seven lengths at Doncaster, finished runner-up at Cheltenham ten lengths in front of the Greystoke star. The result was a travesty but one that was accepted as 'an unfortunate rub of the green'!

Compensation, if that is the word, came in April's Scottish National, but not before connections had faced a worrying build-up to Ayr's annual marathon. Dick Allan explains: 'The Boss was in personal charge of Playlord's feeding. As a regular supplement to his diet he would fold in some dozen raw eggs. Playlord appeared to thrive on the rations, but a week before he was due to run at Ayr he broke two blood vessels. This had never happened before and Gordon was at a loss to account for the burst.

'It occurred to me that Playlord was suffering from a surfeit of eggs! His blood was just too rich. The Boss was doubtful, but to give him his due he always listened to his staff and he agreed to dispense with the eggs as a temporary measure. Playlord never bled again, but for such a thing to happen in the immediate run-up to a big race did little to increase the confidence in a sizeable ante-post wager!'

Fearless Fred, prominent when a faller at the 14th in the Grand National at Aintree, and Roborough, a previous winner at Ayr, were preferred in the betting to Playlord who was a 9–1 chance at the off. In direct contrast to the Gold Cup, the going for the Scottish National was firm – 'firmer than firm', according to Ron Barry, who added: 'Playlord was such a good mover that he acted on a sound surface, but the ground that day at Ayr was faster than he wanted. He had 12 stone on his back, too, a pound more than Red Rum was to carry when he won in 1974. I didn't want to give him too much to do, so we lay handy throughout the race. I saw Fearless Fred fall at the 15th and let Playlord go to the front five out. He was absolutely cooked in the home straight but was such a battler that he wouldn't let anything get to him. His will to win was astonishing. When we got him back home his legs were all swollen up with the effort of carrying 12 stone on that firm ground and there was no question he had to be put away for the autumn.'

After his performances in the spring Playlord was going to be handicapped out of all but the prestige events. Gordon decided that he would be aimed at the Hennessy, with just one preliminary race to sharpen him up. The Wetherby Pattern Chase, ten days before the Hennessy, was the race chosen for his warm-up and Playlord delighted his trainer with a splendid effort at the West Yorkshire course. Only three came under starter's orders and once again the bookies had promoted Domacorn the 5–4 favourite. He was the first to weaken, dropping away well beaten from the eighth. His departure left Arcturus, the outsider of three at 11–4, at the head of affairs until passed by Playlord at the 12th fence. Arcturus rallied on the turn for home and regained the lead four out. It was an advantage he was never going to relinquish. Playlord made him fight all the way to the line but was beaten a bare half length.

The 1969 Hennessy Gold Cup was a fiercely competitive race. Larbawn headed the betting at 4–1 with Playlord, Lord Jim and Spanish Steps co-second favourites at 7s. The official going was firm and Playlord was keen in the early stages. 'That wasn't unusual,' explained Ron Barry; 'he tended to pull one's arms out over the first two fences but once the race began in earnest he would settle quiet as a mouse. He gave me a great feel that day. The Boss had done a grand job with him, and turning out of the back straight for the final time, I hadn't moved a muscle on him. He was running away with me and I have rarely been so confident of winning a big race as I was at that moment. Then disaster struck at the cross fence the fifth from home. Cottager, who had led until six out, crumpled in a heap on the landing side of the fence. There was no way that Playlord could avoid him. We were brought down and Limeburner and Johnnie Haine suffered the same fate. It was a very nasty business and in my view Playlord was never the same horse after that fall at Newbury. The experience seemed to knock all the stuffing out of him. He lost confidence and never again had a proper cut at his fences.'

The formbook would seem to endorse Ron Barry's opinion. Playlord ran three more times during 1969–70. He finished a modest fourth behind Spanish Steps in the Benson and Hedges Gold Cup at Sandown; was beaten into third place when bidding for the Rowland Meyrick at Wetherby on Boxing Day; and trailed home a remote ninth in the Great Yorkshire at Doncaster, before being rested for the season.

After a long summer out at grass Playlord took a deal of getting fit for the autumn of 1970. He dropped out tamely on his seasonal début at Perth and was pulled up at Ayr. A walk-over at Huntingdon didn't serve much of a purpose and on the last day of October he was hardly out of a canter to account for a sole rival at Market Rasen. His first major task of the campaign came a week later in the Doncaster Pattern Chase.

Ron Barry takes up the story: 'Playlord was set to take on Spanish Steps, his old rival, at level weights but he had a definite fitness advantage. Had he been the same horse as he was in the Hennessy the previous autumn, I would have been confident of turning the tables – and to be fair he might still have won if he had stood up. Tragically he took the 16th by the roots and fell heavily. He took a while to get to his feet. Although he walked back to the stables, something was badly amiss and he was in obvious discomfort.'

Playlord never walked again. He collapsed in his box at the racecourse, his back legs seemingly paralysed. It did not take the vet long to diagnose a fracture of the spine. There was no way that he could be saved.

Playlord was still only nine at the time of his death and despite the many famous names who were to follow in his hoofprints at Greystoke, The Boss never failed to mention him in the same breath as the likes of Titus Oates, One Man, Lucius and Hallo Dandy. Without Playlord it is arguable that Gordon would never have left the haven of Beadnell. Without Playlord it is certain he would never have attained the heights he was destined to achieve.

Thirty years on, Weatherbys have countenanced the appearance of a new 'Playlord'. Owned by a patron of Graham McCourt, this modern variety is by Arctic Lord out of Show Rose. He has yet to emulate the early achievements of his illustrious predecessor. I wish him the best of good fortune. But for me, and I suspect for many other traditionalists, there will be only one true Playlord.

EIGHT

Move to Greystoke

The mind doctors tell us that moving house comes a close third in the stress-factor stakes to bereavement and divorce. Unless there are extreme circumstances, this has to be a load of nonsense and the decision to leave Beadnell for Greystoke proved a calculated challenge rather than a pill-popping trauma. There was a degree of sadness and heartache. But from the time that the offer to lease Castle Stables was first intimated, the likelihood of the Richards family turning it down and staying put at Town Farm was remote.

Jean had more to lose by upping sticks and crossing the Pennines. She had been born and brought up in Northumberland and loved the area and the people. For Gordon the county had become an adopted home since he arrived in Chatton Park in the early '50s.

From a career point of view the opportunity to train at Greystoke was akin to receiving manna from heaven. Gordon already had first-hand knowledge of the stables and, more importantly, the facilities. As a jockey he had occasionally stayed with Jack Pearson down in the village at Rectory Farm before schooling in the morning. He was equally familiar with the set-up of Tommy Robson, who had trained at Castle Stables with consistent success since first taking out a public licence in 1953.

The argument against the projected switch was based primarily on the financial risk allied to a degree of disconcerting rumour about the reputation that Greystoke had gained as a gambling unit. Tommy Robson himself had suffered at the hands of the Jockey Club Disciplinary Committee and temporarily lost his licence – the reason in fact behind the availability of the stables.

The safety-first brigade warned that the same circle of owners who had allegedly embarrassed the previous tenant might now transfer their allegiance to the new arrival with potentially worrying results. Their spokesmen also emphasised how Gordon had made such a success of his venture at Town Farm and that with the acquisition of Playlord he was well regarded in Northumberland and more likely to attract local patronage at Beadnell rather than in Cumbria.

Shortly before they signed the agreement to go to Greystoke, Gordon and Jean met George Milburn while enjoying a pub supper near Alnwick. George, about to retire and concentrate his energies on working his locally based poultry farm, invited them back to his home for a dram. The subject of Greystoke soon became a topic for discussion and George was asked to give his opinion. He recalls, 'I was against the move and told them so. I pointed out that they had both made quite a name for themselves at Beadnell. The business was picking up and there was the potential for expansion, while if they moved to Cumbria the expenses would be considerable and there would be no guarantee that the owners would send their horses. I went on to mention the gambling angle and advised them to stay put.

'They were very polite but I sensed they'd already made up their minds to go. I was anxious for them, though. I knew Gordon as an excellent horseman but I seriously doubted his head for business. I had been friendly with Jean from a long way back and with hindsight I had underestimated her strength of character and ability to organise. She was the power behind the throne and she weeded out the bad boys before they could cause any problems. I thought they were making a mistake at the time, but who knows? If they had followed my advice National Hunt racing would have lost one of its finest trainers of all time.'

The attraction of Greystoke was irresistible to Gordon. Even now those who spend their lives south of Watford Gap regard Cumbria as a barren region covered with treeless stretches of boggy wasteland, inhabited by ravenous sheep and constantly swept by unrelenting wind and rain. They also believe that it takes a day and a half to reach Carlisle, which used to be famous for its station and biscuit factory but today receives more notoriety from the publicity surrounding the remarkable Michael Knighton, the chairman and major shareholder of Carlisle United.

The truth is that Greystoke lies some five miles from junction 40 – the Penrith exit – of the M6, an interchange that also connects directly with the A66 trunk road to Scotch Corner and all points east. The motorway network was far from complete in 1967, but construction work was under way and the majority of northern and Scottish racecourses would soon be reached within a comfortable morning's drive.

The suggestion that Cumbria is simply a haven for fellwalkers and sheep is equally unfounded. Much of the county, in particular the area around Carlisle and Penrith, is rich in pasture and bears a passable resemblance to the lush grazing lands of Somerset and rural Gloucestershire. Castle Stables themselves are situated in the 4,000-acre estate controlled by the Howards of Greystoke Castle. The central sandstone block once housed the renowned hunters of Henry Howard, who opened his season by decimating the foxes in his native Cumbria before transferring his whole pack south to the Shires for the remainder of the campaign. 'HHH', the capital letters standing for Henry Howard's Hunters, are still etched into the wall-end of the stables while the surrounding parkland has been the training ground for both hunters and racehorses over the past three centuries.

The dominant influence in this part of Cumbria has traditionally been shared between the Howards and the Lowthers, whose most charismatic scion was the controversial Yellow Earl (the shell of whose unique castle still stands overlooking the site of the annual Lowther Three-day Driving Championship and Country Fair). Matches between the pick of the families' bloodstock were often held at Greystoke, where the hallowed turf has witnessed the thunder of hooves since the times of William the Conqueror.

The history of the sporting Howards was not of any concern to GWR, though some 14 years later he would marry a Howard – namely Joanie, great-granddaughter of the legendary huntsman himself. What really appealed to GWR was an established racing stable with a proven reputation for turning out winners under both codes, magnificent gallops and unlimited access to parkland and open hillside. That, plus a certain feeling in the marrow of his bones that if he could only make a flying start then the horse-loving country folk of Cumbria would provide him with the necessary resources.

This latter proviso was going to be essential as the Richards horse box required no more than two trips east and west from Beadnell to transport the entire stable strength of five horses in training. But this quintet included Phillip Cussins's two hopefuls, Playlord and Vulgan's Pleasure, whom Richards had had fired and rested for a year since he came north from Fairlawne. The duo were soon to be joined by Titus Oates, who was to carry the Greystoke banner with distinction for the next five seasons.

In his wisdom Henry Howard had built into the roof area of his stable enough accommodation for his staff. Since the arrival of Tommy Robson this had been converted into a roomy flat, sufficiently large to cater for the requirements of Gordon and Jean, together with ten-year-old Nicky and Joey who was now rising eight.

Gordon 'lived over the shop' throughout the remainder of his married life to Jean. In many ways it was a convenient arrangement. The Boss was a hands-on trainer until the end. Even during his final weeks as the cancer tightened its grip, he would be down at the farm, popping into one box after another, feeling legs, checking the feed and generally keeping the lads on their toes.

Ron Barry drove across from Pooley Bridge in early September to pay a chance visit. He found The Boss, looking thin and far from well, leaning against some straw bales in quiet conversation with Alistair Duff, owner of The Grey Monk. Ron recalled: 'The best way to cheer up Gordon had always been to rag him along. Get him ruffled and he was great crack. I didn't like the look of him health-wise, mind, but I thought better than to change the habits of a lifetime and called out, "Aha! Taking a back seat, Boss; nice work for some!" Within a flash he was up on his feet and blathering about being up at six and supervising first lot, plus a few expletives about cheeky upstart young jockeys turned Inspector of Courses. He got quite hot under the collar, just like when Jonjo and I would deliberately pull his leg to get a reaction during our riding days. Gordon liked that flat. It meant that he could be down in the yard messing about with the horses all hours of the day. Many's the time I would come into the yard and find him bent over the door of a box just staring at a particular horse and talking softly to it. He had a terrific rapport with the horses and he was happiest right there in the hub of things.'

Ron reckons that there were some 15 horses in training at Greystoke at the time he joined the staff in the autumn of 1967. But to the frustration of their trainer, the quick start did not materialise. Dick Allan remembers: 'They were looking and running well, but not getting any of the breaks. The Boss wasn't a happy man and the pressures were building up all round. The stable still hadn't notched a winner by the end of October but I was due to lead up Vulgan's Pleasure at Kelso a few days later and the more I studied the race the more confident I became that he had to win. They opened up 10–1 or longer before he was backed down to 4–1 and scored in a hack canter.'

Kelso has not proved too lucky a course for the Richards stable over recent seasons – with the exception of Jinxy Jack and Whaat Fettle – but Vulgan's Pleasure will always hold the distinction of landing Gordon's initial victory as Master of Greystoke and a fortnight later he completed an even more spectacular 'first timer' by becoming number one of the 38 wins that The Boss was to saddle at Cheltenham. The race was the three-mile Cowley Novices' Hurdle and Vulgan's Pleasure was to prove even more effective over the bigger obstacles. He won novice chases on the Saturday and Monday of Carlisle's Easter meeting and subsequently landed long-distance handicap-chase wins at Haydock and Wetherby – despite having frequent problems with his legs and being forced to miss the whole of the 1969–70 campaign.

Compared to Playlord and Titus Oates, Vulgan's Pleasure was one of Phillip Cussins's lesser lights, but he was a grand trier who overcame all sorts of problems to keep his head in front. Dick Allan recalls that he had constant bladder trouble: 'Poor fellow, he couldn't hold his water and to prevent him coming out in sores he had to have his hind legs continually greased.' Ron Barry described him as one of the toughest stayers he'd ridden. Reflecting that under today's whip guidelines he would have been up before the stewards more times than not, Ron added, 'I've never known a horse to respond to the stick like Vulgan's Pleasure. The more you got stuck in the harder he'd battle. Sometimes I used to think that I must have got to the bottom of him. Then, the morning after, he'd come out bucking and squealing as though he hadn't even been at the races. For a horse with doubtful legs he did us all proud and he proved a splendid advertisement for The Boss, that first season at Greystoke.'

NINE

Phillip Cussins's Record Purchase

Dedication is an invaluable asset. Combined with outstanding talent it can produce international champions and even on its own it goes a very long way. Christopher Collins was by no means a natural horseman, let alone a polished race-rider, but his determination to succeed could not be faulted. At the time he partnered Mr Jones to finish third behind Jay Trump and Freddie in the 1965 Grand National, he was struggling to make an impact in the unpaid ranks. But his steely resolution, plus an eye for a promising young horse and the money to seal the purchase, was to prevail in the end.

Collins rode 24 winners in the 1965–66 season to land the amateur championship. In 1966–67 he defended his title handsomely with a tally of 33 winners. His goal achieved, Collins opted to change sports and focus on three-day-eventing. The dispersal of his national hunt stock at the 1968 Ascot Sales aroused more than a degree of interest and the star lot coming under the hammer was the six-year-old Titus Oates, an imposing bay gelding by Arctic Slave out of a Cacador mare.

Titus Oates had qualified with the Zetland. He had been trained by Arthur Stephenson, winning once over hurdles, and was already notching up a sequence of victories in top hunter chase company. Gordon sounded out WA, convinced that Titus Oates had the potential to become a serious Gold Cup contender. He realised that the progress of Playlord and Vulgan's Pleasure had whetted Cussins's appetite for big race success and he determined to cajole his wealthy patron into adding Titus Oates to his portfolio.

It proved no easy task. Richards knew that there would be other ambitious trainers with deep-pursed owners keen to get their hands on this quality merchandise. He calculated that 12,000 guineas might secure the prize. The telephone wires hummed between Greystoke and the North-East but Gordon was persistent. Time and again he stressed that Titus Oates had the ability to scale the heights. The opportunity to obtain such a ready-made class chaser might not recur for a decade. Yes, he would be expensive, but in the long term he would be sure to repay the purchase price and in the process provide his owner with years of excitement, pride and satisfaction.

The Boss did not receive the go-ahead until nearly 11 p.m. on the night before the sale. At the ringside the bidding was fast and furious. At 12,000 guineas the tension became palpable and the bidding more deliberate. There was no stopping now until the hammer finally fell in Gordon's favour at

14,750 guineas, a world-record price for a national hunt sale. The Boss had got his horse, but it was an anxious trainer that made the call to the Cussins office to explain the necessity for the additional 2,750 guineas above the proposed ceiling.

In the event Gordon did not have to dip into his own money box and Titus Oates went on to win another 17 chases in Phillip Cussins's colours, most notably the 1969 King George VI Chase and the 1971 Whitbread Gold Cup. Stan Mellor was in the saddle at Kempton when Titus Oates proved too sharp for Flyingbolt and Nicky Richards guided him to a couple of wins in his last season. For the main part, though, it was Big Ron who had the responsibility of chalking up the prize money – approximately £11,000 of which was gained through those major wins at Kempton and Sandown.

My personal memory of Titus Oates concerns his head carriage. Between fences his nose was almost glued to the turf, a characteristic which is said to indicate courage and honesty. I remember the Kent-based hunter-chaser Cauliflower holding her head equally low and that mare was certainly one of the most genuine hunters of her generation. Currently the Mary Reveley-trained Seven Towers shares this style of running, not all to the satisfaction of Peter Niven, and it has to be said that consistency is not one of Seven Towers's best known qualities. Still, perhaps he is the exception that proves the rule!

Ron Barry agrees that Titus Oates needed a bit of knowing. 'It was head down, scraping the grass most of the time, but he had his eyes skinned right enough because two strides or so from the next fence, the old head would come up with such force that if you weren't ready for it, you were in danger of slipping out of the back door!'

The difficulties of partnering Titus Oates on the racecourse were nothing compared with the impossibility of attempting to school him at home. Barry has every reason to remember the first effort. He explains, 'We were all gee'd up by the arrival of this star. He certainly looked the part and The Boss was as excited as any of us – "Take it quietly now, Ron. Just squeeze him up and over. Give him plenty of daylight, son." That was the idea, but I never got the chance to find a stride. As soon as he caught sight of the line of fences next to the wood, he dived violently sideways and crashed straight through the wire fence bordering the gallops. He needed 14 stitches on his very first morning in the stable and Mr Cussins was ringing at 10 a.m. to find out how he'd schooled!'

The Boss was perplexed. WA had not mentioned that Titus Oates was phobic about schooling, though there was a theory that the Crawleas jumpers learned their job on the racecourse rather than on the gallops.

Ron continues: 'We decided to try again, but at the second time of asking Titus Oates flatly refused to take the fence and jumped the wing instead. That was enough even for Gordon. He did make one more effort to educate Titus by putting him through a line of slightly raised poles but to no avail. He just kicked them out of the way and refused to leave the ground.'

From that moment onwards Titus Oates was never subjected to even so much as a hint of schooling at Greystoke. If GWR felt that his jumping needed sharpening then he was taken for a session on the racecourse, where his manners were always impeccable.

The six-year-old made his first appearance of the 1968–69 campaign in the Emblem Handicap Case at Wetherby in early November. The odd whisper about his erratic behaviour on the gallops may have reached the acute hearing of the ring, because he opened up at 9–4 before drifting to 7–2 in the face of strong support for the proven Arcturus. The market support for Neville Crump's good chaser was justified. Arcturus won by six lengths, but not before Titus Oates had impressed race readers. *Raceform's* comment read, 'Led 7th. Mistake 2 out. Promising.'

There was much relief in the Greystoke camp. Titus was far from fully wound up and Ron reflects that he had been delighted with his jumping: 'The horse had been no problem when we had taken him away for a racecourse gallop, but this was the real thing and he jumped super until he got a bit tired in the home straight. The race pleased us a lot. Arcturus, the winner, had already proved an accurate yardstick with Playlord and, perhaps more importantly, he jumped straight. There wasn't even a hint of any ducking and diving.'

At home Titus had to be handled with kid gloves throughout his career. Ron describes him as 'a bit of a nutcase, not nasty, but temperamental. If you cracked him one he would go bananas. In fact you wouldn't even touch him with the stick at home. If he hesitated going through a gate you sat and suffered rather than tap him down the shoulder, because if you did then he was just as likely to dive sideways through the gap between the waiting tractor and the concrete post than to keep straight on.'

The Boss roadworked Titus on a regular basis after Playlord's demise, but tended to leave the fast work to Ron or later to Nicky, his son. On his arrival at Greystoke Titus Oates came under the care of Jimmy O'Brien, the head lad. Jimmy was an artist at preparing a horse. He would have pocketed more than his fair share of 'best-turned-outs' had those deserved awards been the fashion at the end of the '60s. Jimmy had the honour of being The Boss's first head lad at Greystoke.

Titus Oates won three times and was placed second twice in the five outings of his first season in Phillip Cussins's colours and any lingering doubts concerning his class were forgotten after his excellent performance in the 1969 Whitbread Gold Cup, in which he finished a three-length runner-up to Larbawn with a highly competitive field in arrears. Taking on a class field from the front and staying there throughout three and three-quarter miles round Sandown is asking a lot of any horse. Two years later Titus Oates was to win the Whitbread under a more patient ride. On this occasion he led from the 13th until headed by the winner between the last two fences.

The big bay was to reappear in the Mackeson at Cheltenham the following November. If it is difficult to make all the running at Sandown, it is an even more demanding task at Cheltenham. Titus Oates did his level best to sustain the effort until, joined by the subsequent Grand National winner Gay Trip, he was overhauled half-way up the hill and beaten by two and a half lengths. Compensation was immediately at hand. Titus returned to headquarters in December for the Massey Ferguson Gold Cup, again over two and a half miles. On six pounds better terms he reversed the placings with Gay Trip by a hard-fought length: Ron Barry, riding at his most effective to grab back the lead on the run to the final fence, held his old rival at bay on the long uphill grind to the winning post.

That was vintage Barry, but the stable jockey was not to share what was arguably Titus Oates's greatest moment – his triumph in the 1969 King George. In between the Massey Ferguson and the Boxing Day Festival at Kempton, Ron had ridden Playlord in the Benson and Hedges Gold Cup at Sandown. It was Playlord's first appearance since being brought down so savagely in the Hennessy, the memory of which his jockey is adamant stayed with him for the remainder of his career and prevented him ever again jumping fences with his former carefree flamboyance.

At Sandown Playlord was hesitant and lacked zip. He made token progress three out, but never reached a challenging position and ran home fourth, thirteen lengths adrift of Spanish Steps, the winner. Mr Cussins was not impressed. Brilliantly successful in his business ventures, he applied the same principles to his hobby of racehorse ownership. He had invested in top-class talent and he anticipated nothing short of outright victory. Titus Oates *had* to win every time. His belief was that he had paid out a record price of 14,750 guineas at the Ascot Sales for this horse, which, as the most expensive chaser in training, was by simple logic the best steeplechaser in Britain.

Phillip Cussins also entertained friends and fellow business contacts in his box at the races and understandably felt let down if the anticipated success did not materialise. Playlord had proved an anticlimax in the Benson and Hedges. The rider took the blame: Ron Barry was jocked off in favour of Stan Mellor. This vastly experienced pilot had no previous acquaintance with Titus Oates, or indeed with Gordon Richards.

He recollects, 'Shortly before Christmas I got this call offering me the ride on Titus Oates at Kempton. I was available so I accepted, but the first time I laid eyes on the horse was in the Kempton paddock. There was no question of me trailing up to Cumbria to ride him out before the race.'

Mellor was impressed with his big race mount. He continues, 'I knew from his record that he was a force to be reckoned with and as soon as I sat on him he gave me that classy feel. Some horses seem to know that they are special and Titus Oates was one of those, a quality animal with a real presence about him. My orders were to be up in the firing line throughout and make the best of my way home from the bottom bend.'

The substitute jockey had few problems carrying out his instructions. Titus Oates found Kempton a happy hunting ground. He revelled in the level ground and easy turns. Travelling up with the pace throughout, he made a couple of minor errors but led from the tenth fence and held on in resolute style to beat Flyingbolt by three lengths.

'Not bad for a spare ride,' murmurs Stan Mellor with a wry smile. 'And a fine piece of training too. Gordon had the horse spot on for the big one; always the hallmark of a true horseman.'

Titus Oates returned to Kempton at the end of February for the three-mile Coventry Pattern Handicap Chase, with Stan Mellor again in the saddle. The King George winner was sent off a 3–1 chance, second favourite to The Dikler, who headed the market at 9–4. This time round the jockey needed no instructions. He remembers, 'I had no worries about taking him to the front from the off. I knew he would look after himself over the fences and I was keen to draw the sting out of The Dikler, who was sure to be doing all his best work in the finish. I am glad that I was on a true front-runner because we managed to pinch just enough ground turning for home to make things that little bit too hard for The Dikler. He came with a rush from the last but Titus held him off by a neck.'

Next stop the Gold Cup – Stan Mellor retained the ride and the partnership disputed the lead until the 12th. They were not far off the pace when Titus was caught out by the downhill third last and fell. Mellor remarks, 'It was another good run but even before the fall I would have been pushed to finish closer than fourth. Against the cream of the country's three-mile chasers it seemed he didn't quite last home.'

It is a view with which Ron Barry would agree, though of course Big Ron was to persuade him to win the 1971 Whitbread Gold Cup over an extended three miles, five furlongs. Barry goes back to the early days at Greystoke: 'He was a real challenge to ride then, y'know. Titus had some speed. When he wanted to turn it on he could beat all the Flat horses over five furlongs. I often wondered why The Boss didn't try him over two miles. If he had, I don't think they would have known where he went. God, he had some toe!'

Gordon would argue with justification that Titus Oates had experienced no problems staying three miles as a hunter-chaser. The evidence of his subsequent performances certainly suggests that overall he probably achieved as much fame and fortune by sticking to the longer trip than he would ever have attained by restricting his appearances to two or two and a half miles.

With Stan Mellor retained to ride Park Ranger for the Thomson Jones stable, Ron Barry was back aboard Titus Oates for the 1970 Whitbread. Seventeen went to post, with Spanish Steps set to hump top weight of 12st and Titus Oates burdened with 11st 11lb. The consistent Charter Flight was on the 10st 11lb mark, with the remainder carrying featherweights around the ten-stone level. Handicapped right up to the hilt, Titus Oates led to the 15th but was unable to sustain the pace from three out, coming home in fourth place behind Royal Toss. The Greystoke standard-bearer had Spanish Steps behind him in sixth and was giving away an average of 20lb to the first three home!

The season 1970–71 saw Titus Oates at his prime: seven outings, four wins, two honourable defeats under huge weights and one dramatic fall in the Coventry Pattern Chase at Kempton. His titanic victory over Young Ash Leaf in the Whitbread must take precedence, but there was immense satisfaction in the Richards–Cussins camp at his eclipse of French Tan and The Dikler in the Gainsborough Chase at Sandown earlier in the year. Ron Barry dictated the pace from flag-fall and, measuring his fences with faultless grace and power, Titus forged clear in the home straight to win, ears pricked. Sport and General Press Agency captured a splendid picture of Titus Oates breasting the last with Ron motionless but perfectly balanced. The power of the leader conjures up an imaginary comparison between Bucephalus, the illustrious charger of Alexander the Great, and a Second-World-War Centurion tank. A couple of lengths adrift struggles The Dikler, rendered legless by his vain but courageous effort to match strides with the dominant leader. He is about to paddle through the birch – and judging by the expression on the face of Stan Mellor, his jockey, it's going to be a painful collision!

In the Whitbread Gold Cup poor Mellor had an even more remote sight of Titus Oates's substantial rump as he trailed in a distant sixth on Rough Silk, the 17–2 favourite. The headlong gallop set by the lightweights played into Ron Barry's hands. It enabled him to settle Titus Oates, on the heels of the leading pack before making his move at the 14th, and going clear from the 20th. Young Ash Leaf, such a splendid race mare for owner Robert Macdonald and his trainer, Ken Oliver, gave determined pursuit; but a bad mistake two fences later left her with too much to do and Titus Oates lengthened up the notorious final hill to gain a famous victory by a length.

Three wins from ten races in 1971–72 was poor reward for a brave but fruitless battle against the secure grip of the handicapper. Titus Oates actually won the Jack White Chase at Market Rasen after falling at the fourth fence and being remounted. He tried the Gold Cup once more, but blundered at the 11th and dropped away tamely. In between times he ran his best race of the season in the King George, this time partnered by Ron Barry. His jumping was spectacular. A magnificent leap at the 10th took him to the front, a lead he maintained until the 13th where he was headed by The Dikler. Back in front at the 15th, he was rejoined by The Dikler two out and, despite having every chance at the last, could not quicken again under 12 stone. He finally weakened into third place on the flat as old rival Spanish Steps came storming through from mid-division to close on The Dikler all the way to the line.

Titus Oates was to land Newcastle's Swift Chase in each of the following two seasons, the last occasion under the guidance of Nicky Richards. He was also to finish runner-up to Kilvulgan in the 1973–74 Gainsborough Chase, but old age was creeping up. Instead of chasing shadows at 13, connections took the sensible course and he went hunting with Danny Moralee, delighting the followers of The Berwickshire by treating them to some spectacular jumping cross-country in pursuit of the old enemy. Moralee, whom Gordon had first met while riding for Johnny Marshall, was champion amateur in consecutive seasons between 1952 and 1956 and partnered his own Happymint to win both the Cheltenham and the Liverpool Foxhunters. He promised to give Titus Oates a happy home until the end and there could have been no better man to provide such comforts.

TEN

Chalk and Cheese . . .

Just as The Boss had that spurious *W* added to his initials to distinguish him from the reigning champion jockey, a similar arrangement had been required to separate Jack and John Berry, who used to train teams of contrasting size at Cockerham and Newmarket. Jack, by far the senior of the pair, was identified by the simple initial *J* while his namesake used his full Christian name. Physically there was no similarity between them at all, but ironically they both share a common denominator. John's mother, Caroline, was one of Jack's established owners – best remembered for her mare I Don't Mind – but an established patron of Moss Side Stables until her death in 1996.

Caroline, the first wife of Claude Berry, former amateur rider, permit holder and more recently the inspiration behind the Tryon Gallery, saw her light-blue and yellow colours carried to success over 70 times under both codes. At her Firth Stud in the Border hamlet of Lilliesleaf, near Jedburgh, she bred the smart two-year-old Petulengra; the useful Good 'N' Sharp, five times a winner on the flat; and the consistent Top 'N' Tale, who notched 12 wins under rules and broke the track record for a three-mile chase round Ayr. In addition to her racing interests, Caroline enjoyed an international reputation for the resilience of the rare breeds of chestnut and palomino Shetland ponies which were bred at Lilliesleaf and exported worldwide.

During his time of over 30 years at Greystoke, The Boss prided himself on 'doing things his own way'. Owners who attempted to dictate or interfere did not last long at Castle Stables, but there always have to be exceptions to the general rule. Ted Briggs, whose long stream of winners includes such household names as Better Times Ahead, The Man Himself and Another City, was more than capable of ensuring that his demands were met. And back in the early '70s Caroline Berry would stand no nonsense. There was no escape. She was a very direct lady and GWR knew better than to ignore her requests.

Claude Berry had ridden Veronica Bell for Gordon before a desperate fall from his own Majestic Prince at Sedgefield had ended his career in the saddle. He recalls, 'It was down to me that Caroline had her horses trained at Greystoke. Ron Barry had won on Chop 'N' Change for us at Cartmel in the spring of 1970 and the following autumn we sent our horses down to Cumbria. For a while I had admired the way Gordon went about his work. Of all the up-and-coming trainers, he was the one whose horses always looked the best turned out and appeared the fittest in the paddock. If I was no longer able to do the job myself, Gordon was the obvious alternative.'

Chop 'N' Change won four times that first season at Greystoke, but it was Gyleburn who provided the touch of class. This strapping brown gelding by Solar Tickle had started his hurdling career with John Barclay at Kettleholm near Lockerbie. Gyleburn was in fact the postal address of the Barclay stables, where Caroline had often ridden work. Impressed with Gyleburn's form over hurdles, she had bought him privately and her new purchase joined the Richards string at the start of the 1970–71 season.

Gyleburn was to prove the perfect role model for the future generation of three-mile handicap chasers on whose success the reputation of Greystoke flourished. At the time of Roger Cook's notorious attempt to tarnish the good name of the Martin Pipe stable by implying that the amazing strike rate of his novice hurdlers was achieved at the expense of their long-term future, statistics were produced to show which national hunt trainers managed to keep their horses in active training for the longest period of time. The stables run by Gordon Richards, Josh Gifford and Jenny Pitman headed the table by a substantial margin, with Josh Gifford's yard gaining top position and Castle Stables achieving an honourable second.

The welfare of his horses held pride of place with GWR. They were treated as members of a large but close-knit family and nothing delighted the trainer more than to watch one of his 'veterans' give the young upstarts a salutary lesson in jumping ability and innate enthusiasm for the game. Tears were shed at Perth's 1996 August meeting when, at the age of 16, Clever Folly won the 29th and final race of his long career. His racing lifespan may have been the longest, but plenty other Greystoke stalwarts have run him close and Gyleburn was one of the pioneers.

In four action-packed seasons at Greystoke he won 18 races. To finish out of the frame was a rare blemish for this most popular staying chaser. He was the sort of horse on which Ron Barry excelled. Tough and durable, Gyleburn might have lacked a turn of foot but his resolute gallop never wavered. Kicked into his fences by his long-legged partner, he responded with spring-heeled boldness. Carlisle, Haydock and Hexham were his favourite venues and in the autumn of 1972 he put up a typically game performance at Aintree's October meeting to pass the post a competitive third behind Glenkiln and L'Escargot in the William Hill Grand National Trial. Six months earlier Gyleburn had lined up for the National itself as understudy to the injured Red Sweeney. I well remember signing off my Friday night Aintree preview on Border Television with the fatal words, 'One thing you can all be certain of: the bold jumping Gyleburn is sure to give his supporters a grand run for their money and it will be no surprise to see him squeeze into a place at a long price.'

That was tempting fate in a major way, of course. The following afternoon there was just one faller at the first fence and that was Gyleburn! In the car on the way back to Lilliesleaf the disappointed owners amused themselves by working out how many pounds Gyleburn had cost for each yard that he had covered at Aintree before his departure at the first. Taking into account the cost of transport, the trainer's charges, the jockey's fee plus the traditional £100 premium to cover the risk of riding in the National, the amount was substantial. But there were plenty of occasions when Caroline Berry's splendid servant, who just for starters won no less than nine races at Hexham, more than paid for his keep. Other multiple winners in the pale-yellow and blue were Chop 'N' Change, her son Top 'N' Tale and the classy Cromwell Road. The latter ended his days with Ken Oliver, a transfer that ruffled Gordon's feathers but which he was helpless to prevent.

Mrs Berry was the type of owner that The Boss was happy to count among the patrons of his stable. On occasions, though, he had to bite his tongue and keep his natural inclinations under tight rein. For example, Caroline was convinced that Cromwell Road was suffering from recurring back trouble, a condition that GWR had failed to treat effectively. She, in company with a number of other Border owners, had blind faith in the 'magic touch' of George Armitage – the mysterious back man who demanded to be left alone in the box when he treated a patient, so that the tricks of his trade could never be copied. Armitage aroused powerful emotions. You either loved him or loathed him. Caroline was a disciple. Ken and Rhona Oliver were also known to use his services. The Boss was not a follower. Cromwell Road moved to Hassendean Bank amidst much grinding of teeth at Greystoke, where the owner's protective zeal on behalf of her horses clashed with Gordon's own determination to do things 'his own way'.

Caroline Berry was also likely to arrive at the stables unannounced to check on the welfare of her horses. On one such occasion she was aghast to discover that one of her team was suffering from a minor ringworm infection and that no one had seen fit to inform her. Relations between owner and trainer may have cooled after a period of years, but on the positive side the continued success of the Berry horses proved to be an invaluable advertisement for Richards's yard. Claude Berry himself held The Boss in high regard. He says: 'Gordon was a master trainer. I had tremendous admiration for his professional ability; and though he may not have had much of a sense of humour, he could still be a source of much amusement, particularly when it came to mispronouncing names. He was always extolling the qualities of Wrekin Rambler as an ideal sire of jumpers, describing him as "a strong and majestic stallion". All very true, but he rather spoiled the effect of this flattering build-up by constantly referring to his idol as "Weakling Rambler"!'

Jimmy McGhie had a similar number of horses in training at Greystoke during the early '70s. He too could be demanding when it came to the running of his horses, but he regarded them more as business assets than members of the family. The McGhies have always enjoyed the cut and thrust of the betting market. Jimmy's clinical interpretation of the formbook, allied to his razor-sharp assessment of the potential ability, strengths and weaknesses of his horses, enabled him to win the battle of wits with the layers to such an extent that his account was closed with several leading firms. The almost daily struggle to discover bookmakers bold enough to take his bets led eventually to a mood of frustration. In between times, however, he organised a series of daring coups interspersed with the occasional unforeseen disaster.

The most publicised of these reverses concerned the last-fence drama surrounding Proud Stone in the 1972 Mackeson Gold Cup. Jimmy McGhie followed the sensible (though unwritten) law that it was folly to risk substantial money backing horses over fences. The risk factor was simply too serious to ignore, but he forsook his creed in the case of Proud Stone, believing that there were sound reasons for reckoning the gamble to be worth the risk.

McGhie had bought the son of Pampered King out of Sally Hall's stable as a three-year-old. Unlike Caroline Berry, he did not dabble in the breeding business. He had his own ideas about pedigrees and as a proven judge of form and no mean horseman himself, he preferred to select his team on the basis of conformation and ability in the book. Proud Stone was not to be the last money-spinner that McGhie would purchase from the Hall's well-stocked Brecongill stable, but he proved to be the best bargain of the lot. This versatile performer was equally successful over fences as he was over hurdles. Splendidly tough and consistent, his limitations were an open book to both his owner and his trainer. Gordon placed Proud Stone with cool and well planned precision. A minor upwards adjustment in class or distance would be sufficient to keep him out of the winner's circle without awakening official suspicions. Proud Stone had spent much of the 1971–72 season on the sidelines. He had won twice from six outings but his campaign had been aborted after he was beaten three quarters of a length by Irish Rain in a handicap chase at Ayr's December meeting. The following July the gelding resumed training 100 per cent sound with the Mackeson as his autumn target. Backward on his seasonal reappearance in the three-mile Corunna Hurdle at Newcastle in October, and partnered by Jonjo O'Neill, he trailed the field and was pulled up before the third last.

A week in advance of the Mackeson Proud Stone returned to Gosforth Park for the Simonburn Handicap Chase. He still needed the race to put the fine edge of fitness on him for the trip to Cheltenham, and despite the presence of in-form duo Red Swan and Celtic Gold, The Boss left nothing to chance. In addition to Proud Stone, he ran the progressive Chariot Fair with Ron Barry in the saddle. The champion jockey ensured that there would be no hanging around. He swept Chariot Fair into the lead and the combination was never in danger of defeat. Proud Stone gave chase at a respectable distance and stayed on at one pace to finish second. It was enough to satisfy his trainer that he would go to Cheltenham cherry ripe, but not sufficiently outstanding to excite the bookmakers.

Neither McGhie nor his trainer made the trip south. Their absence could be taken as further indication that stable confidence behind Proud Stone was less than enthusiastic. In fact the opposite was the truth. Richards was convinced that Proud Stone was travelling south with a winning chance second to none. He had already conveyed this impression to Jimmy McGhie. Jonjo O'Neill was left in no doubt about the part he was expected to play. He recalls that The Boss had taken him aside before he had left Greystoke, with Jean Richards at the wheel of the Mercedes. In his autobiography, *Jonjo*, he relates how Gordon had emphasised the necessity for patience and the importance of waiting behind the leaders before producing Proud Stone to challenge going to the last fence. 'Produce him, then, and you will win!' the trainer repeated, jabbing his forefinger fiercely into Jonjo's chest.

Those close to the Greystoke supremo frequently assert that one of his most invaluable qualities as a trainer was the ability to produce a horse at the very peak of condition on the day of a big race. This was certainly the case with Proud Stone. He was 110 per cent for the Mackeson and Gordon was in no doubt about his gilt-edged chances of success.

Off-course betting activity in the shops suggested that Proud Stone had his supporters. His early morning quote of 25–1 in places was shaved to 16s but down at Cheltenham lack of interest in the Richards contender lulled the ring into a false sense of security. Shortly before the off, Proud Stone reverted to 20–1 without the layers being knocked over in the rush.

Up in Lochmaben the McGhies settled down to watch the action on BBC *Grandstand*. Hal McGhie, Jimmy's eldest son, recalls: 'Gordon had been bullish about the chances of Proud Stone and we were expecting him to run a big race. It is wrong to say that father had a big bet. By his standards he had a modest investment and it was unusual for him to have a bet over fences anyhow. The vibes had to be extra good for him to break this rule. I am the same. In general I don't like my horses to run over fences, but I made an exception when Noyan went to Punchestown a couple of years ago and the decision proved a profitable one.'

What Hal failed to add here was his visit to the fortune teller shortly before Noyan's win. The lady with the crystal ball foretold that the colours red and green would prove lucky. Impressed with this prophecy, Hal immediately ordered a change of strip. Out went his familiar light-blue and black stripes. In came the green and red with the happiest of results!

In the 1973 Mackeson, however, Jimmy McGhie didn't actually need to strike a major bet to obtain a lucrative return. Even on the day of the race the odds were 20–1, and longer at ante-post, so it was a case of putting on a little to win a great deal. Sit back and enjoy it, as the saying goes. But the old cliché of 'so near yet so far' was unfortunately more appropriate that afternoon with Proud Stone at Cheltenham. He gave Jonjo a dream of a ride and the youngster followed his instructions to the letter. He waited and waited some more before unleashing his mount to challenge at the final obstacle. Only then did the feverish excitement of the moment destroy his cool. Instead of sitting tight and letting Proud Stone do his own work, Jonjo called for the proverbial 'big one'. Surprised by the sudden change of tactics, Proud Stone responded with such a spring-heeled leap that Jonjo was lifted vertically into the air; and when he came down, the saddle and Proud Stone were no longer there. If ever there were a classic example of being unseated, this was it. Proud Stone duly passed the post in front but his rider was down at the last fence and the photographers snapping their lenses to record the winning leap for posterity had all got their picture – Jonjo, stick aloft with a couple of feet of fresh air between his bottom and the saddle and Proud Stone still firmly on his feet with a puzzled expression on his face!

History does not relate the reaction in the McGhies' living room at Lochmaben, though with hindsight Jonjo must have been thankful that it wasn't until some seven hours later that he had to speak to Proud Stone's owner on the telephone in Gordon Richards's office and by then both owner and trainer had had time to cool down.

Jonjo was to go on to ride a stream of winners in the McGhie colours and the incident illustrates the owner's intimate understanding of the jumping game. He might be, and surely was, a fearless gambler. Yet he understood that the best laid plans can always go astray and the only sensible reaction is to say little and look to the future.

Jimmy McGhie was one of the big-time punters whom George Milburn feared would make the Richards' life a misery if Gordon moved from Beadnell to Greystoke. George was acting with the best of motives but his anxieties were misplaced. For starters, Jean Richards had the strength of character and the sound common sense to prevent such a situation arising. She was a powerful influence for the good while Gordon himself was never a serious gambler.

That is not to say that his owners did not enjoy the opportunity to land a touch. In many ways GWR appreciated the presence of a successful gambler on the roll call. As Nicky Richards observed recently, 'Owners who have the self-discipline to bet selectively and make a consistent profit from their investments can prove a help rather than a hindrance. To begin with they will spend money on buying good quality horses. Jimmy McGhie was a fine example. He had horses at Greystoke from the time that Father arrived until his death in 1976. He always bought wisely and the results speak for themselves. Horses like Proud Stone, Tussaud and Ribanco not only won him plenty of races, they also acted as eye-catching advertisements for the stable.'

Jimmy McGhie's father had been a much respected farrier whose services were in constant demand from the hunting and racing fraternity of rural Dumfries-shire. His forenames Christopher, Halliday were passed on to 'Hal' McGhie in the fullness of time and his skill as a blacksmith was shared by his son, Jimmy, who had a natural affinity with horses and never lost the habit of checking his horse's shoes before they went out to race.

Not content with the life of a country farrier, Jimmy McGhie had diversified into the dairy business. By dint of hard work, entrepreneurial flair and shrewd financial acumen, he expanded his interests at Lochmaben into the thriving profit-making concern which enabled him to diversify into racehorse ownership. He began on the hugely popular Border 'flapping' tracks, from which it was a natural progression to the ranks of recognised racing 'under rules'.

The McGhie colours first hit the racing headlines through the lucrative exploits of Magic Court, a canny purchase as a three-year-old from the yard of Noel Murless. Trained at Greystoke by Tommy Robson, the classically bred gelding, a snip at 1,300 guineas, went on to win three races on the flat; finish runner up to Grey of Falloden in the 1964 Cesarewitch; and notch ten races over hurdles, including the 1964 Champion Hurdle in the hands of Pat McCarron.

McGhie and Tommy Robson enjoyed many a skirmish with the 'old enemy', none more so than the occasion that Marsh King landed the Usher Vaux Gold Tankard at Ayr. Hal McGhie remembers picking up £2,700 in winning bets, a sum large enough in 1965 to buy a sizeable property north of the Border.

Gordon Richards and Jimmy McGhie were acquainted well before the former settled at Castle Stables. Hal continues, 'When Playlord won his first race at Bogside, he beat my father's Originator into second place, but losses were retrieved later that year and I have still got the trophy to prove it standing on the mantelpiece here at Lochmaben. The race was the Sheffield Quality Tools Hurdle and Playlord came down at the final flight, leaving Originator to win unopposed. My father and Gordon were always arguing about what would have happened if Playlord had kept his feet!

'Magic Court stayed with Tommy Robson until he retired at the age of 12, but Father moved most of his horses to John Barclay. They then moved on to Gordon after the car accident on the A6 which brought about an abrupt end to John Barclay's training career.'

Tussaud was another multiple winner trained by The Boss for Jimmy McGhie. Like Proud Stone he came from Sally Hall and won over both timber and fences for the Lochmaben owner. Tussaud may have lacked the consistency of Proud Stone, but he certainly had his moments. It was sometimes said by the jockeys who rode the McGhie horses that they only knew if the money was down when they got the leg up in the paddock.

Legend has it – and I stress that the story may well be apocryphal – of a case at an evening meeting at Hexham early in the '70s. Tussaud was already down at the two-mile start, with the jockey still unsure about the type of race he was expected to ride, when a breathless stable lad arrived at his side with the required message, having sprinted all the way from the members' enclosure.

Tussaud was not the most reliable of horses to be entrusted with the task of landing a touch. Nicky Richards never won on him – 'perhaps I was never meant to,' he jokes, 'though no one ever told me not to!' Jonjo O'Neill punched him home several times, but it was 'Big Ron' Barry who was regularly left at the sharp end. Tussaud ran his very best races with RB on board.

Hal continues, 'Father was a shade nervous of going for a touch on Tussaud. The horse tended to decide for himself if he was going to try his hardest. If he got beat people would often think that there had been funny business, when in fact Tussaud had downed tools on his own accord.'

Ron Barry recalls a tricky moment at Kelso with Tussaud on his worst behaviour and the stewards looking daggers as he dismounted in fourth place. Gordon himself is on record as saying that in the seven seasons that he trained for Jimmy McGhie, he was only once called in by the stewards to explain the running of a particular horse. That interview ironically concerned Proud Stone, then a four-year-old and running for the second time over hurdles. Gordon told me, 'Proud Stone had run down the field first time out at Ayr. I think he finished seventh or thereabouts. I knew he'd come on for the race and on the day I reckoned he was "a good thing". I told Mr McGhie and he had a biggish punt with a bookmaker who had always promised to give him a fair price about his horses. My owner wasn't so pleased when Proud Stone did the business and he discovered that he had been "on" at just 4–1. At least his face looked as long as those of the Newcastle stewards when they quizzed me about the improvement in form. To be 'onest, I was a bit worried myself, but I told them that Proud Stone was the sort who always came on a treat for his first run and they took my word. A sound decision, I thought!'

ELEVEN

Not Just a Jumps Trainer

Gordon Richards ended his training career as he began it, focussing his energies on producing winners over fences. Since the end of the '80s the number of runners he sent out on the flat were few and far between, and the number of winners could be counted on the fingers of one hand – four to be precise. The two-year-old Swingaway Lady scored twice in 1990 and the versatile Sweet City picked up a couple of early races at Hamilton in 1994.

It was not always the case. The '70s saw Richards-trained horses in regular action on the level, achieving such a notable strike rate that in the latter part of the decade (continuing through until the end of the 1983 season) Greystoke could be justifiably labelled a genuine dual-purpose establishment.

Nicky Richards explains: 'Father was a workaholic and flat racing kept him busy in the summer. He wasn't a novice, y'know! He'd learnt plenty during his time with Jack Waugh and the gallops here at Greystoke were ideal for the job. Early on, owners like Jimmy McGhie and Andy Scott were actually more interested in running their horses on the flat. Pat Muldoon was another and with the prize money so poor over the jumps by the end of the '70s it made financial sense to keep going throughout the summer.'

Jimmy McGhie's decision to concentrate his forces at Greystoke provided The Boss with promising raw material on which to work. Hal, the owner's son, recalls, 'My father left Magic Court with Tommy Robson but after John Barclay's road accident he transferred the rest of the team to Gordon and never regretted the move. Autograph looked like being a real money-spinner until he broke a leg. Father preferred stayers to sprinters and though he didn't breed any of his winners, he had a sound working knowledge of pedigrees and took a keen interest in the progeny of the French stallion Auriban. Hemon, who landed several nice touches at the beginning of the '70s, was by Auriban and so was Ribanco, who showed good form as a three-year-old and would have won plenty more races if he had stayed sound.'

Ribanco did not win as a juvenile but strengthened up as a three-year-old. Nicky Richards partnered him to a smooth success on his seasonal reappearance in an amateur riders' race at Redcar; and after three subsequent outings in which he finished on the heels of the placed horses, he gained his second win in a long-distance maiden at Ayr.

This victory is indelibly printed on Nicky Richards's mind. He recalls, 'The Boss had got Ribanco in peak condition but Mr McGhie had his sights set on bigger fish. Johnny Greenaway had been booked to ride and it was made pretty clear to him that Ribanco was "not expected"!'

The message fell on deaf ears, though for three-quarters of the race the Malton-based jockey had Ribanco quietly tucked away behind the leading bunch with little room to manoeuvre. Nicky continues: 'With less than two furlongs to go Ribanco was in a pocket, still on the bit but seemingly with nowhere to go. Then, without warning, Greenaway took a pull and switched him to the outside. Once Ribanco saw daylight he quickened clear in a matter of strides, winning cleverly, ears pricked. Mr McGhie's face was black as thunder and Johnny Greenaway made the short trip from winner's circle to the haven of the weighing room faster than any jockey I have seen either before or afterwards. Once inside the jockeys' room, he sensibly stayed put for the rest of the day!'

All this talk of gambles won and lost might suggest that GWR was privy to the 'sting'. Nothing could be further from the truth. Gordon was never a major player in the ring. Early on he did occasionally risk the odd hundred, but in the main he was happy to have played his part in the business by producing the horses cherry ripe for battle. Greystoke's reputation as a gambling yard, if not quite a figment of the public's imagination, was exaggerated. Yes, throughout the '70s The Boss did train for a number of well-known 'faces'. He enjoyed the challenge while it lasted, more so because of the quality of the horses involved rather than the money won. Once the yard reverted to its role as a National Hunt stable specialising in the production of top-class chasers – as was the case from the early '80s – the gambling pre-fix was abandoned and the quest for major prize money, rather than 'bets won', became the priority.

In the '70s Gordon tended to use a spread of jockeys on his flat race runners. The veteran Alec Russell was still a popular choice. Tony Murray got the call at regular intervals with top northern names like Edward Hide and Johnny Seagrave also used when available. Jimmy McGhie, though, was never averse from employing a claiming rider when he thought that a few pounds saved in the saddle could prove a crucial advantage. Nicky Richards himself squeezed home a number of winners in the McGhie silks and for the 1973 Top Rank Club Handicap at Newcastle's July meeting the responsibility of driving home Ribanco fell to the well-regarded northern apprentice Tom O'Ryan. At the time Tom was attached to Pat Rohan's thriving yard at Malton. He swapped the jockey's whip for the journalist's biro nearly 20 years ago. Today he is one of the three northern-based staff reporters on the *Racing Post*, combining daily work at the racecourse with contributing colourful and perceptive features on leading racing personalities.

Tom, whose father rode Distel to win the 1946 Champion Hurdle, rode 85 winners including victories on such familiar names as Alverton and Gunner B. He was 18 and still claiming the seven-pound allowance when he was booked to partner Ribanco. The occasion proved one of the highlights of his riding career. Reflecting on the moment, he says: 'I'd been across to ride work at Greystoke a number of times and was well aware that Ribanco had a lot of ability. He stayed the trip well and had a high cruising rate. The Boss had been confident before the race and everything went as planned. Ribanco did his job like a true professional and we ran out as cosy one-and-a-half length winners from Moire. To make matters even better, the race was on television, which counted a lot in those days.'

Tom O'Ryan enjoyed further success for the Greystoke stable on Hooked Again and Drumdella, but the Top Rank was the last flat race to be won by Ribanco. He pulled up lame and missed the remainder of the season. Although he managed to win four times over hurdles in 1974–75, the leg trouble recurred and he was finally sold on cheaply without ever fulfilling his potential.

O'Ryan remained on good terms with GWR right up to the end. He recalls, 'He was always very helpful when I rang him to ask about running plans or to check a story. Back in my riding days I found him fierce but fair. He would make it clear how he wanted his horses to be ridden and provided that you carried out his orders he would be satisfied. Mind you, if you didn't obey the instructions then he would blow a fuse – win or lose!'

With hindsight, Gordon did more than pick up the odd hint from his teenage experiences with Jack Waugh and Ivor Anthony. Throughout his training career he clearly modelled his behaviour and honed much of his horse management on the lessons learnt at Chilton and Wroughton. In many ways he was absolutely right. Quite apart from their obvious credentials as leaders of their profession, they were both forthright characters whose man management was mightily effective, even if it might not have been politically correct.

Jimmy McGhie's health deteriorated in the mid-'70s. In the months leading up to his death in January 1976, Hal acted as his chauffeur to the races. His last substantial purchase was Asset, a rangy son of Birdbrook. As a three-year-old colt Asset had won four times for Sally Hall. Hal records: 'My father had a close rapport with Sally's mother, Agnes, and on her recommendation he bought Asset unseen for £6,000 with the agreement that a further £2,000 would be handed over when he won his first race in the McGhie colours. Asset was just the sort of horse who appealed to my father. He was as tough as teak, stayed a mile and three-quarters on the flat and seemed sure to make the grade over hurdles.'

Jimmy McGhie was far from well in the summer of 1975, but the chance to land the Northumberland Plate kept the adrenalin flowing and Asset did his level best to realise the ambition. Previously successful in a one-mile, five-furlong handicap at Ayr, he started 14–1 for Newcastle's two-mile marathon. Always prominent in the hands of Pat Kelleher, he came with every chance between the last two furlongs, but could not quite go through with his effort and was beaten less than five lengths into fifth place behind Grey God.

By sad coincidence Asset was to follow a similar fate to Ribanco. He only ran twice more on the flat. Though he won three out of three as a novice hurdler in 1974–75, and was again successful over hurdles at Ayr in 1976–77 he was never allowed to reach his peak. Hal McGhie continues, 'Father died in January 1976. The following year Gordon and I travelled down to Cheltenham, confident that Asset would win the Coral Hurdle, only for the heavens to open on the morning of the race and the ground turn from good to firm to soft. Asset had to have a sound surface and was taken out. He was sent to Liverpool for the long-distance hurdle, but he was over the top by then and was pulled up lame after jumping three flights. He never raced again.'

While Jimmy McGhie was the quiet, ice cool investor, Andy Scott and Pat Muldoon belonged to the extrovert, flamboyant variety. The former had started a timber company near Alnwick with little more than a single 'hired' lorry to his name, but through the sweat of his own brow and his natural flair for salesmanship he had cornered the market on both sides of the Border. Later he was to take out a licence to train over the jumps and, christened the 'Wizard of Wooperton' by the racing media, he was to win a County Hurdle with Hill's Guard and land a series of infectious gambles with the likes of Another Captain, Handycuff and Stop It. Now in his 70s, Andy Scott has returned to the trainers' ranks with stables at Otterburn. Back in the early 1970s, though, Andy was more interested in the Flat. Le Coq d'Or and Downstream, his two best known horses, were both trained for him by Gordon Richards.

Le Coq d'Or won eight times between 1971 and 1973. A compact horse, he inherited his turn of foot from Goldhill, his sire, but he stayed a mile well and was effective at a mile and a quarter. The Greystoke colt proved a model of consistency as a three-year-old, scoring four times and only finishing out of the first four twice in twelve outings.

The year 1972 saw Le Coq d'Or competing in valuable northern handicaps. He picked up a further three victories, as well as being placed fourth in the Irish Sweeps Lincoln and third in the Usher Vaux Gold Tankard (then rated one of the highlights of Ayr's May meeting). Gordon had him sharp and ready for the Lincoln. Frankie Durr, a rare booking for the Greystoke trainer, had the mount but Le Coq d'Or was ignored in the betting. Drawn two and sent off at 33–1, he lay handy on the far side, had every chance between the last two furlongs, but could not quicken when Sovereign Bill and Edward Hide lay down the gauntlet passing the furlong marker and weakened close home. He returned to Doncaster a week later to gain compensation in the Easter Apprentices' Stakes getting up in the shadow of the post to pip Royal Hart by a short head.

Steve Perks, then a five-pound claimer with Reg Hollinshead, gave Le Coq d'Or an artistic ride to land the Ayrshire Handicap at the Western Meeting in September. Gordon had told Andy Scott that he thought the colt was better than ever. He had enjoyed a midsummer break before making a winning return over ten furlongs at Newcastle's August meeting and had been ticking over quietly during the intervening fortnight. Later in his career, when he had progressed to training his own horses, Andy Scott gained the reputation for being a fearless punter. In the early '70s the bookies were not yet running scared and Le Coq d'Or's owner was able to get on at 8–1. The four-year-old went off a point shorter. Fifth turning into the home straight, Le Coq d'Or made his move between the last two furlongs and quickened near the judge to beat Mercia Boy by a head.

As a five-year-old Le Coq d'Or won the Dobson Peacock at Newcastle's big June meeting, gaining revenge on Queen's Fantasy by a decisive three lengths. With just a little more luck in running he would have added the Usher Vaux Gold Tankard to his portfolio. He was beaten a short head by Tripper, but was in front a stride past the post. He was to occupy the runner's-up berth twice more at Ayr in 1973 and defeat by Tack On in the Wills Silver Goblets cost connections dearly.

By 1975 age, and in particular the handicapper, were catching up with the Greystoke money-spinner. He drew a blank and retired to stud in Northumberland, becoming a popular and successful sire of winners under both codes.

Downstream, by Derring Do, was a year-younger half-brother to Le Coq d'Or. He was a neat athletic colt who won at five furlongs as a three-year-old, but with increasing age developed into a smart six- and seven-furlong performer. Placed in all five of his two-year-old races, he broke his duck at the eighth attempt making all the running in the hands of Jock Skilling to win the five-furlong North Berwick Maiden at Edinburgh by five lengths from Princess Karen.

Nicky Richards recalls, 'Downstream was always happiest bowling along in front. The Boss did his best to get him to settle and a couple of times as a four-year-old he was held up with some success. But he preferred to dominate and even at seven furlongs he ran his best races from the front.'

Alec Russell partnered Downstream to easy wins at Carlisle and Ayr and was again in the saddle when the colt ran arguably the best race of his career, beaten a neck by Some Hand in the 1973 Northumberland Sprint Trophy at Newcastle. *Raceform* commented: 'With leader, effort and switched left below distance; ran on inside final furlong; finished 2nd, beaten a neck; disqualified for causing interference.'

The stewards, it seems, had little option. Downstream cut directly across Flintham, the mount of Jimmy Lindley, as he was switched to make his challenge. Flintham, finishing third past the post, was badly baulked and relegation was inevitable. Compensation was sought in the Wigan Sprint Handicap at Haydock with Lester Piggott in the saddle. The maestro did his best, but Downstream lost second place by a short head. Downstream recorded his biggest win as a four-year-old, landing the 1973 Mark Lane Handicap by three lengths from Rock Signal. That was his final victory. He was never right the following season and was sent to the Doncaster September Sales. Though always running in the name of Andy Scott, Downstream was part-owned by

Jack Jeffreys who wished to dissolve the partnership. Scott retained him for 1,750 guineas only to transfer him to Great Habton where Peter Easterby persuaded him to win over five furlongs at Redcar and Thirsk. The effort took its toll. Downstream never raced again and was sold at the Doncaster August Sales for a beggarly 260 guineas.

Despite Andy Scott's lengthy absence from the training ranks, he kept in touch with the jumping game by sponsoring a handicap hurdle at Kelso. He has fond memories of his time with Gordon Richards and, tongue in cheek, prior to shouting home Shinerolla in his sponsored hurdle at Kelso, he paid tribute to the Greystoke trainer: 'Gordon was a fine trainer on the flat . . . Not as good as me over the jumps, perhaps, but he could get them fit for the summer game, no trouble; and he did a right good job with my two horses.'

At the time Scott was piling up the prize money with Le Coq d'Or and Downstream, Pat Muldoon was poised to take over as leading owner at Greystoke. Muldoon hailed from Bo'ness. A successful wine and spirits merchant with a thriving business in Armadale, his appetite had been whetted when Sunny Bay, the family's first horse, had won over hurdles in March 1972 – cheered on by all his staff who had been invited down to Ayr for the occasion. In the summer of 1973 Gordon Richards bought Barrein out of Derrick Candy's, with a long-term view of winning decent races over hurdles but with the immediate target of 'making hay' on the flat.

Barrein became Muldoon's first flat-race winner when he landed a gamble in the Tote Roll Up Handicap at Haydock. Muldoon's McIntyre tartan and red-sleeved colours – made famous through the exploits of Sea Pigeon – were more familiar during the jumps season, but they were seen to good effect on the level through the efforts of Sonnenblick. Gordon Richards had secured this powerful colt by Song for 6,000 guineas as a yearling and word that he was something out of the ordinary had alerted the bookmakers before he made his début at Hamilton in July 1975. Partnered by Jonjo O'Neill, he obliged by three-quarters of a length from Gemina with the rest of the field struggling in their wake. The duo followed up in convincing style at Newcastle, but a rather more ambitious attempt to capture the Solario Stakes at Sandown in September ended in anticlimax when Sonnenblick became very stirred up in the preliminaries and finished down the field behind Over To You.

The regard with which Sonnenblick was held at Greystoke was reflected by his presence in the line-up for the Tote Free Handicap at the 1976 Newmarket Craven Meeting. He may have been flying a shade high in this classy company but he went on to finish fourth in the Northern Free Handicap, then considered a race of some significance and his subsequent performances marked him down as one of the most successful flat-race horses that Gordon ever trained. Sonnenblick dead-heated for second place behind the awesome Roman Warrior in the Canada Dry Shield at Ayr before occupying the same runner's-up berth in the Northumberland Sprint Trophy at Newcastle. He went on to win the Wykeham Handicap at York's Ebor meeting before cantering over his rivals to take the Shaw Memorial at Ayr by seven lengths from King Willi. Sonnenblick ended his three-year-old career beaten a short head by Briarvanter in a competitive sprint at Redcar. By the time the 1977 flat race season got under way Pat Muldoon had transferred all his horses to the care of Peter Easterby at Great Habton.

Rundontwalk was another speedy youngster whose progress persuaded GWR that an expansion of his flat-race interests would be worth while. This son of Takawalk was a diminutive foal. He only fetched 1,600 guineas but this represented riches compared with his purchase price as a yearling. Nicky Richards took a shine to him despite his lack of substance and bought him for chickenfeed; 350 guineas in fact. He chuckles, 'Father's face was a picture when he saw what I had bought, but Rundontwalk was a tough little beggar who had plenty of early toe.' As a two-year-old he proved to be a real pocket battleship, growing sideways rather than upwards. *Timeform* described him as 'small, strong and robust' and he recouped his purchase price many times over before the end of his juvenile career. The colt scored at Ayr and Thirsk early on for Cockermouth hotelier Sammy Romano, but it was his placed efforts in the Chesters Stakes at Newcastle and the Sir Gatric Stakes at Doncaster that underlined his potential.

Rundontwalk hit top form as a three-year-old, finishing second to Delayed Action in the Field Marshal at Haydock, dead-heating with Gold Loom at Ripon, running on bravely to take fourth place behind Urray Harry at York's May meeting and finally making it fourth time lucky – holding on in the gamest possible style to take the Tote Sprint Trophy at the Ascot Heath fixture by a head from his old rival, Pennina. Pat had to dig deep on Rundontwalk to prevail at Ascot and arguably the colt was never again quite the potent force he had been as a three-year-old. Indeed it could be said that while GWR was the soul of patience with his jumpers, he hated to see his flat-race team standing idle in their boxes. Once 'fettled-up' for the season, they were expected to earn their corn. Rundontwalk was brought out at regular intervals in an attempt to emulate his Ascot victory, but he lost his enthusiasm for the fight and never obliged again.

Astute punters also cottoned on to the realisation that by the autumn Gordon was busying himself with his jumpers and that the time to support the Greystoke flat-race strength was in the spring or early summer. There were, of course, exceptions. However a glance at the formbook will show that the majority of his flat-race performers were at their best during the first half of the season.

By the end of the '70s The Boss had increased his flat-race strength to over 20 horses. He had decided to become a 'dual-purpose' trainer on a major scale, and to ease the load on his regular staff he opted for a stable jockey whose responsibilities would be both to look after the flat racehorses at home and to partner a proportion of them on the racecourse. Michael Wood, not long out of his apprenticeship and a well regarded lightweight, got the vote.

Michael had served his time with Steve Norton at High Hoyland near Barnsley. He was still claiming the five-pound allowance when he arrived at Greystoke and with hindsight would never have missed the opportunity. He reflects, 'You were expected to turn your hand to most things. The Boss was a hard taskmaster and his rollickings could be frightening, but they were often deserved and once he had blown his top it was all forgotten. I had some great times in my three full seasons there; and the knowledge which I picked up working under Gordon served me in good stead when I started up my own livery stable.'

Michael remembers riding out three lots most mornings. He continues: 'We had around 20 flat-race horses in the yard and not more than half a dozen lads available to ride work on them. Sometimes I'd go out four times in a morning and then be expected to muck out and turn my hand at anything from breaking-in the youngsters with Tommy Walsh to cleaning them up after they'd enjoyed their daily roll in the mud and sand. The Boss was a genius with the jumpers but he always took a close interest in his flat-race team. He loved to do things "his own way" but was prepared to listen to the opinions of his work riders. He used to hear you out, then go and try out his own ideas first. If they failed then he would act on our advice. If that proved useful, he was always ready to come back and show his appreciation.'

Though Gordon expanded his flat-race team towards the end of the '70s, it proved a case of quantity rather than quality. The stable picked up a series of modest prizes with horses like Hard Held, Black Charmer, Dime A Dancer, and Cumnock Scouse. 'I rode winners on all of them,' adds Wood. 'They may not have been much out of the ordinary, but GWR had few superiors when it came to placing his horses and knowing when they were ready to win. If he told the owner to have "the odd fiver" on his horse, he was never very wide of the mark.

'Home Ground and Man Alive were two of the best horses I rode for Gordon. Man Alive was to go on to win the Mackeson at Cheltenham, but he was a bit useful on the flat and The Boss had his eyes on the 1978 Cesarewitch. I hadn't been at Greystoke very long when he put me up at Chester in the long-distance Black Friars Handicap. His last race had been the Chester Cup back in May. Clive Eccleston had the mount and Man Alive had run a great race to finish eighth behind Sea Pigeon. He'd had a long break but I knew that he was pretty fit and The Boss told me that he was the type to go well fresh.'

Man Alive lived up to his trainer's forecast. Michael had him smartly into his stride and turning into the short straight he had quickened into third place. Wood recalls: 'He gave me a grand ride, but began to tire approaching the furlong post and could only run on at the same pace.' Man Alive finished third to Valuation and the race brought him on well. The Cesarewitch was not beyond his capabilities but Gordon reckoned that he needed one more outing to blow away the cobwebs. Man Alive thrived on a sound surface: with the going described as 'good to firm' for Edinburgh's September meeting, the grey was in the line-up for the Musselburgh Handicap. The Boss indicated to Jim Ennis, the gelding's owner, that he was confident of a good run. But the reputation of the John Dunlop-trained Albeni ensured that Man Alive would go off at a backable price. In the event his starting price was 11–4 and Michael Wood rode a confident race on the Greystoke stayer. Always prominent and travelling keenly throughout, he turned into the straight a close third, made his move between the final two furlongs and stayed on in determined style under pressure to score by a shade over two lengths from the favourite.

Next stop the Tote Cesarewitch. Man Alive had friends in the market, though the leading bookmakers were of the opinion that he did not have the flat-race class to upset either Centurion or Knighthood, the market leaders. Sadly they were proved correct. Man Alive tried his hardest for Michael Wood, holding his position in the leading bunch until being outpaced over the final two furlongs. He was beaten less than five lengths into fifth place. Much to the chagrin of connections, he missed out on fourth position by three quarters of a length. Seventeen had faced the starter and the layers were paying a quarter the odds for the first four past the post.

Compensation was at hand! Three weeks later Man Alive went down to Cheltenham for the Mackeson meeting and landed the Nicolet Instrument Hurdle. Big Jim Ennis had certainly struck a bargain when he went to 8,800 guineas to buy him out of Maurice Camacho's stable at the 1977 Doncaster November Sales. Word passed that the Malton trainer was none too pleased to lose Man Alive and understandably so. He had been a profitable servant for the Camacho stable. The painful lesson was to be rubbed home the following autumn when Man Alive gained a deserved success under Ron Barry in the Mackeson Gold Cup.

Encouraged by the success of Man Alive, owner Jim Ennis invested in a yearling colt by No Mercy. Somehow the name of the sire seemed to rub off on his progeny. Certainly the rub of the green never favoured his compact grey son, who was christened Home Ground. Michael Wood remembers him well. 'He was a tough little barrel of a horse when he arrived at Greystoke,' says the ex-jockey. 'He had plenty of character, hardly ever running a bad race while he was under the care of The Boss, but he never seemed to get any luck. I can't remember the number of times he finished second, only that it was all too often and many of these near misses came in really good class races.'

Wood's remarks are spot on. Home Ground was a splendid advertisement for the skill of his trainer. He did in fact finish runner-up nine times out of the fifteen races that he ran for The Boss. He was only once out of the first four and that was at Thirsk as a three-year-old when he made late headway to finish fifth in the Coral Classic Stakes. Home Ground won three times as a juvenile and the following season, 1980, he passed the post in second place on five consecutive occasions before Jim Ennis ran out of patience and transferred the grey to Barry Hills's Lambourn stable from where Home Ground never managed to reach the frame. During the winter Home Ground was gelded and returned to the north to be trained by Peter Easterby, who campaigned him over hurdles with mixed success.

Jim Ennis likes nothing better than to put one over the bookies – but he is a calculating investor rather than a speculative gambler, and convinced though he was that Home Ground would develop into a money-spinning juvenile, he bided his time. Gordon chose Carlisle as the venue for the grey's first appearance in public. The Blackwell track was the Richards' local course and word that Home Gound was useful had preceded him. The colt went off at 4–1 second favourite with Michael Wood in the saddle. Michael recalls, 'We were never far from the pace, but Tommy Fairhurst's Divetta always had the legs of us. She had run a promising race behind Silly Prices at Ripon and she ran out an easy winner. Home Ground found his stride inside the final furlong and ran on in determined style to dead heat for second place.'

The Boss was well satisfied and Divetta carried the colours of Tom Carrick – not to be confused with Alan Carrick, whose Moybrook had already opened his account at Ayr, a course where both he and his trainer were to enjoy many more happy days. Jim Ennis maintained his watching brief at Newcastle where Home Ground traded at 7–1 and again finished runner-up; this time to the Peter Easterby-trained Bonol. Steve Cauthen had been booked to ride and after being switched to make his challenge, Home Ground was doing all his best work in the finish. Michael Wood was back in the plate at Ayr for the Glen Sannox Maiden. This time the money was down. The grey was supported at 7–4 favourite and the jockey only had to shake the reins in between the last two furlongs for his mount to get the message and storm home two and a half lengths clear.

A visit to Thirsk for the Coral Classic Stakes in early August proved expensive. Michael Wood, once more entrusted with the mount, experienced a frustrating ride. Slow into his stride, Home Ground was last turning into the straight. The colt then hung towards the far rail, passing the two-furlong marker, and despite running on he passed the post in fifth place. This was the only time that Home Ground failed to reach the first four during his two-year-old campaign and Wood lost out for the rest of the autumn in which Greystoke's star juvenile won twice at Haydock; finished a respectable second in the Knavesmire Nursery at York's Ebor meeting; and finally showed his quality by taking fourth place in the Somerville Tattersalls Stakes at Newmarket.

Home Ground's consistency at a most competitive level persuaded The Boss to rate him the best two-year-old to have passed through his hands. He trained on to hold his own as a leading northern three-year-old. After Michael Wood had given him an early pipe-opener at Doncaster, the burly colt ran up a sequence of five consecutive near-misses, culminating in a controversial disqualification in the valuable Norwest Holst Trophy at York's May meeting.

Edward Hide was in the saddle and the competitive nature of the race can be judged by Home Ground's starting price. The grey was sent off at 20–1, but his performance belied the length of his odds. Home Ground ran the race of his life: always prominent, he still held a slight lead entering the final furlong, but under hard driving hung left on the surge to the line and passed the post three parts of a length behind the much-vaunted Moorstyle. It had been a really gutsy effort, but the stewards adjudged that his antics inside the last half-furlong had caused significant interference. He was disqualified and placed last.

To Gordon's dismay Jim Ennis determined to remove Home Ground from Greystoke and send him south to Lambourn, hoping that the change of scenery would lead to a change of fortune. He was proved right, but not alas in the manner he anticipated. Perhaps pining for the soft mists and rugged fells of his adopted Cumbria, Home Ground lost the will to compete. His stay with Barry Hills was short-lived. 1981 saw him at Great Habton with Peter Easterby, gelded and aimed at a new career over hurdles. He proved a useful recruit to the winter game, but his heyday had been with The Boss at Greystoke and his departure coincided with a gradual winding down of GWR's flat-race ambitions. 'Gradual' was the operative word. There was no clear-cut decision and the stable continued to send out its share of winners. The years of plenty, though, lay between 1978 and 1981.

Pinkerton's Man, an above-average two-year-old, won his first two races at Hamilton and Newcastle. Then there was Moybrook, the Ayr specialist. Home-bred by Alan Carrick by The Brianstan out of River Moy, who had won over fences for Carlisle trainer Billy Atkinson, Moybrook won twice as a three-year-old at the West of Scotland course in 1979, beating the speedy Cree Song by three quarters of a length in May and scoring a comfortable four-length success over First Class Mail at the August meeting. Michael Wood was the winning jockey on both occasions. The stable jockey steered Moybrook to his third Ayr success early in his four-year-old career and it was over the same course in July of that summer that Moybrook went close to landing the prestigious Tote Sprint Trophy. Michael Wood recalls: 'Primula Boy made all that day holding on to win by two and a half lengths. I had to ask Moybrook for his effort earlier than I wanted and he used up his effort getting to the leader before the furlong marker. He stayed on well enough but the leader went away again close home.'

Moybrook was back in the winner's circle as a five-year-old, beating Tobermory Boy at Nottingham; but within a month he was dead, the victim of a freak accident in the stalls at Redcar. He reared up in the stalls, hit his head a sickening blow on the superstructure and fractured his skull.

Coriace and City's Sister were admirable race mares. The former won at Thirsk as a three-year-old in 1977, but enjoyed her best season in 1980 when she scored three times, being partnered by a different jockey on each occasion. Edward Hide rode her to win the Cumberland Plate, the highlight of Carlisle's summer meeting by a neck from Credit Centre. The Boss was 'over the moon': Carlisle was his local course and 20 years ago the Cumberland Plate was still a fashionable race to win. Hide, the master tactician, timed his challenge to perfection, bringing Coriace with a long steady run from the bottom of the hill to put her nose in front only a couple of strides short of the line. Gordon had saddled five winners on the same card at the November jumping meeting in 1979, but this victory in Carlisle's major event of the racing year gave him just as much pleasure.

Jonjo O'Neill gained a follow-up success on Coriace at the next Carlisle fixture and Michael Wood did the business at Newcastle later in the season. City's Sister, the dam of Better Times Ahead (the gallant grey who was the last horse on which The Boss ever rode work) liked to dominate. Owned by Garstang farmer Ted Briggs, she made all to win at Thirsk and Haydock in 1981; and the following season Martin Fry drove her right out to win two races in decisive style at Hamilton.

GWR's reputation as an instructor of top jump jockeys was second to none, but it is sometimes forgotten that he was also responsible for doing all the early groundwork towards the education of John Carroll – one of the finest horsemen riding on the flat today. As a youngster John used to spend his summer holidays staying with Ken Tuer on his farm near Tirril. Ken was a successful permit holder, responsible among other things for selling Forest King to near-neighbour Ken Hogg (now of Isle of Man fame) for 125 guineas. He introduced John Carroll to Ron Barry, who in turn mentioned his name to The Boss, then on the look-out for a promising lad to help Michael Wood with the education of the two-year-olds.

Invited by Gordon to come and work in the stables at Greystoke as a holiday job, the diminutive Carroll jumped at the chance. He was only 13 and weighed just under five and a half stone. John recounts, 'I managed to persuade my parents to let me stay with the Tuers and spend my last year at school in Penrith at the Ullswater Secondary Modern. I left at 14 and immediately signed on as an apprentice. Gordon sent me down to Newmarket to attend the British School of Racing under the direction of Johnny Gilbert. It was an eight-week course and did me the world of good. Back at Greystoke I soon settled into the routine of mucking out and doing my "three or four". I was very much the junior member of the team but had a great time. I was given digs in the village and enjoyed the crack with the likes of Martin Todhunter and Ted Stanners.'

John would ride out three lots most mornings. He adds, 'The flat horses didn't do roadwork like the jumpers. The regular routine was to canter quietly up to the top of the gallops, past the all-seeing eye of The Boss, until we reached the level stretch of turf where the fast work was done. The flat horses at Greystoke were doing interval training some time before Martin Pipe perfected the art.'

John Carroll was 17 before he had his first ride in public. He partnered the modest Propus on his seasonal début in the one-mile Craigmillar Stakes at Edinburgh's 1981 July meeting. It wasn't an auspicious start. The partnership trailed in last, but six mounts later Carroll was offered the ride on the useful Helvic in the Game Cock Apprentices' Handicap at Pontefract. The American-bred three-year-old was always close up. He turned into the short straight in second place and got his head in front inside the final furlong.

John was to spend three full seasons at Greystoke. Looking back, he says, 'I was lucky to spend my apprentice days with two inspirational guv'nors: The Boss at Greystoke and then Jack Berry at Cockerham. I got on well with Gordon. You knew where you stood with him. When you received one of his famous bollockings it was usually deserved and quickly forgotten. I shall also remember The Boss as a very successful trainer of two-year-olds; again, he had a great similarity to Jack Berry in this respect.'

John Carroll's indentures were transferred to Jack Berry for the final three years of his apprenticeship. He explains, 'Gordon was winding down on the strength of his flat-race team, so it was time for me to move on.'

Nicky Richards admits that his father had become disenchanted with the Flat – not because he had found the training in any way too tricky or demanding, but because the costs of buying replacements were rocketing. He says, 'When Father finally realised that 30,000 guineas was insufficient to buy a decent yearling, but more than enough to buy a winning jumper, he knew it was also time to run down his interests on the Flat and revert to doing the job he loved – that of training top class three-mile chasers!'

TWELVE

Trio of Champions

The National Hunt season of 1972–73 and the summer of 1973 saw Gordon Richards's stable at Greystoke achieve a unique treble. Ron Barry, the stable jockey, retained his title as the country's Champion Jockey. Jonjo O'Neill was undisputed master of the opportunity rider's table. And Nicky Richards deservedly took top spot in the race for the leading amateur on the flat.

'Big Ron' rode 125 winners in 1972–73. At the time the feat was acclaimed as a historical benchmark that would stand for decades. In fact, Ron's record was eclipsed within five seasons and ironically it was Jonjo O'Neill who consigned it to the shredder by notching a tally of 149 winners in 1977–78. The total would probably have been 150 if the helicopter ferrying Jonjo from Stratford's afternoon meeting to the final evening fixture of the season at Market Rasen had kept to its timetable. Jonjo had been booked to partner Any Second for Cumbrian permit holder Bill Murray in the 8 p.m., the Sprite Long Distance Hurdle. In fact he was circling the course waiting for the signal to land while Phil Mangan, his substitute, was driving out Any Second to a clear-cut success.

RB's major wins in the 1972–73 campaign – the Gold Cup on The Dikler and the Whitbread on Charlie Potheen – may have been for Fulke Waiwyn. But it was his guv'nor who provided him with the bulk of his bread-and-butter rides and together they covered well over 60,000 miles during the gruelling grind from August until the following June.

Travelling certainly was a grind. The motorway network in the early '70s was primitive compared to today's giant stretches of three-lane highways and the A66, the vital trans-Pennine artery from Greystoke to the North-east and Yorkshire was still single carriageway for almost its entire length. Such luxuries as the Racing Channel had not even been contemplated and for 'hands-on' trainers like Gordon Richards, always anxious to watch their horses in live action on the racecourse, time on the road was the bane of their lives. Little wonder that several of them, notably Jack Fawcus and Buster Fenningworth, perished in the process.

Gordon and his stable jockey regularly shared the driving. Gordon took the wheel on the outward journey; Ron was in charge on the homeward run. It was a custom that GWR continued all his training life until the final two seasons when, growing sick of the long journeys, he restricted his travelling to the local tracks and the major races. For the remainder he would settle back in his special 'relaxing chair' and study the action on the big screen. However in 1972 he had just turned 40, still approaching his prime. There was no fitter or more dapper trainer in the business. He looked the part too: soft brown trilby, military-style raincoat, highly polished walking shoes and binoculars dangling free from the crook of his elbow – there was no mistaking The Boss at the races! The older he became, the smarter he dressed. The raincoat was forsaken and replaced by fashionable waxed waterproofs, worn over a selection of elegantly cut suits. At home it might be sweater and cords. At the racecourse it was 'dress order' – and that went for jockeys and staff as well.

Detailed pre-race plans were laid during the journey to the course. The Boss was a stickler for detail and Ron Barry reflects that 'he would be issuing race-by-race instructions from the moment we left the stables, often to the time the car entered the trainers' car park. I never had any orders in the paddock. There weren't any more to give! Either riding out in the morning, or on the trip to the track, we would have been like dogs with a bone. Mind you, if things had not gone well there would be plenty of words exchanged in the unsaddling area and on the way home.'

Gordon's near obsession with 'doing things his way' was rigorously applied to race-riding tactics. The jockey who followed his orders to the letter, win or lose, would at the very least receive grudging approval – even praise. Those who discarded the race plan in favour of personal initiative could expect a roasting, regardless of the result.

Ron continues: 'You knew that you'd be in for a bollocking even if you'd won. The Boss was always thinking first of all about the welfare of the horse. Its best interests would be his major concern and to override his orders was tantamount to disobedience. The trouble was that in many cases the race would not be run in the way that had been anticipated and a new plan of action would be necessary. The Boss was often loath to accept this, and while his own reading of a race grew steadily better, in the early days it could be open to question.'

Discretion was a quality that Gordon took a long while to master. By the time One Man had arrived on the scene he was the model of decorum, fielding awkward questions from the media with an easy assurance born of lengthy experience. Earlier, though, he found it impossible to prevent his pent-up emotions from boiling over in the immediate aftermath of the action. He would say what he felt there and then in front of the Press in the unsaddling enclosure, rather than wait until later and then explode.

Ron Barry explains, 'When the race had not gone as planned he'd react instantly. It wasn't that he was a bad loser; more that he tended to read the race as he thought it ought to have been run. In the early days he'd take me aside the moment I dismounted rather than think what might have happened. He'd just fly off the handle rather than wait for an explanation. Mind, he improved with the job.'

By 1972–73 Ron was no longer partnering the McGhie horses. 'Not that

I'd fallen out with the man,' he adds quickly. 'Mr McGhie hardly ever blamed his jockey. He understood the game very well. But he did gamble massive amounts provided he could get on. They tell me he had a £20,000 bet on Proud Stone when he won second time out at Newcastle – a vast sum in those days. There were times, too, when the money wasn't down. It didn't happen often, but if one of his was just enjoying a breeze round he didn't mind how the jockey managed things. Only, there would be hell to pay if his wishes were ignored. After one such an occasion in a small field at Kelso, I'd told Gordon to put someone else on his horses and from then onwards either Jonjo or Nicky [Richards] rode the bulk of his team.'

Gyleburn won five times for the champion jockey in 1972–73 but arguably his best run came in defeat. Ron, who never won an Aintree Grand National, enjoyed a marvellous ride round the the big fences in the William Hill Grand National Trial at the autumn meeting. Gyleburn survived a mistake at the fifth to give his rivals a jumping lesson. Still well in contention at the final fence, he had no more to give on the run-in and finished third, a little over 16 lengths behind the winner, Glenkiln, and some four lengths adrift of L'Escargot, the runner-up. Golden Fort provided RB with four wins and Titus Oates carried him to a memorable victory in the Swift Chase at Newcastle. Even more important were the regular wins enjoyed by Ron on the Greystoke novice chasers and first-season handicappers. GWR's knack of turning out a succession of exciting young chasers was to my mind his greatest single achievement as a jumping trainer. Season after season, the Richards novice chasers would blitz the bookmakers – often first time out and invariably poised to run up a winning sequence.

The high risk of leg injury to bold jumping chasers of this calibre cost the Richards stable dearly over the years and 1972–73 was no exception. Gordon was never averse from running more than one horse in the same race, a policy that occasionally backfired on him. In the Simonburn Handicap Chase at Newcastle in November, Chariot Fair was marginally preferred in the betting to Proud Stone, but in the race itself there was never any doubt about his superiority. Given free rein by Ron Barry, he dominated the contest from pillar to post, but five days later in a less competitive event at Carlisle this most promising six-year-old slipped up at the fifth fence. He damaged a tendon and was never quite the force that he aspired to become, despite returning to action the following season.

That fence at Carlisle, incidentally, was a frequent source of anxiety. The fourth obstacle in a two-mile chase used to be the water splash, taken right in front of the stands. Horses then faced a mostly downhill run of some five furlongs until tackling the fifth fence, which was sited in the dip on the far side of the track. Judging the take-off stride, often at speed, could be tricky: punters breathed a sigh of relief once their selection had safely cleared the obstacle. Such worries are now lifted. Since 1998 the water jump has been filled in and an extra plain fence built, sited midway down the slope of the hill.

The highly rated Gone With The Wind was another expensive casualty. Ron partnered him to an impressive win at Ayr only for the gelding to begin to break blood vessels and go into decline. Erring Burn was the classiest novice chaser produced by The Boss during 1972–73. Backed down to 10–11 on his chasing début at Wetherby, he came to grief at the first but Ron Barry guided him to decisive wins at Catterick and Newcastle. Though never quite able to fulfil his potential, Erring Burn was still good enough to land a Stone's Ginger Wine Chase at Sandown.

Apart from a short break in the mid-'70s, Ron Barry rode as stable jockey for The Boss from 1966 right through until his retirement in 1983. He remained a close friend until Gordon's death last autumn. Professionally, no one either knew or understood The Boss better. 'He lived for his horses,' reflects Ron. 'As a trainer it was that instinctive rapport that was at the core of his success. At the sales, or on private buying trips, he knew exactly the type of horse he was looking for and his "eye" seldom let him down. Back in the stables and at morning exercise it was a similar story. He was always in and out of the boxes feeling legs and sometimes just standing there, watching and listening. On the gallops he liked to employ the personal touch, often riding work on the "big race hopes" to see if they gave him the right feel. In the early days he regularly had the leg up on Playlord and one summer I remember him partnering one of the least talented horses in the yard, telling everyone that he was getting him ready for "a nice touch at Perth's August meeting". I still didn't believe him when he legged me up for the seller with the advice, "Don't look so worried son; he'll win, mark my words." He was right. The slowcoach sprouted wings and had the race won well before the home turn.'

On a personal level there was no better man than Ron for defusing potentially ugly scenes. He continues: 'Gordon wasn't a great one for telling jokes but he was tremendous value when fully wound up. Simple little things could set him off, like opening the gate at the entrance to the all-weather. One horribly cold January morning The Boss and I had led the first lot out of the yard and had put distance between ourselves and the main pack of freezing cold lads. When we got to the first gate I said to Gordon, "Wait there, I'll open the gate." I dismounted and released the catch. Then, knowing full well what the reaction would be, I added, "It's a pity there are no young lads about, Boss!"

'Gordon looked over his shoulder; and with the nearest lad still some ten paces away, he let out a fusillade of expletives, tearing a strip off all and sundry before cantering off head down towards the second gate. Here the same process was repeated, often to the same unfortunate lad unless he had had the sense to change places! Mind you, they took it in good heart for the most part, knowing I had begun it all!

'The more wound up The Boss became, the greater the crack. He could be so gullible too. I once got him to believe that I hadn't been able to overtake the big stable horse-box on the road to Scotch Corner because Martin Todhunter had his foot down at 70 mph. Poor Martin, he had to put up with a torrent of abuse before he managed to convince The Boss that it had all been a wind up! In the end Gordon would see the joke and calm down. He was the same right up to the end. About a week before he died, I thought I would go over and have a chat. I found him sitting on some bales of hay talking to Alistair Duff, the owner of The Grey Monk. It was a sunny morning but The Boss looked down and far from well.

'"What's all this sitting around, then, Boss; is it a holiday camp or something?" I joked. Quick as a flash the old fighting spirit returned. He leaped to his feet, growling, "Ooh, not so much of that son. I've been up since six o'clock doing the entries and seeing they're doing things properly down at the farm." He was much happier, y'know, when someone wound him up. It didn't take much to get him going and the banter was tremendous!'

Jonjo O'Neill, blue-eyed and bushy tailed with curly hair and fresh complexion, didn't look a day older than 14 when he flew into Newcastle in early February 1972 to take up his first job in Britain as stable lad and claiming jockey. He was met at the airport by Jean Richards, who took the route back to Cumbria across the ancient 'Military Road' built in the mid-eighteenth century as a supply route by General Wade (using many of the stones originally reserved for the construction of the adjacent Hadrian's Wall). The road runs long and straight but, blessed as it is with more undulations than Epsom and Cheltenham combined, it's never been a favourite terrain for those who suffer from the horrors of motion sickness. Not far short of the Roman fort of Housesteads, and a few hundred yards from the stables of George Reed – the Northumberland-based trainer and father of Tim, the north's senior jump jockey – Jonjo was wretchedly sick. Fortunately he had had the presence of mind to issue an emergency warning and the interior of the Richards' Mercedes escaped the flood of bile. It was, though, an unpropitious start to Jonjo's new career and he always remembers the patient understanding with which Jean Richards viewed the incident.

Like everyone at Greystoke, from Gordon himself to the youngest lad, Jonjo owes a lasting debt of gratitude to Jean Richards. At Castle Stables GWR looked after the horses. Jean did everything else, from mundane matters like booking dentist appointments and satisfying the Inland Revenue, to entertaining the owners and – not least – smoothing relations between The Boss and his staff. During his first few months at Greystoke, and then again at a crucial juncture in his title-chasing season of 1972–73, Jonjo recalls two particular moments when Jean's intervention played a vital role in his decision to remain at Greystoke and eventually to break into the big time.

Jonjo's first 'winner' for the Richards stable should have been notched at Uttoxeter's mid-March meeting; but though he was first past the post on Katie-J, the margin was only a short head and in his desperation to gain the verdict Jonjo had barged his way past Pride of Coulter, the runner up. Richard Evans, the latter's rider, lodged a successful objection.

Jean had driven Jonjo to Uttoxeter and on their return to Greystoke Jonjo was trembling with apprehension at the reception he was likely to receive at the hands of The Boss. He was mightily relieved, therefore, to hear Jean argue in his favour. Thanks to her quiet words Jonjo escaped with little more than a rap on the knuckles and the advice that he was no longer in Ireland and that he couldn't get away with strong-arm tactics this side of the Water.

Come November, Jean's diplomatic qualities had to be at their persuasive best to save Jonjo from annihilation after the Proud Stone affair in the Mackeson. Later Jean was to guide Jonjo through the agonies of a badly broken right leg and the excruciating pain of a serious blood clot behind the knee. Hardly surprising, then, that Jonjo regarded her with such respect and affection thoughout his years at Greystoke.

With one disqualification to his name from only six rides, Jonjo had been in two minds about coming back to Cumbria for the beginning of the 1972–73 season. By the end of October he must have wondered how he had ever had second thoughts. Alexandra Parade gave him his first official winner at Stratford's late September meeting, despite breaking down between the last two flights. This gallant success was the opening leg of a remarkable six-timer, a feat that did not go unnoticed in the media – whose coverage then intensified, even if it was for the wrong reasons, when he was unseated in such dramatic fashion at the final fence of the Mackeson Gold Cup (a race in which he only partnered Proud Stone because Ron Barry was unable to draw the correct weight).

For the record, Jonjo's six consecutive winners came on Alexandra Parade, Hallington Burn three times and Stamper twice. Some 48 hours after his Mackeson disaster he scored at Ayr on Kirwaugh; and the following Friday he put the record at least partially right by guiding Proud Stone to a comfortable success in the Emblem Chase at Wetherby. Once again Jonjo delayed his challenge until between the final two fences, but this time he kept a firm seat as Proud Stone cleared the last and ran on well to gain deserved compensation. Other notable winners that season included the much underrated Tamalin in a novice hurdle at Catterick; the talented Sir Garnet on his hurdling début at Ayr; and an 'outside' win for Tony Dickinson on The Chisler.

Jonjo started that season as a raw recruit. By the time it drew to a close he had been acclaimed Junior Champion, his feet already a significant way up the ladder to future stardom. Later he was to have his differences with The Boss. But like Ron Barry before him, these were only temporary hiccups in a relationship that survived the stormy passages and matured into a bond of mutual respect and lasting friendship.

With hindsight, too, he recalls those long hours in the Mercedes, travelling with Ron Barry and The Boss to and from the races, as a learning curve without which his race-riding education would have been incomplete. He says, 'Ron always tells it that The Boss was the one who did all the talking, but that's only part of the truth. RB used to give as good as he got and I sat in the back listening and learning. Exchanges could get pretty heated, but these were the opinions of two of the finest horsemen in the business and the lessons I stored away from those journeys have never been forgotten.

Nicky Richards has not ridden in public for 25 years. As a teenager, though, he was regarded as one of the country's most promising amateurs under both codes; and in an age when records seem to disappear like confetti in the wind, it should be noted that Nicky Richards, the jockey, still retains his own special niche in the turf section of the *Guinness Book of Records*. He is the only known rider to have landed a winner first time out on the flat; on his initial race over hurdles; *and* on his first effort over fences.

While still 15 he partnered Unruffled to score on the flat at the now defunct Teesside Park. The following winter Watermelon provided that first success over hurdles at Ayr in the colours of Jimmy McGhie. The Lochmaben dairy farmer was also responsible for the chasing leg of Nicky's unique treble when his grand campaigner Proud Stone landed the odds in the Gosforth Park Amateur Riders Handicap Chase at Newcastle on 25 November 1972.

Nicky admits that with the passing of the years he has to jog his memory to recall the high spots of his riding career, but a glance at the records shows that his winners included such famous names as Titus Oates, The Spaniard, Canadius and old Whispering Grace (whom Neville Crump trained with such distinction for the Lycett Green family). By the time he was 17, Nicky's reputation as one of the most proficient amateur riders on the circuit was no longer restricted to the Richards camp. He was much in demand for outside rides and the bookmakers viewed his mounts with wary caution. At the same time his weight was increasing steadily. He had to accept that he came a poor third to Ron Barry and Jonjo O'Neill in the pecking order for rides under rules; and of course the opportunities for amateur riders to show their skills on the flat were nothing like so numerous as they are today.

Nicky admits, 'The Boss was not the type to give away rides just because I was his son. I had to earn those mounts in the same way as Jonjo or the lads like Tony Meaney and later Chris Brownless. Father always wanted his beloved horses to be ridden by the best men for the job. Then there was my weight. I was already turning the scales at around nine stone as a lad of 16 and getting steadily bigger all the time. I don't think that I would ever have made the grade as a professional, even over the jumps, and my days as an amateur were probably numbered.'

With hindsight Nicky's assessment is realistic, but at the time he was much in demand from Greystoke's top owners like Jimmy McGhie and Pat Muldoon. He headed the unpaid ranks in 1973; and had he not sustained a badly broken wrist in a fall at Kelso in the spring of 1974, he might well have added the National Hunt amateur title to his portfolio before increasing weight forced him to take a back seat.

Nicky endorses the views of both Ron Barry and Jonjo O'Neill that his father expected blanket obedience to his riding instructions. He adds: 'I was never left in any doubt. I was to carry out my orders to the letter and I always did to the best of my ability. The horses came first and Father wouldn't let anyone loose on one of his string if he didn't think that he'd do the job properly.'

The teenage Richards did have an advantage over the lads and lasses who joined the staff after GWR had become established at Greystoke. Nicky knew what to expect. He had, after all, been riding out with his father since the early days at Beadnell. He also had the support of his mother, who was keen at all times to further his interests and was aware how important his riding achievements had become to his standing within the stable. But, as he continues, 'I was never treated any different from the others. Father was an encouraging influence to all his jockeys. Hard on them, yes, but supportive as well.'

Nicky did not take all that many outside rides over the jumps, but he got on particularly well with Cool Angel, a useful handicap hurdler trained by Hughie Rebanks, the Shap farmer and permit holder. Hughie liked a gamble and Nicky guided Cool Angel to several nice touches at Newcastle and Cartmel. By mischance the chestnut was also responsible for bringing about a premature end to Nicky Richards's riding career.

'Every so often these seasoned old handicappers forget the hurdles are there and take a tumble,' explains Nicky. 'The trouble is that you aren't expecting it and when Cool Angel came down at the first flight at Kelso, I was taken unawares and fell clumsily, breaking my left wrist.'

It was a bad break, but Nicky had fractured his jaw during riding work at Greystoke 18 months earlier, and was confident that the injury would mend. There were no immediate worries. A pin was inserted to help the wrist to bind and indeed some four months later Nicky was in full cry again, partnering Sea Pigeon in the Moët & Chandon at Epsom. Later in the autumn, though, the wrist began to give problems. Nicky takes up the story: 'I had been struggling with my weight during the lay-off and then the wrist started to give me aggro. I tried to shrug it off, but the pain grew worse and Mother insisted that I went back to the specialist. He found that the pin had worked loose and there was a danger of gangrene setting in. He warned that my riding days could be over. We decided to take a second opinion but the news wasn't much better. The doctor told me that the wrist would stand up to normal use, but that every time I fell on it the break would re-open. Father took the view that the risk was not worth taking and he was right. Even now I can't get full movement in the wrist, though it has never stopped me from riding work. I was very browned off at the time, but like Dad my ambition was to train and giving up my riding licence was just another step towards that goal.'

THIRTEEN

The Century Club

Sea Pigeon arrived at Greystoke in the late April of 1974. No new purchase had been received with such excitement and eager anticipation since Titus Oates crossed the Pennines six years earlier. The challenge facing Gordon Richards and his staff was equally intense but also refreshingly different. Sea Pigeon was a classically bred thoroughbred, seventh in the Derby the previous June and bought with The Champion Hurdle as his specific target.

The late Tony Murray was the catalyst behind Sea Pigeon's transfer from the soft sunrise sweeping across the Lambourn Downs to the icy tentacles of a raw January morning on the rugged fells of northern Cumbria. Tony had already ridden Pat Muldoon's Barrein to victory at Haydock and suggested to the ambitious wine and spirit importer and dealer from Armadale that the winner of the Tote Roll Up Handicap would develop into a successful hurdler. At the same time he passed on the hint that Sea Pigeon, whom he had ridden in the Derby, might not only be up for sale but would (in his opinion) also make up into an outstanding timber-topper. The advice was not lost on Muldoon, an avid student of the formbook.

Convinced that the son of Sea Bird would justify Tony Murray's confidence, Pat contacted Jeremy Tree with a possible offer – only to be told that Sea Pigeon was taking longer than expected to recover from being gelded and no decision could be reached until Jock Whitney, in whose colours he had run for two seasons at Beckhampton, had been consulted. Meanwhile the prospective purchaser had discovered that Sea Pigeon was spending the winter at livery with Johnny Carey at Oare in rural Wiltshire. By happy coincidence, Carey had been at Ivor Anthony's Wroughton stable with Gordon Richards and the Greystoke trainer, quick to scent a bargain, agreed to accompany Pat Muldoon on the trip south to get the low-down on Sea Pigeon. He was impressed and despite Carey's warning that Sea Pigeon suffered from 'brittle feet', counselled his owner to take the plunge. Muldoon was of the same mind. But the vet called in to examine Sea Pigeon before any purchase was confirmed warned that the gelding was troubled by deep-seated bruising to one of his feet. The disappointment was short-lived. On a return visit to the Vale of Pewsey the same expert gave Sea Pigeon a clean bill of health and Muldoon's offer of £10,000 was quickly accepted by Jeremy Tree.

Gordon's immediate job was to persuade the newcomer to settle into his strange surroundings and begin to relax and enjoy life. He told Pat Muldoon that there would be no point in doing anything serious with the horse until this had been achieved and that, as far as possible, he would be divorced from the regimental routine of everyday training.

Nicky recalls: 'Father was fascinated with Sea Pigeon. He was convinced that the way to release his latent potential was to get him interested and happy in himself. He always liked to ride work on the stable's star horses, to check that they were giving out the right signals, but he used Sea Pigeon more as a hack rather than a potential Champion Hurdler. On other occasions he would tell either Ron Barry, Jonjo or sometimes myself to walk him along the quiet tracks through the pine woods above Greystoke Castle. To start with he was very suspicious of the wildlife. He veered away from rabbits and on his first day out on the fells stood stock still at the sight of the cattle grazing on the hillside. He'd never seen a cow in his life!'

It wasn't long before the magic of the Cumbrian landscape and the understanding patience of his work riders began to rub off on Sea Pigeon. He revelled in the quiet life, the jogging up hills, the roaming through the woods and the occasional jumping over fallen trees or narrow water splashes. When Jonjo first saw him he described Sea Pigeon as 'frail and small, compared with the big robust chasing types which The Boss usually filled his boxes with'. By mid-June, though, Sea Pigeon was not only putting on condition, he was already showing a natural aptitude for the jumping game.

The Boss may not have been an expert at 'breaking-in' the youngsters, but he liked nothing better than to introduce them to the art of jumping and he prided himself on the thoroughness of his instruction. Lessons began in the sand ring adjacent to the stable block, with the pupil clearing a couple of poles each time he completed the circle. At the next stage the novice would tackle similar modest obstacles in a specially adapted 'jumping lane'. With increasing confidence the student would graduate to more demanding tasks, before finally being allowed to face the line of schooling hurdles set uphill alongside Thornylands Wood. Gordon was at pains to persuade the learners 'to see a stride and gain momentum by jumping off their hocks in the approved steeplechasing manner, rather than by brushing feet-first through the obstacles'. Before long he was able to report to Pat Muldoon that Sea Pigeon had taken to hurdling 'like a duck to water'. At the same time he planned that Sea Pigeon's initial return to the racecourse would be in the prestigious Moët & Chandon Stakes at Epsom's August Bank Holiday fixture. The race is widely known as 'the amateurs' Derby' and always attracts an upmarket entry. Nicky Richards was to have the mount. This booking pleased the owner as Nicky had already forged a successful partnership with his expensive new acquisition – the promising hurdler Canadius, formerly under the care of Arthur Stephenson but bought out of WA's Crawleas stable for a substantial sum the previous autumn.

The Boss and WA enjoyed great crack with one another and there had been a typically late hitch in the sale. It had been agreed that Canadius would be brought to Newcastle races in the Stephenson horse box and, on receipt of the money, would be transferred to the Greystoke transporter for the journey back to Cumbria. What had not been discussed was the fate of the aged nanny goat, an inseparable travelling companion of Canadius both to and from the races.

'You've bought Canadius but you haven't yet paid for the goat or even said you want him,' insisted Stephenson. 'He won't go a yard without him y'know,' he added with a twinkle in his steely eye. Eventually WA relented with good grace. The goat joined Canadius *en route* to Castle Stables, much to the delight of the horse if not of his future lad, who found himself having to milk the wretched animal twice a day for lengthy periods. To his relief the goat did not survive the rigours of Cumbria for long. He passed away within the year and was replaced by a pet pony who could look after himself and was no trouble in the box!

Canadius had not made an auspicious start in the Muldoon tartan. His début was scheduled for the Bertola Sherry Hurdle at Catterick. Pat was in fact sponsoring the race and thought it would be amusing to win back his own prize money. The fates thought otherwise. The horse box bringing Canadius from Greystoke had been delayed by an accident on the A66 and it was a very upset and sweaty horse who arrived in the paddock only minutes before the off. An equally breathless Jonjo O'Neill was hoisted aboard and to the consternation of all, not least his backers, Canadius was unsighted at the first flight and deposited his rider face down in the turf. Jonjo was later to guide Canadius to a number of victories, but in that first season at Greystoke it was Nicky Richards who did the business.

Six weeks after the Catterick shambles, Nicky had the leg up on Canadius in the handicap hurdle at Haydock. The combination were sent off unconsidered outsiders, but given a positive ride by his amateur pilot, Canadius finished a creditable second to the experienced Past Master. Nicky retained the mount for the Schweppes Gold Trophy at Newbury but the race was abandoned because of frost. The partnership made it third time lucky in the Princess Margaret Hurdle at Doncaster. The win over Firefright provided Nicky with a welcome present on his 18th birthday. His handling of Canadius impressed Pat Muldoon and the ultimate suggestion that Nicky should have the responsibility of being the first Greystoke jockey to partner Sea Pigeon in public was well received by the horse's Scottish owner.

Ten days before Epsom's Bank Holiday fixture, Pat Muldoon ran two of his lesser lights on the flat at one of Hamilton's popular evening meetings. The Boss had decided that the Lanarkshire course, with its tight circular loop and downhill bend into an undulating home straight, was something similar to the terrain at Epsom, even if the wrong way round. He included Sea Pigeon in the box for Hamilton together with the useful four-year-old Sun Lion.

The plan was for both horses to cover ten furlongs at racing speed. Jonjo O'Neill on Sun Lion set off well in front of Sea Pigeon, but Nicky Richards had no problem reducing the deficit and swept past the toiling Sun Lion to 'win', easing up by a substantial margin. If the lads back at Greystoke hadn't quite believed in Sea Pigeon's touch of class, they had no doubts after this remarkable piece of work and confidence was high that 'Pigeon' would leave them for dead at Epsom.

The quality of Sea Pigeon's performance at Hamilton was soon to be enhanced by the running of Sun Lion. A maiden at the time of his Hamilton work-out, he proceeded to win both his next two races in the hands of Nicky Richards against competitive opposition at Haydock and Ayr.

Gordon had a number of runners at Cartmel on the Bank Holiday Monday, so Jean drove Nicky south on the Sunday. Nicky recalls: 'Mr Muldoon put us up in the Hilton. We had the best of everything and despite what happened later, I couldn't say a wrong thing about Pat Muldoon. He was extremely generous and always very pleasant to ride for. He liked a gamble, of course, but though he knew the formbook as well as anyone, it would be fair to say that he wasn't a horseman in the same vein as Jimmy McGhie was.'

Sea Pigeon faced no easy task at Epsom. The opposition included experienced handicappers like King Frog, winner of valuable events at Madrid and Ascot; James Young, the Newbury Summer Cup winner; and in particular Laurentian Hills, successful in the Churchill Stakes at Ascot and not disgraced behind Weaver's Hall in the 1973 Irish Sweeps Derby. Robert Armstrong's top handicapper was also ridden by Philip Mitchell, an acknowledged Epsom specialist, whose father Cyril trained adjacent to the course. Philip, now a long established trainer in his own right and a familiar face on the Racing Channel, enjoyed a widely held reputation as the country's finest amateur.

Before leaving Greystoke The Boss had given Nicky detailed instructions, the most crucial being the vital importance of getting Sea Pigeon relaxed and settled during the first half of the race. Perhaps anticipating these tactics, Philip Mitchell dictated the pace from the front, maintaining a powerful gallop from the start and striking for home early in the straight. Nicky Richards had obeyed orders. He tucked Sea Pigeon quietly in behind the leaders before producing him to throw down his challenge approaching the final furlong. Sea Pigeon answered the call in brave style but Laurentian Hills was not stopping and held on by half a length.

Richards senior was not dissatisfied with the defeat. He considered that Nicky had played his part well and tended to blame himself for laying down the law about the necessity to be patient and to keep Sea Pigeon happy and switched off. He said later, 'The boy did well. He got the horse nicely settled but with hindsight probably delayed his finishing effort just too long.'

Back in Cumbria Sea Pigeon's confidence-building education continued. Gordon was emphatic that the horse needed to be sound in mind as well as limb if he was to produce the goods on the track. In between the daily variety of long treks through the wooded Cumbrian hills and lively spells as Gordon's hack, he would be schooled over hurdles by Ron Barry, under whose sympathetic handling his technique grew steadily more assured.

RIGHT: Gladys Richards leading in a West Country winner, accompanied by her father, Arthur.

BELOW: Eleven-year-old Gordon at his father's timber yard near Bath, keeping a tight hold of the reins – and younger brother, Archie.

RIGHT: Young Gordon being led out at Salisbury in the summer of 1944 before his first ride in public.

BELOW: Gordon W. Richards (right) shakes hands with the 'original' Gordon Richards, Salisbury, 1943.

LEFT: Jean Richards in her modelling days.

BELOW: Jean Richards at work in her office at Greystoke.

Doncaster Races: Lady Grimthorpe presents the trophy to The Boss after Playlord had won the 1969 Great Yorks Chase. © Bespix

The Spaniard (Nicky Richards) is first, and Rainborough second, in the 1973 Stratford Irish Amateur Riders' Chase.

Lucius and Bob Davies (near side), clever winners of the 1978 *Sun* Grand National from Sebastian V (centre) and Drumroan (far side). © *Sunday Express*

Lucius being led back after winning the 1978 *Sun* Grand National.
© *Sunday Express*

'Gipsy' Dave Goulding among friends! © *Daily Mirror*

Noddy's Ryde (Neale Doughty) taking the water on his way to winning the 1984 *Sporting Life* Weekender Chase, Aintree.

LEFT: Titus Oates (Ron Barry) in a celebration outside the Greystoke local.

BELOW: Christmas at the stables, mid-1970s: The Boss (front left) with David Goulding and Jonjo O'Neill (centre left & right) at the lads' annual party.

A man for all seasons: The Boss on Lucius, at a meet
of the Cumberland Farmers. © *Daily Mirror*

The policy of giving Sea Pigeon the VIP treatment was never adhered to at the Peter Easterby stable: when Sea Pigeon transferred to Great Habton in the winter of 1976 he was exercised with the main string. Mark Birch was in the saddle the first morning, and though Sea Pigeon did his level best to 'cart' him, Mark forced him to change his mind by aiming him directly into the backside of the horse in front of him. From that day onwards Sea Pigeon went out at the rear of the string and remained on his best behaviour.

It could of course be argued that the patience shown at Greystoke had worked the oracle long before Sea Pigeon had made the trip across the Pennines. In the autumn of 1974, however, Gordon reckoned that Sea Pigeon needed one more outing on the flat before being launched on his hurdling career. The selected race was the East Riding Yeomanry Challenge Trophy for amateur riders at Beverley.

Only five went to post, with Sea Pigeon impossible to back at odds of 1–5. Nicky Richards bided his time as Swirl, the mount of Elaine Mellor, cut out the running at a fast clip. Bearing in mind what had occurred at Epsom, Nicky closed with the long-time leader early in the straight. He sent Sea Pigeon ahead below the distance with every expectation of quickening away from the tiring Swirl to score with comfort. It was not to be! Swirl rallied, Sea Pigeon began to labour and the hot pot was turned over.

Opinions varied as to whether horse or jockey or both were culpable. Most observers, though, maintained that Sea Pigeon had turned it in and that for Pat Muldoon's expensive purchase the future did not look bright. In fact the reason was simple to find, as Nicky is quick to point out: 'Sea Pigeon never gave me the right feel from the start. I had to work to overhaul the leader and when he came back for more inside the last half-furlong there was nothing left in the tank. The next day Sea Pigeon was coughing his head off and he was under the weather for some while.'

The moment for which Pat Muldoon had been waiting with such anticipation arrived in early November. Sea Pigeon made his long awaited hurdling début in the Panama Cigar Qualifier at Newcastle. Ron Barry reflects, 'He was very keen and I had a job to drop him in behind and settle him. To make matters worse, Good Judge fell at the second last and we were left in front too early. In the end I had to drive him right out to hold the late rally of Dutch Sam.'

The Boss knew that he must not rush his star pupil. For someone renowned for his 'short fuse' he was by contrast patience itself when it came to dealing with his horses. Gordon waited until Ayr's New Year meeting before giving Sea Pigeon his second attempt over timber. If patience was one of Gordon's outstanding qualities as a trainer, a possible loophole in his armoury was a tendency to run two of his horses in the same race. There was just a trace of obstinacy in this habit which was invariably motivated by the desire to run his horses in the races best suited to their needs. The fact that the owners involved might be less than keen on taking each other on in this way counted for little with The Boss.

The practice was to gnaw away at Pat Muldoon's equilibrium, but in the first instance Sea Pigeon's owner had no grounds for complaint. Jimmy McGhie had persuaded Gordon to saddle Ribanco in the same division of the Cardhu Novices' Hurdle, reckoning that the greater hurdle race experience of his French-bred gelding would enable him to outpoint Sea Pigeon. Right or wrong, the Lochmaben dairyman would be assured of a decent price. Gordon was happy, confident that Sea Pigeon would demonstrate his class. Pat Muldoon was less than chuffed. He was worried that his horse would be given a harder than necessary race. In the event he shouldn't have worried. Though initially inclined to pull Ron Barry's arms out, his hurdling was always fast and keen, and by half-way he was travelling smoothly on the bridle. Barry allowed Lepidus to lead over the final flight before swamping him for speed on the flat.

Sea Pigeon completed a quick hat-trick in the Shoveller Hurdle at Newcastle. He won in a canter, relaxing from the start and zipping over his hurdles as though he had been bred for the job. All was peace and quiet at Greystoke. Pat Muldoon celebrated by buying another two promising recruits, Highway Rambler from Ireland and Town Ship out of Albert Davison's Caterham yard.

The Rossington Main Novices' Hurdle, then rated a high-profile race for progressive youngsters, was next in line for Sea Pigeon. At Doncaster he was pitted against southern rivals for the first time, but taking the lead at the penultimate flight, he had no difficulty in quickening away from the Fred Winter-trained Brawny Scot. The ease of this win encouraged Gordon to end Sea Pigeon's first hurdling campaign with a searching test in the Grey Friars Hurdle, also at Doncaster, in which he was set to tackle Bird's Nest and Super Nova at level weights. Three-horse races are notoriously tricky contests and Ron Barry had to be at his tactical best to win the battle of wits with Andy Turnell. By now Sea Pigeon was well used to Ron's methods. He consented to being dropped out 'early doors' and to increase the pace steadily from the third last. All was going to plan until Super Nova hung across him on the approach to the final flight. Sea Pigeon hesitated. Bird's Nest got first run, and though it was nip and tuck close home, Sea Pigeon was beaten three quarters of a length. First blood to Bird's Nest in a long-lasting duel; but the final time that Ron Barry was to partner Sea Pigeon.

Ron's decision to part company with GWR was not totally unexpected. However because The Boss and his stable jockey had been so close for so long – literally growing famous together and living with triumph and disaster for so long – it was not hard to foresee that firstly the actual separation would be charged with emotion; and secondly that the split would be short-lived. Thus it proved!

Unrest between trainer and jockey, simmering for a while, boiled over towards the end of the 1974–75 season. Ron had played a vital role in the re-education of Sea Pigeon. He had been champion jockey in the two previous seasons and was still at the height of his powers. Yet the way in which things were going at Greystoke implied otherwise. Ron publicly challenged The Boss to come clean. Feelings ran high. Harsh words were exchanged. In the heat of the moment fists were raised and the immediate upshot was Ron's sudden departure. He would ride freelance for the next two seasons; but his home was still at Roehead high above Ullswater, 20 minutes from Greystoke, and he would be back. By the winter of 1977 the partnership was restored and Ron continued to ride as first jockey to the Richards team until he made the snap decision to retire from the saddle after winning on Final Argument at Ayr in October 1983. Shortly afterwards he succeeded the late Bobby Faulkner as Jockey Club Inspector of Racecourses in the North. And although The Boss had the odd difference of opinion with Ron in his official capacity, the pair of them remained the closest of friends until the end. He reflects: 'I rode for him nearly 19 years. In all that time we had just one serious fall out . . . Not bad when you come to think about it!'

Sea Pigeon needed his first race of the 1975–76 season. He 'blew up' after taking the third from home and weakened into seventh place behind Night Nurse in the William Hill Hurdle at Newbury. A fortnight later he was back at the Berkshire course as odds-on favourite for the Bagnor Hurdle. Jonjo settled him well. He hurdled slickly and outclassed the useful Simon's Pet.

While Pat Muldoon was pleased with progress on the Sea Pigeon front, he was less than pleased with events in the Torksey Hurdle at Doncaster the following Saturday. The Boss had again opted to run two in the same race: Muldoon's promising Highway Rambler; and Lord Greystoke, then running in the colours of Gordon Sandiford, and like Highway Rambler a winning novice the previous season. David Goulding, now riding as second jockey for the Richards team, had the leg up on Highway Rambler. Jonjo O'Neill was on board Lord Greystoke, who went off an unconsidered 15–1 (while Highway Rambler started second favourite at 11–4). For much of the race the better backed horse was in command but he fluffed the final flight and the error allowed Jonjo to grab the initiative. Hard though David Goulding tried on Highway Rambler, he could not prevent Lord Greystoke running out the winner by a head. This was the second time that Pat Muldoon had watched one of his horses, the stable's 'preferred', get turned over by a less fancied stable companion. The outcome rankled but he let the matter rest for the time being.

November was always Gordon's happiest month. From the moment that his operation at Greystoke was up and running, right through his training career, his horses would peak about this time. The ground in November is arguably at its seasonal best, taking in sufficient rainfall to ease the surface and still remaining warm enough to be unaffected by frost. Gordon loved the late autumn. He would strut from paddock to the stands, binoculars at the ready, smiling to himself in that confident style which so often presaged an equally good-humoured return to the winner's circle. Form students frequently complained that GWR was an 'expensive trainer to follow', but those who doubled their stakes in November would be raking in the cash in preparation for the comparatively lean period in January and February.

Another factor that was to become a hallmark of the Richards bandwagon was the 'cluster effect'. Gordon might go several weeks with little more than a trickle of winners; then almost without warning the bookmakers would be bombarded with a rash of doubles and trebles from the Greystoke stable. I use the word 'almost' on purpose, because as the seasons passed the trainer's fondness for certain courses became increasingly apparent. He grew to be dominant at Ayr and Carlisle, while he had a penchant for multiple wins at Haydock, and in the heyday of Caroline Berry's top chasers Hexham was a regular source of success.

November 1975 was a vintage month. Within the space of six racing days The Boss completed consecutive hat-tricks at Hexham, Carlisle and Ayr. Mrs Berry's Lord of the Hills and Cromwell Road were decisive winners on the Yarridge Heights with Two and a Quarter sealing the three-timer. At Carlisle the cheerful grin returned to Pat Muldoon's face as his expensively bought newcomer, Arctic Mist, demolished the opposition on his seasonal début. The progressive pair of Tamalin and Greystoke Rambler added further wins at the Cumbrian venue. Sun Lion, Lucius and Eversholt continued the bonanza at Ayr. Nine winners in six days; and Pat Muldoon looked assured of his personal treble until his 2–5 shot, Dormitor, hit the deck with a careless blunder three out – leaving the less fancied Eversholt to score for Jimmy McGhie.

Sea Pigeon's next outing was the Fighting Fifth at Newcastle, another tilt at the cream of the country's hurdling talent. Comedy of Errors and Night Nurse were both in the field and Sea Pigeon was partnered by David Goulding as Jonjo O'Neill had been required to ride Tamalin in the Hennessy at Newbury. The new combination settled happily. No surprise, this, as 'Gipsy Dave' had an instant empathy with horses and indeed animals of every shape and size. Pat Muldoon recalls: 'They got on famously, but Sea Pigeon did not hurdle with the same fluency as he had done at Newbury and you can't get away with sloppy jumping in a race like the Fighting Fifth. David did well to have him in contention at the third last, but once the leaders began to pile on the pressure Sea Pigeon had no answer. He had used up his energy making good his earlier mistakes.'

Third place was a disappointment, but the enigmatic star put Newcastle behind him on his crucial visit to Prestbury Park for the Cheltenham Trial Hurdle. A second drubbing by Comedy of Errors would be a depressing setback to his Champion Hurdle aspirations. Also among his rivals were Fash Imp and Tree Tangle, second and third at the Festival the previous month. Equally important was the presence of Navigation, the athletic New Zealand-bred front runner who would ensure a fast gallop, allowing Jonjo to drop in behind and be towed along by the tide. Navigation proved more than a pacemaker. He was still tanking along at the head of affairs on the run to the last flight, but Sea Pigeon was now sitting on his tail. Not until the final 50 yards or so did Jonjo ask him to quicken into the lead, posing the question with hands and heels without recourse to the stick. Sea Pigeon produced a decisive burst of speed to score head-in-chest with his big race rivals well beaten.

Muldoon and Richards were walking on air. This, they both knew, was the performance of a Champion Hurdle winner. The Boss planned two further outings in the run-up to the Festival. Sea Pigeon would renew his battle with Comedy of Errors in the New Year Hurdle at Windsor before once more travelling south for Sandown's Oteley Hurdle in February. At Windsor, Comedy of Errors exacted revenge for his Cheltenham defeat. But the margin was a hard-fought head and Jonjo O'Neill confirmed what The Boss had already told Pat Muldoon, namely that the fall of Dramatist at the penultimate flight had cost Sea Pigeon the race. Jonjo explained that he had been tracking Dramatist into the flight and that his impetus had been checked by the fall, causing him to use up Sea Pigeon's reserves of energy to get back on level terms with Comedy of Errors (whose challenge had been unaffected by Dramatist's demise). Sea Pigeon actually headed Fred Rimell's reigning champion half-way up the short run-in, but the energy expended in getting there told inside the surge to the line, and Comedy of Errors rallied to lead in the last stride.

Connections' unanimous view that they had been unlucky at Windsor was endorsed as a result of the Oteley Hurdle. Sea Pigeon took advantage of Lanzarote's fumble at the penultimate flight to pinch a vital four lengths and, staying on stoutly up the hill, landed his third victory of the season. The Boss was a bundle of bluster and pent-up nervous exhaustion. He knew that in Sea Pigeon he not only trained a potential Champion Hurdler but one who was classy and young enough to set up a sequence of wins in the style of Hatton's Grace, Sir Ken and Persian War.

With less than a fortnight left before Cheltenham he decided to send Sea Pigeon across the Pennines to Wetherby with a box load of stable companions for a racecourse gallop. It was a habit that Gordon followed regularly in the immediate build up to a big race. He reckoned that a change of scenery provided a mental stimulus and sharpened the edge.

The party at Wetherby had been well chosen. Speed was provided by Wotdyknow and Highway Rambler, who himself had run with some distinction in the Schweppes at Newbury. Stamina would be tested by the presence of Lucius and Current Gold. Jonjo, on board Sea Pigeon, gave the quartet a 20-length start. He then plotted an intentional course all round the outside of the track – but even using these deliberate delaying tactics he and Sea Pigeon still joined their rivals running away on a tight rein as the group turned into the home straight. Worthy performers though they were, the foursome couldn't hold a candle to Sea Pigeon. He left them flat-footed to scorch ahead and pass the post, ears pricked, a ridiculously easy winner. Jonjo drove back to Greystoke dreaming of Cheltenham glory. Little did he realise that his hopes would be shattered within the space of another 12 hours.

The Boss and Colin Parker, the head lad, were down in the stables at six o'clock each morning to distribute the early morning feed. It was a practice carried out in virtual silence every day of the season. Bowls were checked and refilled and horses given the quick 'once-over'. Gordon's route took him into Sea Pigeon's privileged quarters. As he whispered a quiet 'good morning old fellow', he went to pat him affectionately on the side of his neck and was alarmed to feel the horse shrink away from his gentle movement. Sensing something wrong, Gordon flicked off his rug to reveal an angry swelling on his withers. It was a warble, a hard tumour-like bump similar to an enormous mosquito bite. Sea Pigeon's discomfort increased during the morning. The Boss ordered the swelling to be poulticed. The vet was summoned but the warble was obstinate. Instead of diminishing, it grew more inflamed and the infection began to spread down the shoulder. After 24 hours of frenetic treatment it was all too clear that Sea Pigeon would have to be scratched from the Champion Hurdle. The stable went into mourning. Pat Muldoon was disappointed but staunch in his support for the stable. The Boss was devastated. Nicky Richards remembers, 'It took him a while to recover. He never said as much right out, but it was among the worst moments of his entire training career, and to make matters even more frustrating the weather turned warm and dry and Night Nurse won the first of his two Champions on good fast ground which would have been ideal for Sea Pigeon.'

Speaking recently, though, Pat Muldoon surmised that Sea Pigeon might have been 'a shade immature' to win the race at the first time of asking. Victory in the Champion Hurdle would have promoted Gordon Richards into second place in the trainer's table, marginally above Fred Winter. In the event he had to be content with a best-ever third position on a record-breaking tally of 105 winners, making him at the time only the second trainer to have saddled more than 100 winners in a single season over the jumps (emulating his old adversary Arthur Stephenson).

Strength in depth was the major factor behind the Greystoke success. With over 70 horses in training there was no shortage of ammunition and the spread of quality in the yard meant that almost every opportunity was covered. One pertinent statistic was the comparison between the number of chases and hurdles won during the course of the campaign. GWR sent out 54 winning steeplechasers and 51 successful 'timber-toppers' – a record that goes a long way towards proving his versatility as a trainer, and knocks the theory that he was a chasing specialist firmly on the head. With the departure of Ron Barry the winners were broadly shared between Jonjo O'Neill, who rode 63 winners, and David Goulding who ended the season on the 49 winner mark. Pat Muldoon was the stable's leading owner with 17 winners; apart from Sea Pigeon, other substantial contributors to the memorable campaign were Alan Metcalfe's Tamalin (five wins from eight races), Lucius (six wins from eleven races) in the colours of Fiona Whitaker and Pat Muldoon's Canadius (six wins from eight races).

The latter's splendid season was crowned by victory in the Yellow Pages Pattern Handicap Chase at Kempton. Tamalin was invincible in north-country handicap chases, but was sadly fallible when it came to the big occasions, disappointing connections in both the Hennessy and the Scottish National. Lucius landed competitive handicap hurdles at Sandown and Wetherby, as well as graduating with promise to tackling the major obstacles.

By no means the least part in the outstanding achievements of 1975–76 was that played by the backroom staff – Colin Parker, Malcolm Jefferson, the travelling head lad, and the loyal band of stable lads and lasses who braved the elements all winter and ensured that the Greystoke horses stayed at their peak from October right through to the end of May. Later campaigns were to be spoilt by coughs and colds in the wet months of January and February. In 1975–76 the string boasted a clean bill of health from beginning to end.

The reverse side of the coin was mercifully low profile. Sea Pigeon's warble was top of the list. Nicky's enforced retirement from the saddle was a personal sadness and Jean's heart problems had become an increasing worry to all but herself. She remained a tower of strength and – reinforced against continual bouts of pain by liberal supplies of pills, aided by the occasional cigarette and glass of the amber fluid – she was a constant source of inspiration to the whole stable.

Pat Muldoon had replaced Jimmy McGhie as the yard's principal patron. He had enjoyed much success during the year, but beneath the surface the cracks were just starting to show. GWR's policy of running two horses in the same race did not endear itself to the Lothian wine and spirit tycoon. Sea Pigeon had 'missed' Cheltenham. Town Ship had broken down and the expensively bought Arctic Mist had yet to live up to his inflated reputation.

FOURTEEN

Hard Decisions

Sea Pigeon thrived during his second summer out at grass; this time with Stuart Lyburn on his farm in Perthshire. His return in August coincided with the hottest summer for a decade. The ground was so hard in the early autumn that several meetings had to be called off because the sun-baked going was adjudged dangerous.

The Boss was itching to make his customary early start but, mindful of his horses' legs, kept his runners to a minimum. His first winner of the 1976–77 season fuelled memories of past glories. Playbella, a full sister of the never-to-be-forgotten Playlord, opened her account in the Pringle family colours at Market Rasen. The mare was to win another modest event at Carlisle in late September, but sadly she was pulled up lame on her next outing at Ayr and never got the chance to emulate her formidable elder brother.

Gordon had Sea Pigeon ready for Ayr's opening fixture of the season. He was giving away lumps of weight to all his rivals in the Culzean Handicap Hurdle; but he had no difficulty closing down Homefield, the long term leader, at the final flight and won easing up, breaking the course record in the process. A fortnight later The Boss attempted to kick-start his season with a four-horse raid on Kempton Park. It proved a disastrous venture. Asset was unsighted in the opener. Arctic Mist was beaten a long way out. Cumnock Scouse trailed the field in the final race. Sea Pigeon, meanwhile, was easily put in his place by Lanzarote in the featured 'A Day At The Races' Hurdle. Jonjo reported that Sea Pigeon had travelled badly and was very much on his toes in the paddock. In the race he had never given the rider the same feel as he had done on his seasonal début at Ayr.

Misfortunes continued for Greystoke when both Tamalin and Highway Rambler fell at Newcastle. There was just a hint of desperation about the decision to send six horses to Catterick's late October meeting. Near-drought conditions had restricted the fast work that Gordon could give his horses at home and there was also a suspicion that a nagging bug was doing the rounds of the yard. The only serious contender at Catterick was Pat Muldoon's Justaminute in the novice chase.

Bought out of Paddy Sleator's yard the previous year, Justaminute had won a couple of novice hurdles in good style and Gordon was certain that he would prove even better over fences. He was accompanied to the post by Current Gold, owned by Alec Picken, a well known butcher from Ayr whose Carry Off won the 1971 County Hurdle when trained by Nigel Angus. Current Gold had won four long-distance handicap hurdles in 1975–76 and, like Justaminute, was making his début over the major obstacles. The Asgarth Novices' Chase had no pretensions to fame but in the autumn of 1976 its result was to have far-reaching consequences. The part played by The Boss in pre-race discussions remains confused. One record suggests that he was in two minds about which of his two runners was the superior, though when pressed he advised Alec Picken to 'have his fiver on Justaminute'. Pat Muldoon maintains that Gordon had told him, 'Justaminute will win. Don't you worry. Have a nice bet on him in the morning!'

Muldoon had been both annoyed and unhappy on discovering from his evening paper that Current Gold had been declared in the same race as Justaminute. As mentioned in the previous chapter, he had already suffered twice at the hands of 'the Richards neglected', and after the Doncaster fiasco he had made his views abundantly clear.

Speaking from his Edinburgh home in June 1999, Pat declared: 'I could never understand why Gordon wanted to run two of his horses in the same race, but until Highway Rambler got beaten I kept my feelings pretty well to myself. I knew that my horse was down to run in the Torksey Hurdle at Doncaster, but on the evening before the race I was telephoned by Gordon Sandiford, an old friend from the Midlands, who had a horse in training with GWR called Lord Greystoke. Sandiford was ringing to say that he would be at Doncaster to watch his horse run against mine in the handicap hurdle and to suggest that we have lunch together before the race. I got in touch with The Boss, who told me straight out that Lord Greystoke was useful but that he needed the outing and would be no problem to Highway Rambler.'

The upshot of these two telephone calls was that Messrs Muldoon and Sandiford met at Town Moor and over lunch both agreed to back Highway Rambler. Pat continues, 'David Goulding was on board my horse who went off second favourite. Lord Greystoke was ridden by Jonjo O'Neill and started one of the outsiders. Goulding gave Highway Rambler the ideal ride, holding him up until the home turn before bringing him with his usual steady run to hit the front between the final two flights. All was going to plan until Highway Rambler hit the last hurdle and momentarily lost his momentum. I was watching him through the binoculars and didn't see Jonjo stoking up Lord Greystoke until the last few strides. There was only a head in it at the line, but Lord Greystoke was the clear winner. Not only had I lost my bet, but I had to eat a lot of humble pie with Gordon Sandiford. It was all most embarrassing and afterwards I told GWR that I never wanted to be put in such a situation ever again. If he really thought it necessary to run two horses in the same race then he was to leave mine well alone!'

The Boss appears to have taken this message to heart until Catterick, nearly a year later, and there were mitigating circumstances. The 1976–77 season had got off to an inauspicious start and by the end of October he was searching for any possible chance to give his horses a run in public. The Aysgarth Novices' Chase looked tailor-made for Justaminute and it also provided the opportunity for Current Gold to blow away the cobwebs.

With hindsight The Boss had logic on his side. Current Gold had already shown his liking for distances in excess of two and a half miles over hurdles. He had given no indication of being bursting with vigour on the gallops at Greystoke and two miles around Catterick – one of the sharpest circuits in the north – should have seen him well outpaced by the specialists at this trip. Whether he was inviting trouble by running two horses in this particular contest is open to question, but his motives for doing so had nothing to do with either greed or the intention to deceive.

Gordon wanted to give Current Gold a race to sharpen him up for the more strenuous work to come. He was not cheating Alec Picken when he advised him to put his fiver on Justaminute. He had already convinced himself that Justaminute would murder the opposition.

Pat Muldoon was not so sure. Furthermore, he had been at Newcastle and Kempton and had first-hand knowledge of the manner in which the apparent 'good things' from the Richards stable had been performing like damp squibs. He was far from happy on opening his evening paper to note that Gordon had declared Current Gold to do battle with Justaminute.

He recalls, 'I was unhappy to find Current Gold in the lists because I held him in high regard and I could see very much the same scenario as there had been at Doncaster the previous November. I rang Gordon to express my disapproval and to suggest that Justaminute should be withdrawn if Alec Picken was determined to run Current Gold. Gordon told me to calm down. He pointed out that the only way that he could take out Justaminute without incurring a substantial fine was to provide the clerk of the scales with a vet's certificate, which would be difficult as the horse was in great shape. Gordon was adamant that Justaminute, a specialist two-miler, would come out on top. And he emphasised that Current Gold wanted a more galloping track and at least another mile to show winning form. He ended the call with the advice that I had nothing to worry about and suggested that I have a major punt on Justaminute.

'In fact I was far from convinced and invested a small sum on Justaminute.'

Pat did not go to Catterick. Instead he listened to the race, with increasing misgiving. Justaminute, a warm favourite at 11–8, was always in touch with the leaders. Jonjo asked him to close on the home turn, but he was under pressure before the third last. Current Gold, a 10–1 chance in the betting, was held up by David Goulding, but maintained his pitch throughout the contest. He quickened past tired horses in the straight and taking up the lead at the final fence, scooted home by four lengths with Justaminute beaten 21 lengths into fifth place.

'That was it as far as I was concerned,' stressed a disillusioned owner. 'I had lost confidence in my trainer and it had all been so unnecessary. When I rang through to say that I intended to remove my horses I got Jean on the other end of the line. She was horrified and tried to tell me that I couldn't do this to Gordon; that he would explain what had happened at Catterick on his return; and that she was sure I would see things differently.

'Gordon telephoned me later that night, but nothing he said persuaded me to change my mind. Next day I contacted Peter Easterby. I explained the situation and asked him to take over the training of my horses. Peter begged me not to do things hastily. He said that Gordon was a top trainer and that I should sleep on it. If I still thought the same way afterwards then he would accept my offer.

'I was sad that matters at Greystoke had come to an end like this, but I was adamant that the transfer should go ahead. On receiving my second call Peter Easterby agreed. He said that he would get in touch with GWR and arrange for all eleven of my horses to be collected from Greystoke and transported to Great Habton.'

Reflecting on his actions nearly 23 years after the event, Pat Muldoon sticks to his guns: 'It was a matter of principle. I felt that Gordon's word could no longer be taken at face value and that time had run out as far as the two of us were concerned. The pity of the thing was that I had always liked Gordon both as a person and as a trainer.'

Muldoon's first winner for the Richards stable had been Sunny Bay back in the spring of 1972. Their four-year association had been mutually profitable, with a lot of winners under both codes, and the owner never lost his high regard for Gordon's horsemanship and professional ability as a trainer. He explains, 'I had a lot of respect for him. He loved his horses and was a marvellous trainer of steeplechasers. You couldn't fault the way the horses were turned out. Essentially he was a man of integrity. I always regarded him as a friend, but as time went on he would insist on doing everything 'his own way' and became less disposed to listen to reason. I was sad to leave Greystoke for many reasons, not least because I was living in Dunblane at the time, within easy reach of the stables by motorway. I used to drive down to see the horses most Sundays and we also had a mutual friend in Jack White. The three of us went on a number of buying sprees in Ireland and had some great crack in the process.'

Nicky Richards is supportive of his father. He adds, 'The Boss was always straight with Mr Muldoon. Yes, he did sometimes run two horses in the same race, but there was never any ulterior motive involved. We had a big team at Greystoke and you must remember that there wasn't the amount of racing then which we have today. The Catterick business brought matters to a head, but relations had been under pressure for a while before that.'

The Boss was unrepentant. At no time in his training career did he allow owners to dictate their own terms. If they didn't appreciate the way he was training their horses then they were at liberty to leave. Several did, though few were as influential as Pat Muldoon. The loss of his horses left gaps which would take a while to fill.

Heads down, the lads at Greystoke carved out 50 winners by the beginning of next June. Tamalin took over the baton of stable star from Sea Pigeon. Back in November he had been the moral victor of the Hennessy. Carrying 11st 13lb, he came to throw down his challenge at the second last, only to peck on landing and lose the initiative to Zeta's Son. Jonjo O'Neill rallied the topweight to harry the leader all the way to the line but the concession of 27lb was just too much and Tamalin lost out by one and a half lengths. Zeta's Son, ironically, was ridden by Ron Barry.

In February Tamalin landed the Trout Chase at Newcastle. He was also among the leaders in the 1977 Piper Champagne Cheltenham Gold Cup, all the way to the run downhill to the second last, before that demanding extra quarter of a mile found him out. A much underrated horse, Tamalin was described by David Goulding as about the most exciting jumper he had ever had the privilege to partner.

In contrast Current Gold was 'a bit of a scrapper', a label that serves no disrespect. The formbooks use the adjective 'compact' to classify his physical shape. Head stretched low and forward into the rain and wind, he did however resemble a determined terrier. In his first season over fences Current Gold scored four times, including a hard-fought victory in the Royal Porcelain Chase at Worcester.

Pattern Maker, a half-brother to Bula, was the hope for the future. David Goulding made it a personal target to tame the temperamental gelding, who returned the compliment by winning competitive novice hurdles at Wetherby and Haydock. Jonjo's tally of 65 left him a creditable fourth in the jockeys' list, but the popular Irishman was hungry for futher success and hankered for the greater independence of a freelance role.

Since the departure of Ron Barry, The Boss had come to regard Jonjo as an integral part of the Greystoke set-up, always at hand to give assistance and even advice. His life was inextricably linked with the Richards' machine. By the end of the 1976–77 campaign Jonjo felt that he was facing a personal dilemma. He knew that he owed a huge debt to both Gordon and Jean: The Boss for supplying the opportunities and the guidance that had transformed his career from struggling stable lad to top jump jockey; his wife for her sympathetic understanding in the early months of his arrival and her long-suffering patience during the pain and frustration of his six-month inactivity with that shattered leg.

Jonjo appreciated all these intense ramifications, but at the same time he sensed that his independence was being throttled. He sought advice from family, friends and colleagues. Finally he knew that he had to break loose. On his return from a short break at home in Ireland, he marched straight into the Richards' flat and announced that he was leaving. The Boss was stunned.

FIFTEEN

David Goulding 'Top Dog'

For the first few days Gordon was confident that Jonjo would reconsider his decision to leave his job at Greystoke and ride as a freelance. When the rider's resolution failed to wobble under pressure, the feeling of disbelief changed to disappointed frustration. It was predictable that The Boss should regard Jonjo's departure as tantamount to personal betrayal. He regarded his stable as the best, his horses second to none, and he could not understand that any jockey should not think along the same lines. To aggravate his sense of angry bewilderment he regarded Jonjo almost as 'one of the family'. Ever since his initial arrival at Greystoke Jonjo had been cosseted, encouraged and supplied step by step with the raw material that enabled his reputation as potential champion jockey to spread contrywide.

Cordial relations between trainer and jockey were gradually restored, but all was fire and brimstone at the beginning. Jonjo rode out the storm, believing that once the shock had worn off Gordon would come to accept his reasons. It may have taken a while, but in the long run nothing but good came out of the break-up. Jonjo proved his point by landing the jockey's title with a record-breaking 149 wins in his very first year as a freelance. The Boss trained Lucius to win the 1978 Sun Grand National and continued to turn out a steady stream of big-race winners under the able guidance of such leading jockeys as David Goulding, Neale Doughty, Phil Tuck and Tony Dobbin.

Once the news had been broken Jonjo kept his head down. He recalls: 'At the time I was thankful to be living in Plumpton Foot on the other side of the M6 from Greystoke! I had tried to explain to Gordon that my decision to leave was not because I was fed up either with him or the stable, but because in the long run I wanted to train myself and felt it important to broaden my horizons before that time arrived. I realised that he would find this difficult to swallow, but it was how I felt at the time and I was not going to change my mind. The Boss came round eventually and in recent years we started going to the sales together and all the old "crack" began again.'

Jonjo's absence left David Goulding at the top of the tree. Somehow the combination of 'Gipsy Dave' and The Boss was odds-on to be short and sharp. It was a meeting of opposites: GWR wearing his heart on his sleeve, always out there conducting the show, extrovert and often abrasive; Goulding patient, soft-spoken, the epitome of coolness yet a genuinely funny man blessed with an instinctive sense of timing both in and out of the saddle. Gordon found

David Goulding difficult to understand as a person, too tricky by half. Pat Muldoon, a great supporter, recalls once asking Gordon if he ever gave David any definite instructions: 'The Boss fell silent as though about to produce some profound observation. Then, turning sharply on his heel, he replied curtly, "No. He wouldn't obey them if I tried!"'

The common factor which kept them together, longer than many people had ever imagined, was a mutual love of animals. Gordon's affection and respect for his horses was the cornerstone of his training success. David Goulding's empathy with horses was equally close. He was a natural horseman because he could both read their minds and understand their feelings. In Dave's case the affinity stretched far beyond the horse. He was an animal lover in the widest sense of the word. Not long after his retirement from the saddle he became fascinated with the world of *One Man and his Dog*. Equipped with a couple of Border collies, one of whom he had rescued from a local dog sanctuary, he sought the advice of the real Fellside experts. Their teaching, added to his own intuitive ability to work on the same wavelength as his dogs, have combined to create an outstanding talent. David Goulding is now winning trials throughout the Lake District and beyond.

Goulding was a Cumbrian by birth. He lived at Brigham, near Cockermouth, and gained his early racing experience helping out 'Doc' Macdonald, the local vet and permit holder who enjoyed considerable success on the northern circuit with such familiar names as Avon Bay, Lochar Moss and Allerdale.

Goulding made his mark with Arthur Stephenson at Crawleas, but he maintained links with Cumbria – notably through his association with the Brough-based permit holder Bryan Bousfield, for whom he enjoyed a number of successes on the home-bred Tony. The pair were most effective together at Catterick, where their trademark was to come from a long way off the pace to scythe through beaten horses and get up close home. It was a tactic for which David Goulding became famous and one which caused Pat Muldoon to tear out his hair until he realised that the clock in his jockey's head was finely tuned. Pat explains: 'David rode Highway Rambler for me on a regular basis and there were times that I was certain he was overdoing the waiting tactics. But Highway Rambler got on famously with him and come the last two flights or the final fence there they both would be, poised to challenge, often with the race at their mercy.'

David puts it this way: 'Throughout my career I had this reputation for leaving things until the very last moment. In fact I won plenty of races by riding up with the pace. It all depended how quickly I could get my mount to settle and enjoy the occasion. If they insisted on pulling for their heads then I would try my best to get them switched off and conserve their energy for a late run. From the stands it may have seemed that we were quickening up, but in most cases it was more a question of our rivals dropping back beaten and us staying on at the same pace. I was lucky that the best horses I rode, like Ekbalco and Current Gold, always ran their best races this way.'

Pattern Maker and Mixed Melody also liked patient handling. However both would be put right into the firing line on the run to the second last, while Tamalin often jumped himself to the front even earlier.

David Goulding had ridden 49 winners in Greystoke's record-breaking 1975–76 season. Jonjo had grabbed most of the glory the following campaign and Goulding's final tally of 11 would have looked even thinner had it not been for the consistency of Current Gold and the promise of Pattern Maker. This talented but temperamental half-brother to Bula provided just the sort of challenge that Goulding relished.

Pattern Maker had inherited much of his illustrious half-brother's ability. On the racecourse he was a pleasure to ride and had he stayed sound might have gone all the way to the top. The fact that he actually raced at all was down to Gipsy Dave. He was the only man in the yard brave enough to tackle Pattern Maker's ruthless habit of 'dropping' his rider at regular intervals both to and from the gallops. Every three or four paces Pattern Maker would put in a prodigious buck intended to catapult his rider out through the front door!

David, though, could anticipate the moment to a split second and as Pattern Maker's powerful hind quarters left the ground so would David's bottom lift off his saddle to balance the angle. No quarter was asked or given. Pattern Maker would repeat his rodeo tactics all the way to the gallops. Dave would continue his balancing act without even so much as a harsh word. Once on the hill horse and jockey would work in perfect harmony. Exercise over, and the bucking would begin again – all the way back to the stables, with David Goulding's backside rising and falling in unison with that of his partner.

The jockey never lost patience with his mount. Nor did he alter his opinion that Pattern Maker was a star in the making. Early performances seemed to justify his confidence. After winning novice hurdles in impressive style at Haydock and Wetherby in 1976–77, he delighted connections the following season with two further victories in handicap company. His win at Haydock in the keenly contested Merseyside Handicap was achieved in awesome style but, cruelly, he was to pull up lame and never raced again.

Current Gold, whom Goulding had ridden to victory four times in 1976–77, failed to add to his score during his partner's sojourn as stable jockey, but the pair performed with commendable consistency at the highest handicap level. Third in the Mackeson, the Massey-Ferguson and the Scottish National, Current Gold also galloped home a most creditable fifth in the Whitbread behind Strombolus. David's patient handling of this courageous stayer was to pay a rich dividend in years to come. Not that everyone agreed. There was a school of thought which interpreted matters differently and some people were only too quick to equate David Goulding's patience with their own definition of insufficient effort. Well before he had joined forces with the Richards stable, stewards' secretaries from Market Rasen in the south-east of the region, to Ayr in the north-west, had taken this line and encouraged their well-meaning panels to call the jockey before them 'to explain his riding'.

From the stands their actions might have seemed amply justified, but then they were not in the saddle as David was and his instinct for the welfare of his mount was rarely wrong. If David felt that a horse was losing his action, or in any way distressed, he would ease down rather than press on regardless with the chance of aggravating possible injury. This being said, he wasn't blessed with second sight. There were occasions when officialdom, and even The Boss himself, had cause for complaint.

Goulding rode 52 winners during his stint as number one jockey at Greystoke. Three of these came on Lucius, but to his bitter disappointment injury prevented him from being in the saddle when Fiona Whitaker's bargain buy achieved his famous victory in the *Sun* Grand National. David damaged his coccyx so painfully while in action at Wetherby earlier in the week that he was forced to forsake the chance of a lifetime.

Gordon was in the broad sense supportive of David Goulding. He appreciated his talent as a jockey and applauded his judgement of pace and sympathetic horsemanship. But at the same time he was far from happy at being put in the position of increasingly having to explain away his jockey's tactics, either to enquiring officials or, on occasions, disgruntled owners. The Boss had been able to discuss matters on equal terms with Ron Barry. He had a close working relationship with Jonjo O'Neill. Discussions with David Goulding, though, were somehow more complicated.

As the season progressed The Boss felt a growing sense of unease develop. GWR, we know, liked to insist on 'doing things his way'. David Goulding, it seemed, thought along similar lines. Such independence of thought did not augur well for the permanence of the partnership and so it was to prove. With hindsight, small chinks in the chain were evident some while before the eventual difference of opinion at Cartmel. Back in late November Ron Barry had ridden Bobby Gordon to win at Ayr for Greystoke patron David Scott. Even earlier, a certain young jockey called Neale Doughty was beginning to catch the eye with his promising handling of horses trained at Haddington by Wilfred Crawford. It would not be long before the Commander recommended that Gordon should take an interest in the potential of the determined Welshman.

Meanwhile life at Castle Stables continued untroubled by such under-currents. Excitement about the Aintree chances of Lucius became intense as the time for the Grand National neared. Incoming stars like Man of Steel raised morale in the yard and Mixed Melody was being prepared for the *Daily Express* Triumph Hurdle on the strength of three consecutive victories, the last and most important of which had been a 12–1 win in Haydock's Victor Ludorum Hurdle (postponed until the early March meeting after its traditional date in February had fallen foul to the frost). David Goulding had excelled on Mixed Melody at Haydock, sitting down to ride a power-packed charge for the line from in between the last two flights, and withstanding a sustained attack from the closing pack to score by a hard-fought three lengths.

Mixed Melody was not only the first filly to win the Victor Ludorum; she was also one of the very few horses in the yard to benefit from the attention of

Joey Richards, the trainer's vivacious daughter. A splendid portrait of Mixed Melody hangs on the side wall of the Old Rectory drawing room, much to Joey's delight. She recalls, 'I used to look after Mixed Melody all through the day: groom her, roll her and ride her out. I liked to lead her up at the races too, but for some reason Colin Parker did not send me to Haydock. I was due to lead her up at Cheltenham for the Triumph Hurdle, but half-way down the M5 the message arrived that Cheltenham had been abandoned because of snow and the horse box returned home!'

David Goulding's love of animals, and his intuitive way with them, was demonstrated in one of his most popular achievements during his time at Greystoke. Pat Muldoon tells the story of his intervention in the alliance between Canadius and the nanny goat: 'Both Gordon and I were cheesed off with the obsession that Canadius had for the wretched goat, though I hasten to add that neither of us ever had the doubtful privilege of having to milk her! The nadir arrived when Canadius was prevented from running in a big race at Sandown. I think it was the Tingle Creek, because foot-and-mouth restrictions banned the goat from travelling south. Canadius could travel, of course, but nothing would induce him to leave Greystoke without his constant companion.

'This is where David stepped in. He spent hours talking quietly to Canadius in his box and gradually weaned him away from the goat. The first stage was to convince Canadius that the goat would sometimes like to take a wander in the yard instead of being cooped up in his box all day. Canadius agreed, but with poor grace, and for a long while would not let "nanny" out of sight in case she wandered off. David decided to play him at his own game. Every time the goat went "walkies" outside Canadius's box he ensured that she not only stayed within sight, but returned inside after a pre-set time. Gradually Canadius relaxed his vigil and little by little David extended the time that the goat was absent – until the day finally dawned when the goat did not reappear and Canadius was blissfully unaware that she had gone. The obsession was lifted but to avoid a relapse Little Tiger, the Richards' family pony was introduced as a substitute. Whenever Canadius travelled to the races, the pony went along for the trip and everything was sweetness and light.'

Crunch time for the Richards–Goulding partnership arrived at Cartmel's late May Bank Holiday fixture. David Batey, who farmed some five miles to the north of Greystoke, had Bell Colleen, his home-bred mare, in training at Castle Stables. She was a modest firm-ground performer and duly scored in a novice chase at Hexham in the last week of April. David Goulding held her up until safely over the final fence and persuaded her to quicken sufficiently on the flat to get her head in front close home. Bell Colleen then finished third in a similar contest at Sedgefield. The Boss knew full well that the owner's ambition was to see the mare win at Cartmel. With this in mind, he declared Bell Colleen for the Broughton Novices' Chase on the Saturday of Cartmel's two-day holiday meeting. The mare was backed down to even-money favourite on the strength of optimistic noises from GWR. The proud owner and his party watched The

Boss give David Goulding the leg-up in the paddock before hastening to the primitive grandstand which provides Cartmel racegoers with the one vantage point of sufficient height to make it possible to follow about half the race. This luxury was not required, as Bell Colleen ballooned the first fence and was pulled up before the next – impervious to the catcalls from a hostile bunch of frustrated favourite backers, and the even longer faces of the owner's entourage.

Goulding said that Bell Colleen was feeling the firm ground and to save her legs he'd decided to pull her up quickly. Unamused, the stewards called an enquiry. It had been the last race of the day. Faced with conflicting versions of the circumstances leading to Bell Colleen's sudden departure from the action, the officials decided to adjourn the enquiry until before racing on the Monday.

In the interval tempers became frayed in the Richards camp. David Goulding maintained that the mare had been suffering from sore shins and that she should never have been allowed to race on the prevailing firm ground. He added that if Bell Colleen was declared to run again in the handicap chase on the Monday, he would pull her up before she got to the first fence. GWR, almost incoherent with pent-up fury, accused Goulding of talking 'bollocks' and insisted that the mare was sound as a bell. Goulding, he said, should stop his nonsense and put her into the race with every chance on the Monday or he would take the consequences.

By Monday the warring factions had shown no signs of reaching a negotiated peace. Bell Colleen had been declared overnight with riding arrangements undecided. A glorious day in the Lake District brought holiday racegoers out in their hordes, hell-bent on breaking the bank at Cartmel. Traffic on the narrow lanes to the course was at a standstill fully two hours before the first race. The Boss, desperate to attend the re-opened stewards' enquiry to put what he insisted were the only true facts of the case before the panel, and at the same time rubbish his jockey's theory about sore shins, was forced to abandon his Mercedes and run through the beer-toting masses to reach the course on time. Breathless and puce in the face, he took no prisoners. Taken aback, but not brow-beaten, the stewards called David Goulding back in and advised him of GWR's explanation. Goulding in his turn pulled no punches. He accused the trainer of twisting the truth and vociferously defended his version of events. The stewards adjourned the enquiry, as David Goulding's tenure as stable jockey was at an end. And the three-pound claimer T.P. Walshe took the mount on Bell Colleen.

As for Bell Colleen, she started at 7–2 third favourite and made no show. The following autumn she managed two outings over fences in the hands of Ron Barry, weakening from three out in a handicap chase at Market Rasen and falling at the 14th when under pressure at Cartmel. David Goulding never changed his mind about the sore shins. It cost him his job at Greystoke, but his high-profile association with Roger Fisher's brilliant hurdler Ekbalco kept his name in the headlines. Later a run of bad falls left him suffering from a recurrent bout of bad headaches, causing a premature end to his riding career in the winter of 1984.

The Boss opted for a simpler life. The start of the 1978–79 season saw Ron Barry back once more as top man at Greystoke.

SIXTEEN

The National: Both Sides of the Coin

Aintree was not an immediate magnet to Gordon. Later, with two Grand Nationals under his belt, he was rated almost in the same league as Liverpool specialists like Neville Crump, Fred Rimell, Tim Forster and Ginger McCain. But it took him 11 seasons to make a serious impact on the National scene and after his second victory with Hallo Dandy, in 1984, the Aintree pinnacle was to elude him for the remainder of his career.

GWR was fond of labelling chosen individuals from his team as 'Grand National types' – though when he first described Lucius in these terms at Kelso in the spring of 1976, cynics might have pointed out that his previous record in this specialised event had been nothing out of the ordinary. That is, if the example of Red Sweeney is overlooked. This versatile performer would definitely have fitted Gordon's Aintree model. Who's to say he wouldn't have justified the label?

A careful jumper, tough, durable, blessed with unlimited stamina and not devoid of acceleration, Red Sweeney seemed a worthy ante-post favourite for the 1972 National – only to be withdrawn 48 hours before the race. His sudden exit remains etched on the Budden mind.

I had been sent out to Greystoke with a film crew from Border Television to interview The Boss and obtain visual coverage of Red Sweeney for transmission in Friday evening's *Border Sports Lookaround*. Gordon had been called away, but Red Sweeney's lad was with the horse in his box and agreed to walk the chestnut round the outside of the stable for the benefit of the cameras. He was not a talkative type, but his walk-on role did not require conversation. Mission accomplished – or anyhow, the photographic part of the job in the can – we returned happily to the studios.

Hardly had the Volvo film unit estate wagon entered the car-park than figures dashed out to meet us, asking in eager and excited tones, 'Well, then, have you got the story? What are the close-ups like?'

Puzzled by their uncharacteristic enthusiasm, we played for time until the producer cut in testily with the direct challenge: 'Well, then, is he lame or not?'

One glance at my blank expression told him the answer before I had managed to find my voice. In truth I hadn't even bothered to watch the filming, as I had been chasing around the stables in the vain hope of finding GWR to do his interview. It didn't take long for the whole sorry story to emerge. ITN had been in touch to say they had heard a whisper that Red

Sweeney would 'miss' the National and wondered if Border, the local station, knew anything about it.

A short trip to the darkened editing room revealed the disaster in detail. There was the Grand National favourite making a very passable stab at a 'three-legged race' as he limped round the stable block. We had missed the news scoop of the week and we hadn't even realised it. There were red faces all round. To make matters worse ITN sent their own reporter round to Greystoke to interview The Boss. Red Sweeney, it transpired, had trodden on a stone and had badly bruised a foot. There was no hope that he would be sound for the National.

This was the year that Gyleburn, the safe jumping armchair ride, became the late substitute. He fell, however, at the first fence.

In 1974 Richards was confident of a good run from Straight Vulgan, the property of Mrs Gordon Sandiford. His build-up had been most satisfactory. A powerful galloper, he would last out the four miles and his jumping had caused no serious problems. Ron Barry, hungry for his initial Grand National success, had Straight Vulgan handily placed on the heels of the leaders throughout the first circuit and the partnership was still prominent when Straight Vulgan fell at the 18th.

Greystoke had no runners in the next two Grand Nationals but the lightly-made and athletic Sir Garnet, a useful hurdler in his time, revived his trainer's enthusiasm for the race with a promising effort in 1977. Sir Garnet, three times a winner over the drop fences at Haydock, was well in touch; but perhaps he was just beginning to feel the pinch when Jonjo O'Neill was knocked out of the saddle as the partnership swung round the Canal Turn for the final time. As always in racing, opinions about the way he was going at the time of his departure differed according to who was telling the story. The Boss was typically bullish, maintaining that Sir Garnet had to be asked the question, but had bags of stamina and would surely have been in the shake-up. Jonjo was less adamant, but admitted that Sir Garnet was travelling as well as any horse he had ridden over the National fences. Nicky Richards takes the pragmatic view: 'Of course Jonjo was unlucky to be shot out of the saddle, but the way I read it was that Sir Garnet was tiring at the time'.

At the start of the 1977–78 season The Boss had Tamalin at the back of his mind for the National experience. David Goulding regarded Tamalin as one of the finest jumpers of a fence that he had ever had the privilege to ride. If Tamalin was the obvious choice, Lucius had certainly not been forgotten. Gordon still reckoned that his toughness, his ability to look after himself and his proven record in long-distance handicap hurdles all combined to give him a chance second to none – provided his owner was in favour of the attempt.

Lucius was the property of Fiona Whitaker, wife of David, a highly respected Edinburgh-based chartered accountant. The Whitakers lived in Fife at St Colme House, a beautiful eighteenth-century mansion at Aberdour overlooking the Firth of Forth. They had been introduced to the thrills of ownership through the modest exploits of the lovely Arctic Dawn, originally owned by Fiona's family (the Dewhursts, who had the mare in training first with Fred Winter and then with Gordon Richards at Greystoke. Arctic Dawn was to be the cornerstone of Fiona Whitaker's breeding operation. In the spring of 1972 David and Fiona asked GWR to find them a decent jumping prospect at the sales. Gordon went to 1,800 guineas to secure an unbroken three-year-old by Perhapsburg out of Matches – a well-bred Irish mare who had won two races over fences.

Lucius won twice over hurdles in the 1973–74 season. On both occasions he was ridden by Ron Barry, who recalls being torn apart by The Boss in the winner's circle at Ayr. 'That was typical of Gordon,' reflects Ron. 'He was furious because I had picked up the stick and given Lucius a couple of smacks to keep his mind on the job. Gordon always put the welfare of his horses before everything else, even on occasions the interests of his owners. He thought a lot of Lucius and so did I. The difference between us at Ayr was that I felt Lucius required to be educated in the art of winning. If that required a bit of gentle persuasion, so be it. The Boss was still looking to the future. In fact, Lucius never turned a hair and he went on to win again at Catterick under hands and heels.'

Lucius came into his own during the 1975–76 season, scoring four times over hurdles before being introduced to fences and winning at Perth and Carlisle. The transition to chasing had not been an immediate success. On his début at Newcastle he was far from fluent: he needed a couple of reminders from Jonjo O'Neill before the 11th and pecked on landing at the 14th. He finished a staying-on third behind Roystar. Brought back to two miles for a second attempt at the Newcastle fences in mid-March, Lucius blundered at the seventh, found himself in front too early as long-time leader Sharina fell at the ninth, and went down by four lengths to Mr Midshipman.

David Goulding took over the reins at Kelso a fortnight later. Once more, Lucius was sent off a warm favourite; but of much greater importance was GWR's pre-race assertion that the Whitakers' bargain buy was a natural for Aintree. Kelso's novice chase took place 45 minutes after Rag Trade had triumphed at Aintree. Fiona remembers Gordon giving David Goulding the leg-up and saying, 'Ooh now Fiona, I wouldn't be surprised if we weren't doing this in the paddock at Aintree in a couple of years' time. Lucius is just the type to jump those big fences, yes he is!'

The idea left Fiona nonplussed and its accuracy could have been questioned after Lucius fell three out. Gordon, though, was unworried. Disputing the lead at the time, Lucius had jumped safely until his downfall and The Boss reckoned that he would learn from the experience. His opinion was quickly endorsed. Lucius and David Goulding came good with two effortless victories, before ending the season with narrow defeats at Hexham and Perth at the hands of battle-hardened duo Shalimar and The Gent. With hindsight these early reverses were a blessing in disguise. Lucius learned from the start to look after himself and his riders learned from experience that Lucius was a much better proposition when held up for a late run.

The learning curve continued throughout 1976–77. Lucius won three times, though he was an unlucky loser at Perth where his reins broke and Jonjo was unseated before the last. In his remaining four outings Lucius tasted defeat. The frustrating habit of making one bad mistake per race was proving costly.

Gordon may have had the Grand National as the seasonal target for Lucius in 1977–78 but there was no question of keeping him under wraps for the big event. Lucius had run nine times before he reached Aintree. Several of these races were gruelling affairs. The campaign began brightly enough with wins at Sedgefield and Carlisle in the hands of David Goulding. Lucius then went to Ayr and met his match in the shape of Flashy Boy, the highly rated Irish chaser. Michael Dickinson, an unusual booking for the Greystoke stable, kept him handy from the start. But the partnership was left for dead once Flashy Boy moved up a gear in the home straight and galloped clear to score by 12 lengths. Dickinson retained the mount for the Staveley Handicap Chase at Wolverhampton and Lucius was travelling strongly in front until he came to grief at the tenth. David Goulding's return breathed new life into the Whitakers' enigmatic performer. At Carlisle he jumped with bold precision, but could not quicken from the front, and was overhauled by The Last Light on the run to the line.

Early in the new year, Lucius threw away a possible winning chance in the Holmston Chase at Ayr by blundering and losing momentum at the last fence. He recovered, but could not peg back Jack's Flutter on the short run in. By the time that the National weights were published, Lucius had regained winning form in the Wike Handicap Chase at Wetherby. There was quiet confidence in the Greystoke camp and the belief that Lucius would be a viable National contender was boosted by a brave display in the Wlliam Hill Yorkshire Chase at Doncaster.

Michael Dickinson was back in the saddle. He did well to sit tight at the tenth before persuading Lucius to join issue with Autumn Rain on the run to the second last. The leader, though, had the greater reserves of energy and surged clear over the final fence, leaving Lucius to run on at one pace. Autumn Rain was in fact trained by the Dickinsons and Michael was generous in his praise for Lucius, remarking to the Whitakers as he unsaddled that he felt their horse would 'go very well in the National'.

Gordon had never lost faith in Lucius as a live Grand National hope. Fiona Whitaker recalls that The Boss was purring with pleasure after Doncaster and announced without delay that Lucius would finish his Aintree preparation with a run in the Greenall Whitley Chase at Haydock. David Goulding set a swinging gallop and Lucius was an early leader. He continued to hold a prominent pitch until quickening to join issue with Rambling Artist on the run to the last fence. Lucius showed marginally ahead at the final fence, but he could produce nothing extra on the run to the line and was beaten by three parts of a length. It was another eye-catching performance and the bookies shaved his Grand National odds from 40–1 to 25s. David Whitaker had invested £5 to win at 40–1 after Lucius had finished second at Doncaster. Fiona never bets, but her accountant husband was so impressed by GWR's enthusiasm in the unsaddling enclosure at Haydock that the following Monday he slipped down to the nearest betting shop and doubled his stake.

The Boss had done his work. It was now just a case of keeping Lucius on his toes and free from injury or illness. Nicky recalls, 'Father took it in turns to ride out Tamalin and Lucius on the gallops. He reckoned they would both go close, but although he never actually said so in public, he was bullish about the way Lucius had worked since coming back from the Greenall.'

Tamalin had turned 11 on New Year's Day. He had been a wonderful advertisement for Greystoke and a fine servant to owner Alan Metcalfe. Unlucky not to have won the Hennessy in 1976, he had run with credit in the Gold Cup. In 1977–78 he had won three times from nine starts, scoring by a decisive three lengths from Alpenstock at Doncaster in late February, and improving on that effort in the Wetherby Handicap Chase to finish a close second to the classy Gay Spartan. An earlier form line through Rambling Artist indicated that Lucius should finish in front of Tamalin at Aintree, but the 11-year-old was far from being a pushover and Graham Thorner had been asked to ride.

Riding plans should have been no problem for Lucius. David Goulding, who knew the horse so well, was poised for the big chance; but to his chagrin he bruised his coccyx so badly when riding at Wetherby's Easter meeting, at the beginning of Aintree week, that his availability was suddenly in doubt.

The Boss was in no mood for charity. He made it clear that his jockey must be 110-per-cent fit by Friday if he was to take the mount. Poor Goulding could not guarantee that level. He surrendered the ride and such was his dismay that he couldn't even force himself to watch the National the following afternoon. GWR turned to Ron Barry but Big Ron was caught between a rock and a hard place. He was booked to partner Forest King for Ken Hogg (who now trains with commendable originality in the Isle of Man, but at the time was an entrepreneurial permit holder in the village of Tirril outside Penrith). Forest King, bought for only £125 from neighbouring farmer-breeder Ken Tuer, had won nine times over fences in 1975–76. Reg Crank had ridden him into fifth place behind Red Rum in the 1977 National. A former Eider Chase winner, Forest King had shown signs of returning to his best. He had come back from a lengthy absence to finish fourth in a three-mile chase at Catterick in March and 'Hoggy' was prepared to back his confidence with hard cash. In Cumbria, strangely enough, Forest King was attracting as much support in the betting shops as either Tamalin or Lucius. But, to the disgust of his backers and to the distress of his trainer, the local hope developed a corn 48 hours before the race. Emergency treatment from the equine chiropodist raised hopes.

Forest King was declared overnight and Ron Barry ruled himself out of contention for the mount on Lucius.

Ron's refusal left GWR scouring the lists to unearth a suitable substitute. The only top-flight jump available was Bob Davies. Three times champion jockey in the late '60s and early '70s, Davies, at the age of 31, was no longer competing for major honours. But he was still a fine horseman, averaging around 60 winners a season. Davies met Lucius for the first time in the paddock before the National (sponsored that year by *The Sun*). The Boss did not attempt to confuse his new jockey with a surfeit of orders, but stressed how important it was not to hit the front too early – in particular not to boot him into a six-length lead at the last, or Lucius would think he had done enough and pull himself up.

Fiona Whitaker confirms that Lucius did indeed have almost a phobia about being isolated. She explains: 'After he had retired we hunted him every season for a long while and he was an ideal mount for my teenage daughters in every way except one. If he found himself separated from the field he would down tools. It didn't matter who was riding him – he had to have company.'

The 1978 Grand National remains fresh in the memory. The day dawned dank and misty. I had reached Aintree by mid-morning together with James, my elder son, who was paying his first visit to the National and was determined to back Lucius. My own preferences were for Master H and Tamalin. The Whitakers drove down from Fife. They were encouraged, if a bit surprised, by the volume of support for Lucius: once as long as 50–1, he was now as short as 20s and as low as 14–1 in some papers. From being a viable outsider, he had emerged as one of the better-backed horses in the race and had been 'napped' by several shrewd sources. Tamalin, by contrast, was passed over and 25–1 or longer was readily available about his chances.

The race attracted a huge attendance, caused in no small measure by the public's determination to cheer home Red Rum in what was widely considered to be his swan-song. His admirers were aghast to hear the overnight news that he would no longer be in the line-up. (He would, however, parade in front of the stands before the race.)

David and Fiona Whitaker had been down in the paddock to watch Lucius being saddled, but on the way back to the stands had become detached. Fiona recalls, 'David had been walking with The Boss and I had been following with Jean. We were heading towards the section of the stand that had been reserved for owners and trainers, when Jean said that I had better go on with the others – she couldn't risk climbing to the top of the stairs with her "dicky" heart. By the time I had looked round for Gordon and David they had been swallowed up in the tide. I thought I knew the way, but in the near-stampede found myself being swept up entirely the wrong entrance. Half-way up the stairs a gateman was shouting, "No more room up on top". But I was so determined to watch Lucius, and though I am usually rather polite and obedient in such matters I thought, "To hell with this" – so, head down and elbows out, I pushed and shoved my way to the top tier.'

Wrong stand or not, Fiona had no problem keeping tabs on her beloved Lucius. Rather to the dismay of Bob Davies, he went with the pace from the start. Mindful of GWR's instructions, Davies was concerned, but by a stroke of good fortune Lucius was not alone in his determination to adopt an aggressive role. For much of the first circuit he was surrounded by a small group which included Double Bridal, Sebastian V and Master Upham. Lucius lost a couple of lengths jumping the Chair, but Fiona remembers thinking how much he appeared to be enjoying himself as he passed the stands with a circuit to go. For one brief moment her mind went back to the scene in the paddock at Kelso, where The Boss had first forecast that Lucius could be the ideal type for Aintree. Over 20 years later she uses the memory to demonstrate Gordon's knack of instinctively assessing the potential of each horse under his care. 'It may have taken a while for his ideas to surface, but he was very rarely wrong,' she insists.

Such reflections were fleeting as the 1978 *Sun* Grand National began to unfold down the back straight for the final time. Lucius had joined issue with Sebastian out in front a few lengths to the good of a group that included Lord Browndodd, Mickley Seabright, The Pilgarlic, Coolishall, Drumroan and The Songwriter. Tamalin was further adrift but, to the delight of at least one biased supporter high in the press balcony, he was inching closer to the leading bunch with each fence safely negotiated. The orders had been specific. Graham Thorner had been told to hold him up and not to make his move until after crossing Bechers for the second time round.

There was to be more than a touch of passing irony in this instruction. Tamalin's stealthy advance towards the leaders was halted in its tracks by as dramatic a case of the 'equine splits' as any photographer can ever have captured. In a remarkable sequence of consecutive images, Tamalin was first pictured in a steep head-first dive to the landing side of Bechers Brook. In the second frame Tamalin's stomach is flush with the ground, his four legs splayed and Thorner apparently rowing the saddle like a member of the Oxford boat race crew about to sink. The last of the collage shows Tamalin back on his feet, his rider half over his neck but about to thrust himself backwards into the plate and prepare to resume pursuit. So effective was this vain chase that, with a sustained run from the Canal Turn, he had almost reached the heels of the leading quintet at the third last; but the effort finally told and Graham Thorner accepted the inevitable, allowing him to come home in his own time. Tamalin finished 12th. However, had he jumped the second Bechers with the same fluency as he tackled all the remaining obstacles, who knows, he could well have been there with a shout from the final fence! As it was, Tamalin got home in one piece and Graham Thorner won the Ted Dexter *Sun* award for the best riding performance in the 1978 Grand National.

Lucius had never been an extravagant jumper, a habit which served him well when it mattered the most. Bob Davies could allow him to pop his fences, happy in the knowledge that Sebastian's flamboyant jumping would give him a lead for as long as he wanted. Indeed Lucius's one mistake – a slight misjudgement at the third last – made his jockey's task that bit simpler because it checked his forward progress at a time when it was crucial that Lucius should not be given his head. Sebastian still had the call on the run to the final fence, but the pack was snapping at his heels.

From the stands any one from five could have quickened to take the prize. Out there in the thick of the action, though, Bob Davies knew that the race was his, always providing he could press the button at exactly the right moment. With all about him shouting and shoving he remained ice cool, silent and poised to pounce. He moved a bare two strides past the elbow. Lucius pounced on the courageous Sebastian. The acceleration was short, sharp and sudden. Poor Sebastian tried to rally. Drumroan was hard on his heels but Davies had judged his challenge to the second. Lucius was home by half a length and The Boss had won his first Grand National.

Up in the stands Fiona Whitaker had her own particular battle to fight. Not yet convinced that her pride and joy had actually surpassed her wildest dreams, but assured of the fact that he had to be in the first three, she fought her way down through the heaving masses with ever-increasing desperation. Back at ground level she almost fell foul of the legendary arm of the 'Liverpool law' – but something about Fiona's moist-eyed sincerity must have struck the right note, because with one awesome surge of power the policeman divided those swirling hordes and guided Lucius's ever-grateful owner to the haven of the winner's circle.

Amidst all the congratulations and back slapping, it was typical of the man that The Boss should be just as concerned with the plight of the vanquished Tamalin as he was with the delight at the performance of his winner. Emotions did however run high. Fiona Whitaker confesses to bursting into tears. Lucius's faithful stable lad David Dods – or 'Dodsy', for short – was similarly affected. And there was an audible croak in the trainer's tones as he described his feelings to David Coleman in the traditional post-race television interview. The following morning the people of Greystoke, and it seemed the whole of Cumbria, crowded the village square in front of The Boot and Shoe to pay tribute to both horse and trainer.

Lucius never won another race after his National triumph, but Fiona rubbishes any idea that his experience round Aintree was to blame. She says, 'Gordon was never hard on him but the handicapper wouldn't relent. Wherever he ran he was set to carry top weight and the real trouble was that he often went close to winning – or at the least was never beaten very far. The plan had been to take him back to Aintree for the 1979 National, but he got the virus and wasn't able to run. He had one more season at Greystoke and was then retired.'

Lucius was then hunted with the Fife by various members of the Whitaker family. In the spring of 1986, his last serious season with the hounds, he took part in the members' race across natural country and was ridden by Joanne, the

Whitakers' eldest daughter. When the family moved to Glenfarg Lucius assumed control of the younger horses, acting as resident tutor and seeing that they came to no harm out in the paddocks. He hated being brought back inside for any length of time. He spent the rest of his days relaxing in the open with plenty of food, a comfortable outside shelter and plenty of tender loving care.

Lucius was 27 when he died and the manner of his passing was in keeping with his character. Fiona reflects, 'He was just a lovely genuine horse, kind to the last. He had been happy as Larry when we left him the evening before, but the next morning there he was, lying dead in the middle of his favourite field. The vet said that his heart had just given up and that he had gone peacefully in his sleep. It was almost as though he had made the decision himself to avoid any of us needing to go through the trauma and distress of one day having to see him put down.'

The Whitakers have been ever-present owners at Greystoke since the beginning of the '70s. Arctic Dawn, the mare who had first torched their enthusiasm for National Hunt racing, also lived to an advanced age. In 1987 she was honoured by the Thoroughbred Breeders Association with their outstanding National Hunt Brood-mare award. Not before time, either, as Arctic Dawn had been responsible for the winners of 40 races – a tally which had risen to 66 by the time of her death. The great majority of these were at some time of their careers in training with The Boss at Greystoke: household names like Cape Felix, Pyjamas, Primrose Wood and (most recently) Macgregor the Third.

Arctic Dawn's two daughters, Arctic Ander and Primrose Wood, have ensured that the line continues today. The former produced the useful Candlebright, who has given birth to four foals, the last of which is a lovely sort by Bob's Return. Primrose Wood was the dam of The Whirlie Weevil, who herself has mothered three attractive youngsters.

Fiona Whitaker remembers The Boss with a combination of affection and admiration. She regards him as an outstanding trainer: 'Gordon had so many important qualities, it is hard to quantify them. But he was a wonderfully old-fashioned trainer of jumpers. I had complete confidence in the way he trained our horses. If pushed, I would pick out patience and care for the individual as his two most important attributes. Time and again he would say to me, "Ooh, I could give him a run, y'know, Fiona – but then he would be better with another summer under his belt." Such judgements were instinctive but born of long experience and they were nearly always right.

'No one knew his horses better than Gordon. He treated them all as special individuals from the first moment they arrived in the yard. It didn't take him long to establish an affinity with the horses in his charge. He used to wander round the boxes, watching them at close quarters and discovering what made them tick. He did the same on the gallops. His observations enabled him to place his horses with such skill and, even more importantly, to recognise when one of his team was either trained to the minute or not at his best and perhaps sickening for a virus. He accepted that today's methods of "scoping" and checking blood-counts had a vital role to play in assessing the fitness of a horse; but equally, it would be his instinctive "eye for the individual" that would have triggered the question in the first place.'

Fiona also counters GWR's reputation as the 'hard man' of northern racing. 'Yes,' she continues, 'Gordon did demand perfection. He would never accept second best and if he thought standards were slipping then all hell would break loose. At the same time he was immensely proud of his staff and they were intensely loyal to him. Some might get fed up with his treatment and reckon that the grass was greener elsewhere. But more often than not they would be asking for their job back by the end of the season. On a personal level he was always ready to listen. Many a time I'd be at the stables when one of the lads would come to him with a problem, perhaps marital or more often financial, and I was amazed how Gordon would react with such understanding. There is little doubt that he could be a hard man to please, but there was a warm, private side to him that the public only began to appreciate in his latter years.'

During the '90s the Whitakers went on several holidays to the West Indies at the same time that Gordon and Joanie Richards took their annual break in February. Fiona remembers being astonished at how relaxed the trainer became, once removed from the pressures of Greystoke: 'Most of the outrageous stories about The Boss are unprintable because they almost always came in the heat of the moment, either on the gallops or at the race-track. But out of his daily environment Gordon was excellent company. He enjoyed his golf and loved lying on the beach in the Caribbean sun – though he'd seldom go far into the sea as he wasn't the best of swimmers.

'A lot of trainers seem to take their work with them when they go away, but Gordon was quite the reverse. We were on holiday together in 1991 at the time Twin Oaks was running in the Greenalls. We all knew that if the horse won, Gordon would also pick up the £50,000 bonus offered by the Haydock executive to any stable winning more than a certain number of steeplechases at the course during the season. The press had hyped up the occasion all week, but out on the beach Gordon refused even to ring home to find out the result. Instead he insisted that someone get in touch to tell him the news one way or the other – there wasn't anything he could do about it anyway!'

After the withdrawal of Lucius from the 1979 Grand National, GWR was not represented in the big race until Current Gold and Man Alive went to post in 1982. Over two years had elapsed since Jim Ennis's grey had won the Mackeson, and at the age of 11 Man Alive made little appeal to punters, even though The Boss had once regarded him as natural Aintree material.

Man Alive started at 33–1 and deposited Andy Turnell on the turf at the first fence. Current Gold had been regarded as too small for the National fences but, given a grand ride by Neale Doughty, turned for home in third place before tiring over the last two fences to finish fifth behind Grittar.

Current Gold returned with an Aintree collector's item protruding from under his saddle. He had ploughed through the top of Bechers second time round and galloped the remainder of the way with a sizeable piece of spruce as a memento! Doughty was unstinting in his praise for Current Gold's courage, reporting that if it had not been for his near-disaster at Bechers he would have been competing for a place in the frame. Nine years later Alec Picken was to have a fancied Gold Cup contender in Carrick Hill Lad, but few owners have been lucky enough to have the services of such an indomitable little battler as Current Gold, to whom all obstacles came alike and who was regularly 'in the money' for seven successive seasons.

The 1983 renewal saw Hallo Dandy make the first of four consecutive Grand National appearances. Ginger McCain, who originally trained Hallo Dandy for Jack Thompson, had recognised the Aintree potential of this powerfully built gelding from the start and had trained him to win a novice handicap chase at Haydock when he was only six. Further victories in minor races at Market Rasen and Cartmel followed in 1980–81, before Hallo Dandy moved from Southport to join the Richards team. In spring 1982 he distinguished himself over the Mildmay course with a promising third to Silent Valley in a sponsored handicap chase.

The 1982–83 season was difficult for Gordon Richards. Results in the autumn were encouraging and by the time that Little Bay won the Castleford Chase at Wetherby's Christmas meeting, Greystoke had nearly 30 winners on the scoreboard. The final tally of 39 indicates how matters fell apart during the second part of the campaign. The weather, never very agreeable at Greystoke in the early months of the year, was partly to blame. But the virus was the real culprit. The Richards string was struck down in February and the yard was never free of the infection for the remainder of the jumping season.

Hallo Dandy, meanwhile, had changed hands. Richard Shaw, an insurance tycoon in the City of London, bought the gelding from Jack Thompson in the autumn of 1982 for an undisclosed but very substantial sum – with the specific ambition of winning the Grand National. Though he had to wait a year to recoup an outright success from his purchase, Richard's hopes of achieving his ultimate goal were significantly raised by the progress made by Hallo Dandy throughout 1982–83. The son of Menelek did not win, but at Kelso in November he delighted his new owner by finishing third to Captain John and Peaty Sandy in the Arpal Conquest Chase. The resolute stayer then reached the frame in two of his next three outings. Nevertheless, with his stable out of form and little outward confidence in his chances, Hallo Dandy was an unconsidered outsider for the 1983 Grand National; and any serious expectations of success were dashed with relentless rain which changed the official going to soft on the day of the race.

Richard Shaw was entertaining guests at Aintree. Despite the unfavourable conditions he was keen for Hallo Dandy to run. In any case, this first taste of the National fences was always regarded as being the 'dress rehearsal' rather than the 'first night'. The Boss gave Neale Doughty orders to go for the better ground on the outer, give him a clear view of the fences, and above all let him enjoy himself. Doughty achieved all three objectives in the grand manner. Given his head on the wide outside, Hallo Dandy put up an exhibition round of bold, clean jumping. He nosed in front starting out on the second circuit; maintained a narrow lead jumping Bechers; and from there on in matched strides with Corbiere, the eventual winner. The pair of them provided an exhilarating spectacle until the effort told on Hallo Dandy, approaching the second last, and he weakened into fourth place. But that was quite good enough to reward his optimistic owner with a rewarding each-way return at the quaint starting price of 60–1.

The performance excited everyone at Greystoke. If this was the way Hallo Dandy could treat the National fences, on going that he detested, how much better would he fare in 1984 if the ground were to ride in his favour? As for Richard Shaw, he hadn't become one of the most successful figures in the cut-throat world of the insurance market by sitting on his hands. Taking calculated risks was part and parcel of his working routine. So impressed had he been with 'Dan the Man' and Neale Doughty that he began backing the partnership for the 1984 National almost from the moment the pair had passed the post the previous year: nothing too large to awaken the bookmakers' mutual warning system – but a wide spread of modest bets, at odds from as long as 66–1 down to the 20s which he was quoted until only 48 hours before the actual race.

The layers were generous to a fault, particularly in view of the fact that many well-respected pre-season National Hunt annuals highlighted his Aintree chances. No less an authority than Timeform's *Chasers and Hurdlers* for 1982–83 began Hallo Dandy's notes as follows: 'Given top of the ground conditions, Hallo Dandy represents more than an outside bet at this stage for the 1984 Grand National.'

As if to advertise this view, Hallo Dandy opened his winning account for the 1983–84 season first time out at Ayr in – wait for it – the *Timeform* Chasers' and Hurdlers' Handicap Chase. It was the first race that he had won outright in Richard Shaw's colours and he achieved the victory by a decisive six lengths at 14–1 on soft ground. The Boss outlined his plans to Richard Shaw: Hallo Dandy would have a further two outings during the autumn and then be rested until the spring. The chosen races were the Arpal Conquest Chase at Kelso, followed by the Hennessy.

In the event he was beaten by Cockle Strand at Kelso and was pulled up behind Brown Chamberlain in the Hennessy. By the time that the National weights were declared, Hallo Dandy still had not reappeared – a state of affairs that again lulled the bookmakers into a false sense of security. As Hallo Dandy lined up for the Scottish Farm Dairy Foods Handicap Chase, his price for the National still stood at 33–1. He finished runner-up to Good Crack and the run brought him to racing fitness. A relieved Gordon Richards would put the final polish on Dan the Man's condition by giving him a final spin on the hillside gallops of former owner Alan Carrick. On National Day itself the Greystoke star was finally backed. Opening up at 20s, he was supported down to 13–1 by the time of the race. This time round Neale Doughty rode a patient waiting race. Top racereaders noted a forward move jumping Bechers second time round.

Down south at Parham in Sussex, J. Budden was commentating on the Crawley and Horsham point-to-point, whose executive had arranged an hour's gap between races to listen to the big race from Aintree. Stretching the ears to listen to Peter Bromley's rounded tones, far from clear over the crackling of the ageing public address system, it seemed that every horse in the field had been mentioned bar Hallo Dandy. Then, approaching what emerged to be the 23rd fence, Bromley's voice suddenly slid into overdrive with the frenetic message that Hallo Dandy was right there on the far side. Even through the battered loud speaker precariously fastened to the central pole of the weighing-room marquee, it was apparent from Bromley's enthusiastic repetition of the magic words 'Hallo Dandy, Hallo Dandy' that events were going the right way. Then, seconds after the plummy tones had told us that Hallo Dandy was four lengths in front over the last and showing no sign of stopping, the broadcast was interrupted by a fearful squawking sound – ear-splittingly loud and rising to such a pitch that all commentary was drowned in a flood of noise. I gathered later that the crescendo in Peter Bromley's excited delivery had finally overloaded the fraying wires. For some 20 seconds the Parham crowd was left open-mouthed. Then, to undisguised delight from at least one heavily biased Cumbrian 'incomer', sanity was restored as those wonderful words filled the airwaves: '. . . Hallo Dandy has won the 1984 Seagram Grand National.'

Back home, as I sat watching the recording of the race with a celebratory gin and tonic to hand, the reason behind Peter Bromley's dramatic crescendo after the last fence became only too obvious. The head-on camera highlighted Hallo Dandy's sudden and exaggerated lunge to his right, a deviation that seemed to have lost him a deal of ground and might have allowed Greasepaint to close the gap. In those few raw seconds Neale Doughty's ice-cool nerve and outstanding horsemanship stood the test. Realising that the proximity of the stands-side running rail would automatically halt Hallo Dandy's right-hand swerve, he had let things take their natural course before driving his mount inside the last half furlong to maintain his advantage. It had been a momentary blip in an overall performance of sustained brilliance. Hallo Dandy's faultless jumping had allowed Neale Doughty to ride the race he had planned beforehand: to avoid trouble, centre to outside and come from off the pace to pile on the pressure inside the final mile.

Gordon's part in the victory had been crucial. The long-term strategy of giving Hallo Dandy a complete mid-season break was eminently sensible; but it had been put in jeopardy by the prolonged bad weather in the north, and the chance to provide Hallo Dandy with his one preliminary race at Ayr had arrived in the nick of time. Dick Allan and Ron Barry are both agreed that the greatest of GWR's qualities as a trainer was his ability to produce a horse 'absolutely spot-on' for his intended target. Never was this ability put to a sterner test. The Boss had balanced out the need to keep Hallo Dandy 'fresh and firing', yet still fit enough to last out the extended four miles to perfection. It had been a masterly exhibition by horse, jockey and trainer.

The only people muttering in their beer were the bookmakers. The major firms had to satisfy the not inconsiderable claims of Richard Shaw, while the local Cumbrian layers were faced with a massive pay-out. For Hallo Dandy had not been the only Aintree Saturday winner for the Greystoke stable. The wonderfully enigmatic Little Bay had won the Captain Morgan Chase in the hands of John Francome, while Jennie Pat, ridden by Denis Coakley, completed the 471–1 treble by winning the Glenlivet Hurdle in the colours of Jack Thompson (the former owner of Hallo Dandy). It wasn't surprising that the villagers of Greystoke were in jubilant mood as The Boss paraded Hallo Dandy on the Sunday morning.

Richard Shaw's money-spinner returned to Aintree in 1985, but descended from the sublime to the ridiculous by exiting at the first fence. Neale Doughty was sidelined through injury and despite warning words from the trainer, substitute Graham Bradley was unseated. The Boss was not amused. He claimed he had stressed to the replacement rider that Hallo Dandy took a tremendous hold and tended to over-jump at the opening obstacles. Graham Bradley dismissed the implied criticsm: it wasn't a case of Hallo Dandy over-jumping, he said, but that he came down so steeply that there was no way he could retain his place in the saddle.

Neale Doughty was back in charge for 1986 when Hallo Dandy was 12 years old and had lost his edge. Dan the Man could never go the pace but he stayed on with customary resolution to come home in 12th place. The Boss announced that Hallo Dandy would be retired at the end of the season. He was hale and hearty and Richard Shaw handed him over to Lord Onslow to go hunting in the shires with the Fernie. The decision was initially an unqualified success. 'He could pull like a train,' explained Onslow; 'but he was unadulterated magic to ride and loved his days' hunting in Leicestershire.' In 1994, at the age of 20, he went out to grass looking 'in marvellous condition' according to Lord Onslow.

By September the opposite was so. Whatever the rights and wrongs of the case, Hallo Dandy was a pitiable sight: painfully thin, his coat badly scored by exposure to the rain and his feet in serious need of attention. The media cried 'neglect'. The charge was denied by the Earl, who admitted that Hallo Dandy 'wasn't a happy sight' but claimed that he had 'gone downhill with a wallop'. Real fears that Hallo Dandy would have to be put down were alleviated by Yvonne Shaw, who had heard of the splendid work done by Carrie Humble in restoring the health of former racehorses in similar desperate circumstances.

Carrie's highly regarded Thoroughbred Rehabilitation Centre, near Kendal, is not normally used as a sanctuary for sick horses. But this was an emergency and, as Carrie recalls, 'Hallo Dandy had to be an exception. Frankly, I was pretty appalled with what I saw. He wouldn't eat, his ribs were protruding and I was worried that his liver and kidneys might be irreparably damaged.'

Much to the relief of The Boss, blood tests revealed that although Hallo Dandy was anaemic, his vital organs were sound. He had been rescued just in time. Thanks to the individual care of Carrie and her staff it wasn't long before he began to take renewed interest in life, regaining his appetite and rebuilding his muscles.

The Boss had been outraged at Hallo Dandy's predicament. He had to be restrained from jumping to the instant conclusion that his old servant had been the victim of shameless neglect and a visit to Carrie Humble's centre did little to relieve his feelings. However he was persuaded by Carrie that Hallo Dandy would recover. Given her assurance that the 21-year-old would spend the rest of his days as standard bearer at the rehabilitation centre, Gordon agreed to let matters rest. Dan the Man is now in his late 20s and still enjoying every minute of the day.

SEVENTEEN

The National: Continued

The Thoroughbred Rehabilitation Centre, run by Carrie Humble, has recently moved from Kendal to property between Lancaster and Preston, some eight miles from Jack Berry's Moss Side stables outside Cockerham. Carrie reports that Hallo Dandy is no longer being worked, but remains in rude health: 'Perhaps a little portly, but in tremendous condition. I just wish that Gordon could see him now!'

To say that The Boss had improved Hallo Dandy on his arrival at Greystoke would be quite unfair to Ginger McCain. Ginger had started him off on his chasing career, won three races with him and, given the chance, might well have trained him to win another National to add to the triumphs of Red Rum. For a top trainer GWR took charge of remarkably few horses from other yards. The exceptions, of course, were those who came from Ireland, either bought privately from the sales or – as in the case of Dark Ivy – switched by the owner from her Irish trainer to take advantage of the greater opportunities this side of the Water.

Dark Ivy was just one of the increasing number of successful jumpers running in the familiar maroon-and-grey colours of Mrs Stewart Catherwood from Co. Antrim. The grey had been in training with Dundalk handler John Cox, for whom he had performed with modest consistency for several seasons. Two-and-a-half-mile handicaps were his *métier*, but these were few and far between in Ireland and the handicapper would not relent.

The Catherwoods decided to let Dark Ivy try his luck in Britain, so at the comparatively advanced age of ten the gelding joined Gordon Richards, who had already delighted the same owners with his handling of Little Bay. Over the coming months The Boss improved Dark Ivy to such an extent that as an 11-year-old the following spring he was to start a well deserved 11–2 second favourite for the 1987 Seagram Grand National.

There was a touch of the Sea Pigeons about Dark Ivy, without quite the class of that most popular of Champion Hurdlers. The common link was confidence, or rather lack of it, when both horses moved to Cumbria. The Boss, quick to recognise the signs, opted to give Dark Ivy a couple of spins over hurdles to regain his self-esteem.

The first of these was the Thorpe Sackville Hurdle at Leicester in mid-November. Gordon sent Music Be Magic down to the Midlands as well. Stable jockey Phil Tuck rode the latter, while Dark Ivy was partnered by the Irish claimer Jerry Quinn. Music Be Magic went to post at 9–4, while Dark Ivy attracted very little support at 10–1. Quinn allowed the grey to race with the leaders from the start. The combination took up the running between the final two flights but, strongly challenged by Music Be Magic and Quilantaro (the eventual winner), Dark Ivy failed to quicken and was not asked too serious a question. The Leicester stewards were not impressed with Quinn's display, considering that he had not ridden his mount out to the line with sufficient vigour. Under cross-examination the rider admitted that he had been told not to hit the horse behind the saddle, as he had turned sour back in Ireland. This explanation was 'recorded'. Horses trained by The Boss – hurdlers in particular – were at the time coming under the scrutiny of the stewards' secretaries, apparently on the grounds that they were non-triers or at the very least were not being ridden to achieve their best possible placing.

The Boss became overheated at the action of the officials, a reaction which was understandable. The implication was that the horses involved were being 'kept for another day'. Indirectly this was true but definitely not in the manner that the stewards believed. The Dark Ivy incident was a good example. The betting indicated that he was not expected to finish in front of Music Be Magic. He was described as 'backward' and it shouldn't have taken much thought on the part of either punter or official to realise that he was being given an 'educational' run to boost his confidence for an imminent return to the chasing ranks. The Boss may have been breaking the letter of the law; but to equate this with the idea that he was cheating the racing public is stretching the imagination.

Dark Ivy was to race once more over hurdles. He finished second, beaten eight lengths by Rocky's Gal, his market rival, in a handicap hurdle at Southwell. Phil Tuck was in the saddle and the grey was ridden in a similar fashion to the method employed at Leicester. The time was ripe to switch Dark Ivy back to fences. He was declared for the Tairlaw Handicap Chase at Ayr's pre-Christmas meeting. The distance of two miles was short of his best. He blundered at the seventh and made a further mistake three out before weakening into fourth place behind Norton Cross.

Dark Ivy's rehabilitation was now complete. He returned to Ayr for the New Year fixture and, upped in distance to two and a half miles, made every yard of the running to upset the odds laid on The Ivider. A significant win was to follow at Wetherby where, tackling three miles for the first time since arriving at Greystoke, he was caught by Durham Edition after taking the last in front, only to hit back close home and snatch the verdict near the line. Perhaps even more important was his effort in the four-mile, one-furlong Tote Eider Chase at Newcastle. Given a most positive ride by Phil Tuck, the grey overcame a mistake at the 16th to hit the front at the third last. Taken on by Peaty Sandy approaching the final fence, he was unable to quicken, but stayed on in dour style to keep the deficit down to three lengths.

Dark Ivy travelled north to Ayr for his last race before the National. He was set to renew rivalry with The Divider on worse terms, but slaughtered Trish Calder's decent chaser by 25 lengths easing up. The Boss had done a remarkable job with a battle-worn 11-year-old whose form was exposed for all to see. Dark Ivy had been rejuvenated and optimism soared in Cumbria that Greystoke would win the Grand National for the third time in ten years. The public agreed. Dark Ivy, quoted at 20–1 (longer in places) on the day that the Aintree weights were revealed and was sent off the 11–2 second favourite, half a point longer than West Tip.

Phil Tuck carried 2lb overweight at 10st 2lb, but GWR was more than happy. He never wanted his jockeys to go hungry before the National. Dark Ivy took the early fences comfortably in his stride, but sandwiched between Altitude Adjuster and Why Forget on the heels of the leaders, he was unsighted at Bechers, fell heavily and broke his neck. The tragedy was played out in full view of the cameras and Dark Ivy's fatal fall was to trigger off a radical redesign of the National's most famous obstacle.

Phil Tuck reflects: 'Dark Ivy was the best horse that I ever rode in the National. He had more class than Mr Snugfit but we couldn't be sure that he would take to the National fences. In fact he jumped the first very deliberately, but after that he was brilliant. He'd got the measure of them and he was beginning to enjoy himself. As we approached Bechers, we were in the middle of the course, tracking towards the outside. Nial Madden on Attitude Adjuster was on our outside and Why Forget and Chris Grant on our inside. Just yards from Bechers, Why Forget swerved right across us. Dark Ivy was completely unsighted and galloped straight into the ditch.'

Two blank years elapsed before Rinus appeared on the scene. Having drawn attention to GWR's reluctance to take on talent from other stables, one has to admit that Rinus – like Hallo Dandy – had begun his career with Ginger McCain, who won a couple of novice hurdles with him at Carlisle before Albert Proos (his owner, a timber importer and roofing contractor from Darwen) transferred him to Greystoke. Bought out of Ireland as a three-year-old, the gelding was already named Leggykelly; but Mr Proos, whose second Christian name is Marinus, had him re-registered as Rinus.

The Boss won a couple of handicap hurdles with him, but always regarded him as a chasing prospect. In 1987–88, his first season over fences, Rinus won eight races including the valuable Heidsieck Dry Monopole Handicap Chase round the Mildmay course at Liverpool. Many observers were surprised that Rinus was not among the starters for the Sun Alliance Novices' Chase at the 1988 Cheltenham Festival, but Gordon's placing of Rinus on his initial campaign as a chaser emphasised what a shrewd judge of the programme book he had become. He wasn't exactly in the Arthur Stephenson 'little fish' league, yet at the same time he would never overface his horses. I recall his answer to my query as to whether Rinus might end up at Cheltenham, while I was mapping out a Festival preview in February. 'Nope, John,' he said. 'He goes to Ayr for the Scottish Dairy Foods and then we'll find a nice little race before sending 'im to h'Aintree in h'April.'

He was absolutely spot-on in his selection of races, if not perhaps in his correct use of the vowel sounds. By the '90s, regular interviews on TV, and later for the Racing Channel, had polished up his delivery; but earlier he often had the engaging habit of dropping Hs when they should have been in place, and vice versa. It only happened when he was off guard, but "'orses to h'Ayr' was always a favourite expression. As statistics will also prove, Ayr was his most successful course and I have known the occasional self-disciplined Cumbrian who has made a tidy profit by keeping his bets solely to 'the Richards selected' at the West of Scotland course.

Rinus's eventual appearance in the 1990 Seagram Grand National had an inevitable ring about it. He had shown his ability to cope with the drop fences at Haydock by finishing runner-up to Southern Minstrel in the 1989 *Timeform* Chase, before taking advantage of Willsford's last-fence blunder to purloin the 1990 Greenall Whitley Gold Cup only five weeks prior to Liverpool. The extra-firm ground at Aintree which delighted connections of Mr Frisk and Durham Edition, the first two home, was met with misgivings by those closely concerned with Rinus. Though he was widely reported to act on all types of going, it was feared that the Greystoke stayer might be tapped for toe by the dyed in the wool firm-ground specialists.

So it proved. Neale Doughty had Rinus on the heels of the leading group throughout the first circuit, but in the effort to hold his place Rinus made a couple of mistakes. Pushed up into fourth crossing Bechers for the second time, Rinus stayed on with gritty resolution, but could never quicken sufficiently to close with the two leaders. He did well to finish third and maintain Doughty's remarkable 100 per cent record for completing the course. Rinus was the seventh mount that Neale had taken in the Aintree spectacular; all seven had passed the post with their rider still very much in the saddle.

The Boss was satisfied. Rinus had been down with the cough for much of the season. He had enjoyed only a light preparation for the National and there was every hope that, like Hallo Dandy, he would benefit from the experience and be competing for outright victory in 1991.

In the event Rinus caught a viral infection shortly after finishing fourth in the Edward Hanmer at Haydock in November. He did not reappear until *Racing Post* day at Kempton in late February, when by coincidence he also occupied fourth position behind Sabin Du Loir. To freshen Rinus up, The Boss brought him back to two miles at Ayr in March and despite the presence of Jim Thorpe, his stable companion and a recognised expert at this trip, Rinus ran out a decisive winner. There was just time to give Rinus one more warm-up race over three miles before the big day. He finished a creditable second. On the strength of these promising runs and his encouraging third in the 1990 National, Rinus was again a warm order for his second attempt at the National fences. His starting price of 7–1 joint second favourite with Garrison Savannah put him only half a point longer than Bonanza Boy, the market leader.

Timeform indicates that Rinus jumped 'sketchily' during the first circuit, but turning away from the stands to start the second lap, Neale Doughty allowed him to improve into second place. Fluffing the 19th, he had appeared to be full of running as he levelled up to the 20th.

Neale Doughty remembers, 'We were very hopeful that he would "do a Dandy" and win second time round. Rinus was a lot keener after his light preparation, almost flippant at some of the early fences. But he put in a tremendous leap at the Chair and, turning out on the second circut, he was absolutely cantering. Perhaps he was going too well and we might not quite have lasted home – but anyway, that turned out to be just guesswork. He fluffed the 19th and this might have affected his confidence, because he didn't seem to be concentrating at the next and hit the top so hard that I had no chance of staying in the plate.'

Rinus was young enough to try to make it third time lucky. However his first three races in the 1991–92 season resulted in him being pulled up, unseating his rider at the sixth fence and dropping right out from the second last to finish eighth of eight. The Boss then aimed him at Haydock's Premier Long Distance Hurdle, sponsored by Jim Ennis, owner of Home Ground and Man Alive. The move was partially successful as Rinus raced with much of his old *élan*, leading the field until tiring over the final two flights. Rinus raced once more. He contested a two-and-a-half-mile handicap chase at Bangor, in which he was lying close up until he went badly lame approaching the ninth fence and was immediately pulled up. Every effort was tried to save him but to no avail. There was no alternative to having him destroyed.

Greystoke was still powerfully represented in the 1992 Grand National (sponsored for the first time by Martell). Neale Doughty and Twin Oaks had attracted solid support in the ante-post market. And the Haydock specialist, whose last outing at the Merseyside course had seen him finish an honourable third under topweight to Cool Ground in the Greenalls Gold Cup, was sent off 9–1 third favourite to supply Gordon Richards with his third National triumph.

On the day that the 1992 National weights were to be announced, The Boss had made two points quite clear: he would be unhappy about running Twin Oaks if the going at Aintree looked like turning firm; and he would be far from confident about Twin Oaks's chances were he to carry more than 11 stone. In fact the gelding was lumbered with 11st 7lb and GWR was not a happy trainer. His message was simple: 'People say that Twin Oaks is built to carry big weights, but that is over park-type courses. The Grand National is altogether different and I believe in the old racing saying that in the National every pound over 11 stones counts double. In my view he is carrying too much weight.'

Though officially rated 'good' the Aintree going was drying out by the hour and a combination of these factors did not bode well for Neale Doughty's mount. Worse was in store. Twin Oaks was down at the start when the stitching gave way on a girth strap and there was a significant delay while a substitute saddle was fixed. The early pace was frenetic and Twin Oaks, unable to reach his customary pole position, gave a very good imitation of being in the sulks. His jumping was far from fluent and a bad error at the 17th cost him a deal of ground. Much to his credit Twin Oaks staged a brave recovery after landing over Bechers for the second time. So strongly was he travelling on the run to the third last that a place in the frame appeared probable. In reality Twin Oaks was being weighed down by the impost of 11st 7lb and he weakened from before the third last to cross the line in fifth place.

A vociferous minority felt that Neale Doughty had lain too far out of his ground. Tempting though it might be to concur, the fact was that Twin Oaks had brought about his own downfall with too many expensive mistakes on the first circuit and Neale had his work cut out to get him back in the race after his blunder at the 17th. The jockey adds, 'Immediately after the race The Boss reckoned that I hadn't had the old horse in the best of positions. However when he had listened to my explanations and watched the tape for himself, he had no complaints. From early in the race Twin Oaks had not been enjoying the experience, but that didn't stop him giving it his best shot, and if the going had been softer he would have been a lot closer.'

Neale rode On The Other Hand in 1993's void race. The ten-year-old had been bought out of John Mulhern's yard earlier in the season to give Adam Ogden a competitive mount in the *Horse and Hound* Grand Military Cup. Adam made best use of the opportunity to win the 'Soldiers' National' at Sandown and, as a former winner of the Harold Clarke Chase at Leopardstown, On The Other Hand had sound each-way claims at Aintree. A 20–1 chance, he enjoyed himself on his freebie round the big fences, but weakened in the last half-mile and the suspicion was that he didn't stay the full distance.

The Boss entered General Pershing in the 1995 Martell National with David Bridgwater up, but this useful handicapper unseated his rider at the fifth. General Pershing was the final runner that The Boss sent to Aintree for the National. His spirit, though, would have been with Feels Like Gold, who carried the Greystoke banner in April 1999. The 50–1 shot, produced in tremendous shape by Nicky Richards and given a dashing ride by Brian Harding, raced with the leaders throughout. Feels Like Gold held every chance turning for home, but began to feel the pressure approaching the second last and weakened into fifth place. There were again shades of Hallo Dandy's 1993 performance about this introduction and his liking for the Aintree fences was further advertised by his clear-cut victory in the 1999 Becher Chase.

EIGHTEEN

Pursuit of Cheltenham Glory

Ron Barry's return to Greystoke before the start of the 1978–79 season had brought a welcome stability back to the yard. Ron had never been far away during his stint as a freelance and though in his mid-30s he was still up there with the best of them, unanimously respected as one of the finest horsemen in the game. He was to resume his position as stable jockey, although there was a tacit understanding between trainer and rider that The Boss would be scouting about for a suitable youngster to act as his understudy with the eventual aim of taking over as Number One. Tony Kennedy, Chris Pimlott and Chris Brownless made up a promising trio, but satisfied though he may have been with their progress, Gordon was keen to cast the net wider in the search for outstanding talent.

Meanwhile spirits were high. Lucius had won the National in April. The flat-race horses had kept the stable ticking over profitably during the summer and prospects were appetising for the autumn. In the event the 1978–79 season was to prove a bitter disappointment on the track, while off the course a long feared but still tragic death left the stable in deep mourning at the turn of the year.

Greystoke's seasonal tally was only 33. There were sound reasons for this modest total, the weather playing a major role. Firm ground in the early autumn led to a slow start. Frost decimated the cards in the new year and the string was troubled by widespread virus problems in the spring. Lucius, trained very much with a second National in mind, appeared to be approaching his peak at the right time with a most promising performance behind Alverton in the Greenall Whitley. But he succumbed to the infection and missed Aintree. Mixed Melody, for whom much was anticipated, broke down at Wetherby's Christmas meeting, never to race again.

Man Alive and Lord Greystoke did their best to lighten the gloom. A bargain buy at the Doncaster Sales the previous November, Man Alive repaid Jim Ennis, his new owner, with a comfortable victory under Ron Barry in the Nicolet Instruments Hurdle at Cheltenham's Mackeson meeting. Switched to fences, the grey ran out a decisive winner of an 18-runner novice chase at Teesside in February. Lord Greystoke was even more impressive, winning handicap chases at Carlisle and Ayr before proving his quality with a length victory over Alverton in the Castleford Chase at Wetherby on Boxing Day. A bad mistake left Lord Greystoke tailed off in his only subsequent outing in the

Embassy Premier Chase Final at Haydock in March; but arguably he was sickening for the virus at the time.

Jean Richards's heart trouble had been a constant source of pain and worry since the early '70s. Jonjo O'Neill had to grab the wheel and bring the Mercedes to a halt when Jean collapsed *en route* to Cheltenham. Her doctors had emphasised with some regularity that the problem was 'life threatening' unless she reduced her work-load and ceased the intake of alcohol and nicotine. In typically forthright manner, Jean had never heeded the advice. She worked non-stop, often under intense pressure to tackle the mass of paperwork in the office; was always on hand to attend to the requirements of the owners; and at the same time combined the duties of matron, confidante and financial adviser to all the work-force in the yard. Above all, Jean gave a lifetime of love and understanding to her husband and family. On occasions her invaluable support had literally kept the show on the road and despite the ominous strictures about the worsening heart disorder, Jean soldiered on regardless.

In late February 1979 Gordon and Jean were guests at the Leeming House Hotel on the banks of Lake Ullswater, to celebrate the wedding reception of Jimmy and Joyce Bendall – old friends and supporters of the Greystoke stable. The Grand National Trophy, won by Lucius the previous April, had been on display in the ante-room and Jean had told the others to go into dinner while she organised the return of the silverware to the security of the hotel safe. The fatal coronary attack struck without warning. One moment Jean was joking, champagne glass in hand. The next she was unconscious on the carpet. Liz Barry recalls that Ron had the thankless task of going to break the news to Nicky and Joey, while The Boss went with Jean to the Cumberland Infirmary in Carlisle. She had died before the ambulance reached the hospital.

Back at the hotel the guests continued to enjoy the evening, unaware of the cruel drama being played out in the adjoining room. Jean's death was a shattering blow to everyone at Greystoke. She had been hugely popular and a tower of strength. The Boss disguised his sorrow at her loss by devoting even more energy to his consuming passion, the welfare and training of his beloved horses.

Towards the end of the jumping season, with the majority of the string roughed off because of the virus, GWR had time enough to follow up an important lead in his quest for a second jockey to Ron Barry. Wilf Crawford had been in touch to say that he'd had a 'half-decent young lad' who had gone south to Newmarket. His name was Doughty and he had joined up with Bill Marshall. The Boss had always respected Crawford's judgement, not least because it was the Haddington-based trainer who had employed Ron Barry before his transfer to Greystoke. Word from Newmarket was also encouraging and it had not escaped Gordon's notice that Bill Marshall, much better known for his exploits on the flat, had been enjoying his best ever season over timber with a small team of novice hurdlers – all ridden by the selfsame Neale Doughty.

The Boss decided to take a personal look. He drove down to Warwick for a late-season evening meeting at which Doughty was due to ride. Reliving the lesson which he had gleaned from Ivor Anthony all those days ago at Cheltenham, he walked down to the final flight of hurdles to study the Welshman in action at close quarters.

Neale was partnering Fools Rush In for Hugh O'Neill, the former Dorking trainer, in the Opportunity Riders Selling Hurdle. Only three finished, but Doughty had the chestnut up in the firing line throughout and The Boss was impressed with his positive style and the powerful manner in which he drove his mount into the last hurdle to win going away by five lengths. After the race he sounded Doughty out on a possible move to Greystoke. Neale recalls, 'He asked if I would be interested in the job of becoming second jockey to Ron with a view to taking over as Number One in the long term.'

Flattered as he was to be asked, Doughty didn't actually leap at the chance. He explains, 'I was very happy at Newmarket and didn't want to leave. Bill Marshall had been a second dad to me and even now we still speak to each other on a regular basis. It was Bill who made up my mind to accept, pointing out that he could never provide me with the sort of horses to ride that I would find at Greystoke, and that I would be foolish to refuse the offer.'

Not only did Neale Doughty find leaving Newmarket an emotional upheaval, he also discovered that life in Cumbria was very different from the friendly warmth of the Bill Marshall stable. He continues, 'Bill and The Boss were as different as chalk and cheese. Bill was always generous with his praise if he thought that you deserved it. Gordon was the other way about. He might tell the owners that you'd ridden a good race, but he would never think of saying so to your face. Like everyone else, I came in for my share of being slagged off in public! The only thing that Bill and Gordon had in common was their capacity for hard work. They never asked you to do anything that they hadn't done themselves and they expected it to be done equally well.'

Neale admits that his first full season at Greystoke brought its own problems. He remembers the travelling leaving him shattered. 'I was trying to be in two places at the same time. Officially I was working for Gordon, but at the same time I hadn't severed all links with Newmarket. This meant that all too often I was doing more miles than a flat-race jockey, doing afternoons and evenings in the north before driving back to Newmarket to ride work at the crack of dawn. In my case I was mucking out and riding work at Greystoke before rushing down south to partner one for Bill Marshall at Plumpton; then calling in at Newmarket before hightailing it back to Cumbria in time for next morning's stable routine. After three months of this double life I was both mentally and physically drained. It was obvious that I would crack up completely under the strain unless I cut out the driving. I finally opted to remain full time in the north and never regretted the decision.

The Boss was as good as his word. Neale rode 15 winners during 1979–80, his initial season at Greystoke, recording his first victory on Harvest Day at

Carlisle on 1 October. The win was the first leg of a five-timer for The Boss, whose record at his local course was second to none. Go Jack and Chris Brownless completed the double, leaving Ron Barry to land the last three races with Man Alive, Royal Nugget and Burelor. The five-timer paid accumulative odds of 2,199–1 with Man Alive being sent off at the shortest price of 2–1 and Burelor, the final winner, being returned at 4s – a quite remarkable starting price considering the circumstances. Statistics indicate that punters did not get rich by slavishly following the Richards horses, but sifting through the records it is clear that the yard made a habit of picking up doubles and trebles at its favourite courses like Ayr, Carlisle and Haydock.

Ten days later Neale proved his strength in the finish with a sustained drive on Vat Man, who scored at Perth in the trainer's own colours after looking booked for third place approaching the last flight. It was a determined piece of jockeyship on Doughty's part, but for an exhibition of horsemanship and tactical race-riding of the highest quality few could better the display produced by Ron Barry to win the Mackeson Gold Cup on Man Alive at Cheltenham in November. Glued to the inside rail throughout the race, Ron made his move on the downhill run into the home turn, persuaded the grey to throw a match-winning leap to lead after the last and chased him up the final hill to hold the late flourish of The Snipe by three quarters of a length. Jovial Jim Ennis was laughing all the way to the bank and not just with the winning owner's cheque of some £7,220. Man Alive was returned at 6–1 and the Knutsford construction company boss had been happy to avail himself of a sizeable chunk of the action.

While Big Ron was calling the shots at Cheltenham, his understudy had been entrusted with the mount on the consistent Stay Quiet at Catterick. The partnership was backed down to 11–4 and the favourite was in close contention as the field headed towards the stands with a circuit to travel. His supporters were on good terms with themselves, but their confidence turned to disbelief as they watched Neale Doughty knuckle down to ride a finish. Too late he realised his mistake, but the damage had been done and Stay Quiet trailed in ninth.

The Boss was in a benevolent mood. Neale escaped with a 'general bollocking' and the matter was soon forgotten. Neale reflects, 'The Boss accepted that mistakes would be made. He made his feelings pretty clear, but once he'd got it out of his system, that was it and what's more he'd stick by you. Ron made very few mistakes, but Jonjo wasn't blameless, and later on Tony Dobbin also dropped the occasional clanger. We all received a few wallops and a volley of four-letter words, but we learned to take it in our stride and just get on with the job.'

No one was better at rousing The Boss's hackles than Ron Barry. He relished the crack, always giving as good as he got, but less quick-witted members of the team had to develop thick skins. GWR rarely bore a grudge for long, though, and despite their earlier differences both Jonjo O'Neill and David

Goulding had rides for the stable during 1979–80. Jonjo won on Stay Quiet and partnered Current Gold into the runners-up berth in both the Great Yorkshire and The Welsh National. Gipsy Dave also came in for mounts on Current Gold and substituted for Ron Barry on Man Alive when the grey finished fourth to Ballet Lord in the Rowland Meyrick at Wetherby's Christmas meeting.

At Teesside in late November the lads at Greystoke took the opportunity to collect their expenses well ahead of the yuletide rush. Only Money had been off the course with leg trouble since he had returned home lame after winning a novice handicap hurdle at Haydock in January 1977. No one at Greystoke doubted his ability. It was simply a question of whether his fragile joints would stand the test. Patience with his horses, if not with his fellow humans, was a byword with The Boss and he refused to give up on Only Money. The nine-year-old gelding had fallen at the fifth on his racecourse reappearance. He then completed the course in remote sixth place at Wetherby, before being twice pulled up in quick succession. Many would have given him up as a lost cause but this was not Gordon's *modus operandi*. He persevered and, in the week between being pulled up at Ayr and going to Teesside for the Diamond Hill Novices' Chase, the penny suddenly dropped. Only Money was a revelation on the gallops. He schooled immaculately and confidence in his ability to open his account over fences at Teesside was infectious.

About the only person less than happy with the situation was Ron Barry, who would have to field the stewards' probing questions if Only Money were actually to win with the previous form figures of 'FOPP'! He recalls, 'I was so anxious about the possibility of him winning, I told The Boss that I didn't want any part of the business and that he had better put someone else up or run the risk of the horse being pulled up.' Ron's worries increased when he heard what was happening in the ring. Only Money had opened at 20–1, even longer in places, but such had been the interest in the gelding's chances that by the time the jockeys mounted in the paddock his price had shrunk to 5–1. The Springer would have started at even shorter odds if the confidence behind Kelso Chant, the favourite, had not been so solid. In the race itself Only Money led at the seventh and, but for belting the second last, never put a foot wrong. Kelso Chant made a token effort to close in the straight but to no avail. Only Money recovered quickly from his blunder at the penultimate fence to win going away by two and a half lengths with the third horse 20 lengths further adrift.

Questions, as Ron had feared, were asked; but the explanations were accepted and there was much celebration in the betting shops of Penrith. The lads had all 'been on' at first show. The Boss, alas, had left instructions with the man who placed his occasional cash bets, to invest a small wager on Only Money. Sadly for Gordon, his punter had failed to 'take a price' and The Boss had to be content with the starting price of 5–1. So much for the widely held belief that GWR was the scourge of the betting ring!

If Gordon was a little miffed by his return on Only Money's shock success, he was genuinely distressed at the demise of Tamalin. He had not been party to the owner's decision to send the 13-year-old hunter chasing, believing that Tamalin had achieved more than enough to warrant a peaceful retirement. Though never quite fulfilling his potential at the highest level, Tamalin had won 20 races under the care of GWR. Transferred in the twilight of his career to David Barron at Maunby near Thirsk, he gave David Metcalfe, his owner's son, a memorable start to his career under rules: he ran a promising second to Spartan Missile at Warwick before gaining a decisive success over Codwar at Nottingham. Tamalin was driven clear on the flat, but collapsed and died on his way back to the winner's circle.

On a happier note Lord Greystoke maintained his progress. In addition to finishing fifth in the Queen Mother Champion Chase, this striking individual won four times in handicap company, the last of these wins coming at Carlisle in April when Neale Doughty guided him to a seven-length success over Crown Court.

The Boss was quintessentially a man of habit. The advent of summer jumping, for example, was of little interest. He believed that his horses needed their summer out at grass and nothing was going to stand in the way of their annual treat. He too enjoyed the break. He spent much of June and July doing odd jobs around the farm, checking on the hay and attending local shows. More important were the buying sorties to Ireland, where he met private contacts and visited the sales. The summer of 1980, though, was memorable for affairs of the heart rather than the continual quest for potential Cheltenham winners. The Boss had formed a close friendship with Joanie Lacey (née Howard) who had recently returned to Cumbria from America where her first marriage had ended in divorce. Happiness in each other's company soon developed into a warm, loving relationship. On 18 June 1980, at the Penrith registry office, Gordon and Joanie were married.

Accommodation proved a problem. Joanie had no intentions of living in the flat above the stables. Finally they moved into a comfortable modern bungalow close to the Old Rectory farm. The Boss was living away from the stables for the first time in his training career, but if any of the lads were anticipating a few minutes extra in bed, they soon had second thoughts. GWR might be pulling up at the yard in a Land Rover instead of bustling downstairs from the stable flat, but rest assured he would be reporting for duty at exactly the same time.

In 1980–81 Neale was firmly established in his new role at Greystoke. He rode Caroline Berry's Top 'N' Tale to five wins during the season and was entrusted with the responsibility of partnering Current Gold and Lord Greystoke on a regular basis. Both had entries at the Cheltenham Festival at which The Boss had hitherto drawn a blank, despite sending out 11 winners over the Prestbury course at the supporting meetings. Sea Pigeon, of course, might have won him a Champion Hurdle in 1976 and Current Gold himself had finished a brave second in the National Hunt Chase in 1980. Back in the same race a year later, Alec Picken's stalwart went one better at the expense of Gandy VI whom he beat by 15 lengths after taking the lead two out.

The Boss had had to wait 15 years for his first Festival winner. Neale Doughty had achieved this milestone in only his second full season at Greystoke and with the ice broken, both trainer and jockey doubled up within the hour. Lord Greystoke, well supported at 7–2, won the Cathcart Challenge Cup by seven lengths from Hot Tomato, having hit the front at the tenth fence and steadily increased his advantage.

Neale was to partner Current Gold in the William Hill Scottish National a month later when the combination finished a three-length second to the runaway leader, Astral Charmer. There was a school of thought that Current Gold needed to be held up for a late run and his jockeys were sometimes criticised for laying too far out of their ground. Neale is adamant that this suggestion is far from the truth, insisting that Current Gold was simply a genuine but one-paced stayer. He says: 'It took The Boss a while to accept this, but Bill Marshall spotted it as soon as he watched me riding the horse in the Ritz Club National Hunt Chase. He saw me pushing and shoving before the leaders had gone a mile and recognised the signs straight off. I can tell you that I was travelling as fast in the first mile as I was galloping up the hill from the last fence. It wasn't a matter of holding him up for a late run, but more a question of driving him along to keep in touch and then staying on past tired and beaten horses. The leaders had to come back to Current Gold if he was to win and of course they didn't always oblige as they did that afternoon at Cheltenham.'

Neale also points out that both he and The Boss would have sent Current Gold to Aintree for the National at least a couple of seasons before he actually competed there as an 11-year-old in 1982 if he had been eligible. He adds: 'The Boss was tearing his hair out trying to get him qualified, but although he had finished placed in major staying chases like the Great Yorkshire and both the Welsh and Scottish Nationals, it wasn't until he had won at the Cheltenham Festival in 1981 that he became eligible to run and by the following year he was past his best.'

In 1980–81 Ron Barry rode 42 winners, six of which were provided by the talented Little Bay, who had yet to be lumbered with the adjective 'enigmatic' (a description of which the Catherwoods had become heartily sick by the time he had won his 21st and final race at Perth in May 1988). Little Bay and RB ended the campaign with four consecutive victories, culminating in the Red Rum Novices' Chase at Aintree and the London and Northern Group Future Champions' Chase at Ayr's Scottish National meeting. Remembering the desperate efforts of the jockeys who partnered him during his later years to prevent him seeing daylight until he was half-way up the run-in, it is interesting to note that Ron had no such worries early on. Little Bay made all the running to win at such demanding venues as Ascot and Doncaster and it wasn't until his last victory of the season at Ayr that he was actually held up until after the final fence.

Also competing at that Scottish National fixture was a maiden four-year-old called Noddy's Ryde, trained by Sue Chesmore and ridden by Steve Charlton (then a rugged and successful north-country freelance and now a popular and much respected jockeys' valet). Noddy's Ryde made much of the running in the Torranyard Novices' Hurdle that afternoon, but was beginning to weaken when he was brought down at the penultimate flight. This imposing half-brother to Celtic Ryde had already caught Gordon's attention. The Boss had a remarkable eye for recognising scope and in particular chasing potential in a young horse. During the summer this exciting prospect made the journey south from Melrose to Greystoke.

Tom McCormack, his lad, made the journey with him; a useful addition in many ways not least because Tom was 100 per cent dedicated to the welfare of his charge. He had been with Mrs Chesmore since the heyday of Stay Bell and he had looked after Noddy's Ryde since the gelding had come into training. He was convinced that the horse had the potential to go to the very top, but was not blind to his shortcomings – most immediate of which was his volatile disposition. Noddy's Ryde was highly strung and it was noticeable how hard he pulled in his early races. There was no doubting his turn of foot, but this would be of little value if the acceleration was wasted in a fruitless attempt to race his rivals off their feet before the half-way point. Right from the start Neale Doughty was directly concerned with the progress of the new arrival. He rode work on Noddy's Ryde. He schooled him over fences and he partnered him in all his races. Not that he was given a free hand in administering these responsibilities: The Boss always kept his finger on the pulse and when it came to the stable stars his 'hands-on' role was never in question.

Noddy's Ryde would not be five until the turn of the year. Clearly he would have to continue his education over hurdles; but everything about him, his physique, his breeding and his style of racing, cried out for an early transition to fences. Just thinking about his future made the blood tingle. Once Neale began to work him upsides with older and more experienced horses the message was plain for all to see. Noddy's Ryde was not only powerful and fast. He was also blessed with that competitive urge that required him to take on all comers, regardless of their age or reputation. Neale remembers the first time that he worked with Little Bay: 'Ron was in the saddle and nothing in the yard had been able to match strides with Little Bay on the gallops. There was a suspicion that he had turned it in at the racecourse but never on the gallops. To Noddy's Ryde, though, he was just another horse and once the pair of us started to go head to head there was no holding the chestnut – he had Little Bay's measure well before half-way and if Ron hadn't called a halt Little Bay would have been slaughtered. It was the last time that the two of them exercised together. Noddy's would have shattered his confidence if they had!'

Back in action at Perth's October meeting, Noddy's Ryde lost his maiden certificate first time out for the Richards team in the Haig Whisky Novices'

Hurdle Qualifier, handing out a 15-length beating to Allten Glazed, the 9–4 favourite. Easy victories followed at Catterick and in the Comedy of Errors Novices' Hurdle at Newcastle. Defeat in Ayr's Panama Hurdle Qualifier came as an unpleasant surprise until tests showed that Noddy's Ryde had raced with the virus on him. The gelding was on the sidelines for four months and in the circumstances acquitted himself with much credit when finishing a close fourth to Allten Glazed in the Haig Whisky Final at Newcastle on his reappearance in late March. Neale was hurt and John Francome stood in for him at Ayr when Noddy's Ryde made his final appearance of the season. The partnership passed the post in front, but was adjudged to have caused accidental interference to High Hills, the second, and the positions of the first two were reversed.

Doughty ended the 1981–82 season on the 33 winner mark, five ahead of Ron Barry – a changearound reflecting the steady swing in the balance of power at Castle Stables. Among the other good winners Neale partnered during the year were Pounentes; Little Bay, who fell two out in the Greenall Whitley when holding every chance; and the ex-Dick Hern inmate Rushmoor, who seemed a high-class recruit to hurdling, winning two of his three outings and looking a shade unlucky to lose his unbeaten record to Prince Bless in the Ladbroke Hurdle at Aintree.

The 1982–83 season was frustrating for The Boss. The stable started brightly, but a bug swept through the yard in the middle of November and most of the horses were troubled by the infection for the rest of the campaign. Noddy's Ryde was no exception, but even before he had reappeared at Cheltenham in mid-October there had been sadness. His owner had died during the summer and despite being assured by The Boss that Noddy's Ryde was potentially champion class, the Hicks family were determined to send him to the sales.

The outcome left Gordon in the depth of despair. Noddy's Ryde was due to come under the hammer at the Doncaster August Sales. He hadn't yet managed to find a new owner for the big chestnut and his own finances had been stretched by the sound but expensive decision to lay a state-of-the-art all-weather gallop. The initial cost of this strategically vital project had been around £60,000. The mile-long wood chip gallop, in the lee of a sizeable evergreen plantation of fir and pine, was wide enough to allow a wave of horses at least three deep throughout its length and it was being laid alongside the centuries-old turf gallops. The work had been completed, but teething difficulties had led to further expense. The Richards' bank manager might well have baulked slightly at the request to forward an anticipated sum of around £30,000 to buy back a horse who – though rich in talent and potential – had yet to prove his ability over fences.

Neale Doughty recalls that The Boss was really down in the dumps. 'He said to me, "Son, I can't find the money to buy him myself and unless I can find an owner before he goes to Doncaster, I'll have to let him go."'

Neale himself was aghast at the thought. He continues: 'I had saved up a few grand to buy a new car and was so sure that Noddy's Ryde would go to the top that I offered to hand over the money to The Boss if he felt it would save the chestnut from being sold.'

Gordon left for Doncaster praying for a miracle. He found one in the shape of businessman Peter Hincliff, who received a tremendous marketing patter convincing him that Noddy's Ryde was a gilt-edged investment certain to reward his owner with a rich return. Hinchcliff had to go to 28,000 guineas. But Noddy's Ryde returned safe and sound to Greystoke and within 19 months had won his connections no fewer than nine races, amassing over £45,000 in win and place prize money.

Noddy's Ryde recouped the initial instalment of his purchase price first time out at Cheltenham, running out a three-length winner from Al Kuwait. However after a sub-standard performance in similar handicap company next time out, he was 'rested' for the remainder of the campaign. The Boss was never going to take any risks with this outstanding recruit and in any case there was little point in pursuing a career as a handicap hurdler when steeplechasing was his true *métier*. Too much hurdling could teach a potential chaser bad habits. So, frustrating though it was to have such an exciting prospect doing little but eat his head off over ten months, this patient policy gave Noddy's Ryde the opportunity to grow into his full strength at his own pace.

1983–84 saw Ron Barry bow out with a winner; Neale Doughty take over as stable jockey; Hallo Dandy give The Boss his second Grand National winner; and Noddy's Ryde emerge as the finest two-mile novice chaser this side of the Irish Sea. Ron Barry's inspirational presence as top jockey at Greystoke for upwards of 14 seasons, with a break of just three years between stints, cannot be underestimated. Quite apart from his outstanding feats in the saddle, his ability to defuse potentially difficult situations with his own particular brand of Irish humour, and his ready understanding of the day-to-day problems experienced by the younger members of the team, played an invaluable part in raising morale and maintaining standards throughout his long association with the stable

The horses, though, owed Ron the biggest debt. As The Boss might have said when caught off guard,"E 'ad lovely 'ands, did Ron. There was nobody better at teaching a difficult 'orse to settle.' Ron's last ride was on the aptly named Final Argument in the Glentrool Handicap Chase at Ayr's early October meeting.

Looking well forward for his seasonal début, the 3–1 joint favourite led at the ninth and ran on strongly from two out to score by six lengths. Ron announced his retirement on dismounting in the winner's circle. Shortly afterwards he was carried shoulder high by his fellow jocks to receive a case of champagne from the Ayr executive. Ron went on to become the only professional jockey to be rewarded with a public testimonial. Happily, too, he was to remain active in the industry – first as the proprietor of his own firm which specialised in the construction of timber-framed boxes and horse shelters; and later as the Jockey Club's Inspector of Courses for the North. In both these capacities he was to keep in close touch with The Boss, with whom he remained on the best of terms right up to the end.

The team at Greystoke had waited two whole seasons for the chance to watch Noddy's Ryde over the major obstacles and now that the time had arrived, there was to be no hanging about – always assuming that he proved as good as anticipated and that he was enjoying the action. A play-safe policy was adopted on his chasing début at Wetherby. The Boss was keen that Neale should give him plenty of time to see the obstacles, an instruction which the jockey carried out to the letter despite the efforts of Noddy's Ryde to pull his arms out of their sockets. Given his head jumping the seventh, the chestnut relaxed and cruised home ten lengths clear of Beamwam.

Facile victories followed at Ayr and Cheltenham and the four-timer looked assured in the November Novices' Chase at Sandown until he slipped on landing over the sixth fence and gave Neale no chance of staying in the saddle. Neither horse nor jockey came to any harm and a week later Noddy's Ryde headed to Cheltenham to put in an exhibition round to win the Coventry Novices' Chase by ten lengths from Leading Artist.

By early December Noddy's Ryde had yet to be seriously challenged over the minimum distance and it was decided to tackle the two and a half miles of Newcastle's Dipper Chase. Similar success over this longer trip would widen the options available. The experiment was inconclusive. For a start Neale was injured and Jonjo O'Neill took the ride with orders to settle his mount and conserve enough energy for the extra half mile. Noddy's Ryde proved amenable to the change of plan and joined the leaders at the third last, but then he surrendered all chance of winning by losing his footing in dramatic fashion on landing over two out. Jonjo sat tight and the combination passed the post a well beaten third. At the debriefing opinions were unanimous. Two miles would be the distance and the target would be the Arkle at Cheltenham in March. Noddy's Ryde appreciated the decision. Reunited with Neale Doughty, he ran his rivals ragged in both the Freebooter Chase at Doncaster and the Nottinghamshire Novices' Chase.

Tom McCormack had Noddy's Ryde looking a treat for Cheltenham. The Boss was delighted with the build-up to the big race and Neale was itching to get out and do battle. The race was billed as a titanic head-to-head between Bobsline, unbeaten in Ireland, and Noddy's Ryde, the pride of Cumbria. Too often these predictions misfire, but not so in this case. The struggle for ascendancy between Bobsline and Noddy's Ryde over the final two fences was reminiscent of the Bustino–Grundy duel over the last two furlongs of the 1975 King George at Ascot.

Neale had seized the initiative at the sixth but, calculating that Frank Berry would not commit Bobsline until he had jumped two out, he knew that he must keep enough in reserve for the final charge to the line. Sensing Bobsline at his heels, he set Noddy's Ryde alight running into the home turn and the chestnut responded with a further surge of power which held the challenger at bay and momentarily strangled the rising crescendo of Irish acclamation and fanned the frenzy of the home supporters. Stride for stride into the last, Bobsline was marginally the quicker through the air and the greater impulsion pinched him that vital half-length on landing. Crucial though it proved to be, Noddy's Ryde never flinched. Responding to Neale's ceaseless driving, he rallied. Amidst a tumult of cheers and counter-cheers – yes, even the Tuscans were on their feet – the pair of them duelled for glory. Bobsline took the spoils but Noddy's Ryde lost nothing in defeat. The Boss might have lost an Arkle, yet visions of revenge in a Queen Mother were far from fantasy. Noddy's Ryde put flesh on that dream by throwing off the exertions of Cheltenham to finish his season with two more wins, in the Red Rum Novices' Handicap Chase at Aintree and the London and North Group Future Champions' Chase at Ayr.

Noddy's Ryde enjoyed his summer break and came back into work in mid-August carrying plenty of condition. The Boss was under no illusions that finding suitable races for his potential 'champion' would be simple. One, however, did stand out as being the perfect contest for his seasonal reappearance. The Plymouth Gin Haldon Gold Cup, at Devon and Exeter's first October meeting, was ideal in at least three different ways. The race came at the right time; the distance of two miles, one furlong was spot-on; and the venue provided The Boss with a splendid opportunity to return in style to his old stamping ground in the West Country.

Gordon had not had a runner in Devon since first taking out a licence to train. He had told his family in Bath that he wouldn't bring a horse down unless he was confident of victory. After nearly 20 years he had no excuse to stay away. The Haldon Gold Cup was tailor-made for Noddy's Ryde. The Boss was 'up for the cup' in a big way and Neale was equally determined not to let him down. Only four runners went to post, but the Fred Winter-trained Fifty Dollars More was a worthy adversary – a high-class handicapper with a notably good strike rate in the autumn. The bookmakers did not subscribe to this view, sending off Noddy's Ryde as they did at 1–2. They were quite justified in their opinion. The Greystoke star steadily warmed to his task, jumping straight and well and opening up a clear lead as Doughty asked him to quicken while entering the final straight. The answer was immediate. In a matter of strides Noddy's Ryde had quickened clear. The crowd had already begun to acclaim their hero when, unaccountably, the chestnut slipped on landing over the final fence and could not get to his feet. It was obvious to Neale that Noddy's Ryde had shattered his offside hind leg. The course vet confirmed his worst fears and there was nothing to be done but put him out of his misery.

Neale admits breaking down in tears at the tragedy. The Boss was in tears too. However seeing his jockey in such distress he pulled himself together and, putting his arms around Neale's shoulders, said, 'Don't upset yourself, lad. We'll go out and find another one just as good.' There are those who say to this day that The Boss never succeeded in this particular mission; that Noddy's Ryde himself was the best horse GWR ever trained. Meanwhile, National Hunt racing had been prematurely deprived of the most exciting front-running chaser of the decade. The Boss never ran another horse south of Cheltenham until Unguided Missile contested the Jim Ford Challenge Cup in 1997.

NINETEEN

Doughty at the Helm

By the time he rode Hallo Dandy to triumph at Aintree in 1984, Neale Doughty was established as one of Britain's top jump jockeys and, together with Chris Grant and Jonjo O'Neill, was a household name in the North. He had ridden 48 winners in 1983–84 and the following season his tally was 45 – a total which would have been swollen to well over the 50 mark had Neale not picked up a number of troublesome injuries.

The bond between trainer and his now fully committed stable jockey was already close knit. The two of them had developed a most effective working relationship, cemented by mutual respect for each other's ability. Both were driven by a fierce determination to accept nothing but the best. Neither suffered fools gladly and both possessed quicksilver temperaments which could ignite into fiery reaction under provocation. Neale explains, 'The Boss loved the game and lived it to the full with such intensity that we were bound to fall out at regular intervals. We both felt so passionately about the way things should be done that differences of opinion were inevitable and noisy. Life couldn't continue for long without a sudden burst of "effing and blinding". We would shout at each other every so often, but on a day-to-day basis our relationship was strictly professional. Ron did much of his talking in the car, either to or from the races. Gordon and I had most of our discussions in the office. We used to meet there after morning exercise to consider the entries. The Boss would want to know my opinions about whether a certain track would suit a horse, or if another one would benefit from a drop in distance or perhaps from a different method of riding. I wasn't slow in coming forward with my views and as The Boss didn't like changing his ideas, the sessions were usually pretty lively affairs.'

Hallo Dandy's Aintree victory acted as a catalyst to Greystoke's improving fortunes. Despite the tragedy which befell Noddy's Ryde the influx of new owners, horses and riders provided renewed stimulus to the yard's efforts. Gordon had finally turned his back on the flat-racing scene to reaffirm his standing as one of the country's top National Hunt trainers. The decision was wholly supported by Joanie, who had a wide circle of friends, several of whom liked to have the odd jumper in training. Joanie took over the office, a duty which she carried out with increasing confidence. She combined an easy approach to the owners and the press with a valuable understanding of the computer age and the growing demands that the Jockey Club secretariat required from its trainers and staff.

Substantial additions to the ranks of owners included Norman Mason, later to become the most successful permit holder of his generation; property developer Keith Darby; and the Edinburgh Woollen Mill, whose beige-and-brown strip and orange cap were to become a familiar sight on courses throughout Britain. Clever Folly was to win no fewer than 29 races in the Mason colours, the last of which came in a four-horse event at Perth in August 1995 at the age of 16. Keith Darby, whose Triumph Properties have done much to modernise and improve the central shopping area of Penrith, found early success with Glory Snatcher and Colourful Paddy before No Lemon, his most expensive purchase, ultimately proved a disappointment. The Langholm Dyer began the fun for the Edinburgh Woollen Mill, who were to become a lynchpin of the Richards team for over a decade.

Denis Coakley and Jayo Kinane now joined John Hansen and Jerry Quinn as understudies to Neale Doughty. Jayo, yet another of that multi-talented family of horsemen from Co. Kildare, threatened to make a niche for himself but never quite achieved the breakthrough. He left Greystoke to run his own stable near Edinburgh in company with Donal Nolan before finally returning to continue his career with more profitable results in his home country. Coakley impressed The Boss: had he remained at Greystoke for longer than the couple of seasons in which he rode 22 winners as a conditional jockey, in addition to the handful he picked up as an amateur on his arrival at the yard, the quietly spoken Irishman had the potential to make the grade as a fully fledged professional. Instead he opted to resume his association with William Hastings Bass, for whom he had been working in Australia before coming to Cumbria. Denis was to share plenty of success with the royal trainer, better known as Lord Huntingdon. He held the position of assistant trainer until Huntingdon retired at the end of the 1998 season, at which point he leased a yard from his former boss and took out a licence to train on his own account.

Among the horses, Final Argument and Little Bay continued to thrive. Jim Thorpe appeared as an exciting prospect, but the most consistent money spinners were Another City and The Man Himself – both home-bred by Ted Briggs, the Garstang farmer, who later saw his colours carried to even more popular success by the aptly named Better Times Ahead. In 1984–85 The Man Himself won three handicap hurdles, but it was Another City's forcing tactics that really caught the eye. The bold jumping, headstrong mare landed an early season three-timer with novice chase wins at Carlisle, Worcester and Stratford. After a brief loss of form in mid-season, Another City returned to account for The Divider by 30 lengths at Ayr in March. The Boss liked his jockeys to give their mounts a clear view of their fences and to be positive in their guidance from the saddle. Neale Doughty never disappointed him in this respect. He was always asking horses to be bold rather than to fiddle and to float and was seen at his steeplechasing best on brave front runners like Another City.

Neale was sidelined for over a month after Spider Kelly, his mount in a 24-runner novices' hurdle at Worcester's late March meeting, unseated him on the approach to the first flight and threw him to the ground directly in the path of the following pack. Neale explains: 'I wound him up at the start and, going lickety spit for the first flight, the reins broke. I tried to slip off sideways but collided with the rails and dislocated my shoulder.' He was forced to miss the ride on Hallo Dandy in the National and was still out of action for Ayr's Scottish National three weeks later.

For much of the time GWR used his second-line jockeys Denis Coakley, Jayo Kinane and John Hansen to plug the gap, only booking a 'name' jockey for prestige races. At Ayr the choice was Phil Tuck, who recalls the occasion well: 'I had my first-ever ride for The Boss on the day of the 1985 Scottish National. I finished third on The Man Himself in the long-distance hurdle and then won the handicap chase on Final Argument. I was freelance at the time and was delighted to get the chance.'

Gordon was more than satisfied and the following Saturday he booked Tuck to ride The Langholm Dyer in the novices' hurdle at Hexham. The Edinburgh Woollen Mill's gelding obliged by four lengths and Phil gained a third straight strike for the Richards stable with a clear-cut win on Rejuvenator in the handicap chase at Sedgefield a fortnight later. 'I remember that I had to jock myself off Jimmy FitzGerald's Paka Lolo to accept the ride,' adds Phil Tuck, 'so I was pretty pleased that he won so easily.' Before Neale resumed, Phil also partnered Primrose Wood and Scottish Dream for the Greystoke stable. He had only helped out while the stable jockey was unfit, but had taken the opportunity with both hands and in little more than a year he moved permanently to Cumbria.

For The Boss 1985–86 was a frustrating year. He trained 56 winners, a total only exceeded by Arthur Stephenson in the North, but his top horses failed to produce their best when it mattered the most. Bad weather curtailed the racing programme in the new year and the spring brought further turmoil with Neale Doughty leaving the yard before the end of the season.

Music Be Magic ran up a sequence of four novice chase victories in the autumn. The Brave Invader gelding carried the colours of Norman Mason and, together with Centre Attraction who ran in the name of his wife, represented the owner's first venture into jump racing. Three times a winner over hurdles the previous season, Music Be Magic was in his element on the early-season fast ground. He opened his account over fences with a fluent win in the Bobby Renton Memorial at Wetherby's October fixture and followed this encouraging début with exhibition rounds at Cheltenham, the second of which came in the Coventry Novices' Chase in the hands of Phil Tuck, once again substituting for an injured Neale Doughty. With Neale back in the saddle, Music Be Magic had to be kept up to his work to overhaul the front running Charcoal Wally on the flat and win the Freebooter Novices' Chase at Doncaster by half a length.

Gordon gave his leading novice chaser a mid-winter break, bringing him back for Cheltenham without the precaution of a preliminary race. This ability to prepare a horse on the gallops for a particular target remains the hallmark of a true trainer and The Boss achieved this balancing act to a nicety on countless occasions. Much of his success in this department grew from his determination to discover what made his horses tick. He made it his business to study the habits of his horses, the good ones in particular, so that he would be able to tell from almost a cursory inspection whether the individual was at his best, below par or perhaps in need of more work.

They said that GWR had 'an eye for a horse'. He had this quality in abundance, but it wasn't acquired simply by instinct. He built up a mental dossier of the horses in his care by watching them both at close quarters in their boxes and also by carefully assessing their reactions on the gallops and the racecourse. Discussions with work riders and jockeys played their part, but The Boss took his own decisions and these were rarely wrong. Racecourse experience was a vital ingredient in the learning curve. It was the patient 'education' of his youngsters which sometimes brought him into conflict with the stewards and their secretaries, a clash that is worth further expansion. Gordon could be accused, and on occasions be found guilty, of educating his horses on the track; but when this was the case it was always with the intention of preparing them for their proper job over fences and never with a betting coup in mind.

Music Be Magic was produced in great shape for the 1986 Arkle Trophy. Despite his lengthy absence from the course, he was sent off at 9–2 second favourite and might have been an unlucky loser. Doughty had him tucked away in mid-division, travelling comfortably on the heels of the leaders when he came down at the seventh. The race went to Oregon Trail with Charcoal Wally, the grey whom Music Be Magic had beaten twice before that season, three quarters of a length behind in second place. Just as important in the long term were the after-effects of Music Be Magic's fall. His confidence was impaired. He certainly did not jump with anything like his old dash on his return to action at Aintree, where he started favourite for the Woodlands Stud Novices' Chase. Neale had him under pressure before half-way, but the reminders failed to provide any improvement and he was well adrift when pulled up between the last two fences. Music Be Magic progressed to become a useful handicapper, often performing with credit in major sponsored events during the next two seasons. Yet he never reached the heights that his exploits as a novice suggested he would.

From comparatively early in the 1985–86 season The Boss had to contend with problems about the riding arrangements at Greystoke. The concerns might never have arisen if Neale Doughty had remained fit, but the stable jockey was having little luck with injuries. A fall from Easter Brig at Newcastle in late October kept him out of the saddle for five weeks. He had sustained three crushed verebrae. A further short spell on the sidelines in the spring triggered major trouble.

Phil Tuck was drafted in to take the bulk of the rides while Neale was recovering from injury in the autumn. He already had his admirers among the

Greystoke patrons. With Denis Coakley also riding winners, a few of the owners were beginning to express preferences. This was a situation which the trainer could well have done without.

Phil Tuck it was who came in for a wonderful run of success at Ayr's two-day November meeting. Throughout his career GWR used this fixture as a platform for launching his potential stars and in 1985 there was no stopping the Greystoke team. Tartan Triumph and The Man Himself gave the Richards–Tuck combination a winning double, but this was only an aperitif. The pair returned on the Saturday to delight their supporters with a four-timer from Centre Attraction, The Langholm Dyer, Final Argument and Doronicum. The six winners paid accumulative odds of 1,566–1 and Tuck's popularity continued to grow.

Gordon's much canvassed 'eye for a horse' was well advertised at Ayr. Back in 1983 he had told the journalist who compiled his *Timeform* interview that he had bought a quartet of unraced four-year-olds for whom he anticipated a particularly bright future. Unnamed at the time, they were identified by their stallions. One was by Brave Invader, another by Little Buskins, the third by Crash Course and the last was a son of Deep Run. The final trio, Centre Attraction, The Langholm Dyer and Tartan Triumph respectively all obliged at Ayr while the Brave Invader gelding, Music Be Magic, was about to record his third consecutive victory of the autumn in the Coventry Novices' Chase at Cheltenham's Mackeson meeting.

Neale Doughty bounced back from injury with a winner on Tullamarine at Catterick on 9 December. He remained in top form over Christmas and the new year, but a prolonged spell of hard frost resulted in virtually all of February's racing being cancelled. A treble at Ayr put the stable jockey in good heart for the Cheltenham Festival where the falls of Music Be Magic and Little Bay were only partially retrieved by the brave run of Another City in the Mildmay of Flete. Neale had been seen at his most powerful when driving out Ted Briggs's consistent mare to a short-head win over Donegal Prince at Market Rasen in mid-January. Nine days later Doughty and Another City again dominated the race to give Karenomore a six-length drubbing at Ayr. In the Mildmay, Another City either led or shared the lead until making an error at the 12th. She had every chance jumping two out, but weakened up the final hill and finished fourth to The Tsarevich.

Another City's next outing was at Wetherby on the last day of March. The trip was three miles but the mare looked well in command until taking the third last fence by the roots. Doughty sat tight and the mare recovered her breath to outstay You're Welcome and win going away by seven lengths. Next stop the Scottish National! At Liverpool Neale was on board Hallo Dandy in the National, but was not required for either The Langholm Dyer in the Whitbread Best Mild Novices' Chase nor Little Bay in the Captain Morgan Aintree Handicap Chase. Ridley Lamb and Graham Bradley took the rides while Bill Peacock, the owner of Preben Fur used the services of Phil Tuck.

The Boss remained fiercely loyal to Neale Doughty, his number-one jockey, but Joanie was less supportive. She alluded to rumblings of discontent from a group of owners. It was no secret that relations between Neale and Joanie Richards were strained. Matters came to a head at Ayr's Scottish National meeting. Neale Doughty was down to partner Another City in the big race but Ted Briggs, the mare's owner, needed to be convinced that he had made a full recovery from his fall from Doronicum and insisted that the jockey proved his fitness by race riding at the meeting before taking the mount on Another City. This was not a problem as far as Neale was concerned. On the Friday he partnered Greystoke's Katie-Mac in the novices' chase. There he proved that there was little wrong with either his confidence or his strength, by rallying his mount on the flat to such an effect that she narrowly failed to regain the lead from Royal Bowler after being headed at the last. If any doubts about his well-being still lingered on, Neale took the ride on Scottish Simbir for Wilf Crawford in the opening race on Saturday's card. The six-year-old was held up, took the lead four out and ran on strongly from the penultimate flight to score by two lengths.

The win satisfied connections that Neale was in prime condition to get the best out of Another City. The mare had become a major fancy for the four-mile marathon and confidence in her chances was reflected in the on-course betting market. The opening price of 14–1 was quickly taken and by the time the tapes rose, Another City's odds had been cut to 17–2.

Ted Briggs recalls: 'Gordon had the mare jumping out of her skin. After Wetherby we were very hopeful that she would stay the trip and backed her to do so. Gordon reckoned everything was right for the mare. She was fit as a flea, she had a fair weight and the ground was ideal.' As the field passed the stands with a circuit to go, Another City, who had been disputing the lead from the outset, took a definite advantage. Perhaps the racecourse commentator's observation that 'Another City was just cantering on the inside' put the mockers on her, but she had been jumping so boldly and well that disaster struck without warning. At the sixth from home the leader appeared to take the fence cleanly enough before seeming to twist in mid-air and the unexpected impetus shot poor Neale out the side door.

Another City galloped on riderless and in the immediate aftermath feelings ran high. Neale became the scapegoat with 'those expert riders in the stands' claiming that if he had been 100 per cent fit he would have been able to correct the mare's sudden change of direction and arguably have gone on to win. The benefit of hindsight is a marvellous help, but Another City was still 'travelling' at the time of the incident and Ted Briggs remains adamant that she would have gone very close had Neale stayed in the plate. He admits, 'I did think before the race that if we were ever going to win a Scottish National this would be the day and the mare looked to be going so well. I thought at the time the sudden jink she gave must have "sprung" Neale's ribs and shoulder and that if he had not had that previous injury then he might have stayed with the horse.

But that's racing, as they say, and you just have to grin and bear it. Certainly there were no hard feelings towards Neale on my part.'

The Boss was less easy to satisfy. The post-mortem continued into the Sunday with the pressure mounting on both parties. Neale understandably refused to accept the blame, but the atmosphere was thick with recrimination. 'I wasn't going to back down,' asserts Neale. 'I was unseated right enough. I always put my hands up to that, but what The Boss wouldn't accept was that the saddle had slipped . . . No doubt about it. The video shows that the mare twisted in mid-air. I put my right foot hard down. The saddle gave way and I went out the side door. I had been struggling to make the weight and was using my lightest saddle with no breast girth.

'Martin Todhunter backed me up, pointing out that when he caught up with Another City, the saddle was right round her side and there wasn't a mark on her. The Boss, though, insisted that the saddle had slipped while the mare was galloping loose after I had been unseated. He wouldn't budge and neither would I!'

Finally The Boss and his jockey agreed to part. Neale blames outside parties for stirring the flames. He stresses, 'The Boss never sacked me. A lot of harsh things were said in the heat of the moment that would have been best left unsaid, but in the end I made my own decision to leave. It was a dreadful wrench to go because I was genuinely fond of The Boss. But at the time it seemed the only sensible course to follow.'

Another City would seem to have sympathised with her erstwhile jockey. Though unharmed in the incident at Ayr, and indeed successful at Market Rasen next time out, in the long term she never again reproduced the same sparkling form that she had shown in the build-up to the Scottish National. After a handful of undistinguished runs over the next two seasons, she was retired. Ted Briggs surmises, 'Another City was a nailing good mare with just a touch of class. I thought that she would prove ideal to breed from, but she never got anything of any note and then very sadly died in foalbirth some four years ago.'

By contrast City's Sister, who won nothing more than a seller on the flat, has prospered. Her best known son, Better Times Ahead celebrated the 20th victory of his career at Cartmel in August 1999 at the age of 13.

Ted Briggs numbered The Boss as a friend as well as a sparring partner. He explains, 'We went back a long way together. The great thing about Gordon was that he told you straight what he thought and you could rely on his word as being the truth. Mind you, we didn't always agree on the whys and wherefores and often spent some time telling each other what we felt about things. He was a grand trainer, though, always doing his best for the horses and being engrossed in his job right up till the end.'

TWENTY

Woollen Mill Prosperity

'In a question of succession, possession is nine tenths of the law.' What applies to history is equally relevant to racing. Phil Tuck had substituted for Neale Doughty when the stable jockey was injured with conspicuous success over the past two seasons. He was happy to play his part and he was the obvious man to fill the void. Mind you The Boss kept him dangling on the hook and in the end it was Phil who had to pose the question.

Reflecting first on the fabulous two days that Gordon and he had enjoyed at Ayr the previous November, Phil recalls that he might have been fortunate to win two of those races. He explains, 'In the Tartan Triumph race, Kevin Jones was riding Camroc for Arthur Stephenson. Turning into the straight, I called across to him, "Kevin, you've got me beat. Let's hunt home." So Kevin sat in behind me and my fellow tapped him for toe from the last.

'Almost the same thing happened the following afternoon with The Langholm Dyer. Kevin was on Durham Edition and he appeared to be going much the best on the home turn. I yelled across, "You've won this, Kevin" and was delighted to see him take a pull. Then between the last two fences I asked The Dyer to stretch and Durham Edition was left flat-footed. I couldn't believe that it would work for the second time!'

In that same meeting at Ayr, Phil also remembers being called before the stewards to explain the running of Tartan Tomahawk who had dropped out tamely behind Absonant to finish a well-beaten fifth. 'They had Gordon in as well, and after listening to both our stories they "recorded" our explanations. On that occasion I was entirely on the side of The Boss. The horse just wasn't any good!'

GWR tended to turn his horses away in plenty of time for the spring grass and Phil only had the opportunity to pick up a couple of winners at the back end of the 1985–86 season, one of which ironically was Another City at Market Rasen. He then took the place of Keith Darby on Glory Snatcher at Perth's mid-May meeting. 'He jumped from fence to fence and we were flat out to hold on from the last, if my memory isn't playing tricks,' says Phil. He was quite right. Glory Snatcher made all to hold the sustained late challenge of the Maurice Barnes-ridden Purple Beam by a neck.

Three days later Phil Tuck was driving The Boss from Cartmel's afternoon fixture to partner Glory Snatcher at Hexham in the evening and he raised the subject of riding arrangements for the following autumn. 'It had been mooted that he might want me to take over, but nothing had been said for definite and time was running short. I asked him straight out if he wanted me to ride for him.

'"Ooh", he said, "I've got to speak to my h'owners, son."'

That didn't really answer the question and Phil pointed out the need to get things sorted as he would have a house to sell if he wanted him to move to Cumbria. 'Well, the stable jockey has always lived fairly close by,' was Gordon's reply, which Phil took to mean that GWR expected him to move up.

With the benefit of hindsight Tuck realises that it might not have been the smartest of moves, pointing out that he and The Boss had probably got on rather better when there was a bit of distance between each other. In the event the Tucks sold their house in Yorkshire and moved into the lodge at the entrance to Greystoke Castle Drive as a temporary base while they looked for more permanent quarters – a search which was short-lived, as both Phil and his wife, Maria, soon found the ideal setting at Hill House, a mile out of the village of Calthwaite and within 20 minutes' drive from the stable.

'He was a hard old man,' says Phil. 'My mother came up for a brief stay early on. As Thursday was "roadwork day", I rang The Boss to ask if he could manage without me until the Friday. His reply is etched on my mind:

'"We can always do without you, son" – and he put down the telephone.

'He probably didn't mean any harm, but as I was the new stable jockey it set me back on my heels a bit. Gordon could be the master of the cutting one-liner.'

Any misgivings were quickly forgotten as Phil made a remarkable start to his new job. His initial winner was Norman Mason's Norval at Cartmel's Bank Holiday meeting. The win sparked off a sequence of victories which was to put Johnny Gilbert's long-standing record of ten consecutive wins (achieved in 1959) in serious jeopardy. Phil relates, 'That win on Norval came on the Saturday. I was back there for the Monday to ride a four-timer – Doronicum, Easter Brig, St Colme and Atkinsons – all for The Boss. I didn't begin to think about the record until after I had partnered Golden Fancy for Ian Vickers at Perth the following Friday, and completed the double with Norval later the same afternoon. I made it nine in a row with Master Lamb (for Sally Hall) and Atkinsons at Perth on the Saturday.

'By now the media had fanned the flames and there was quite a scrum at Southwell the next Wednesday. I had just the two booked rides for Gordon: Doronicum in the handicap hurdle and Easter Brig in the last race. Doronicum was always going to win and I was more than a touch hopeful that Easter Brig would make it 11 out of 11 to set a new record. But he had a ten-pound penalty and was very much on his toes. He dashed into the lead but made mistakes and dropped back well-beaten before two out. It was a bit of an anticlimax, but I had equalled the record and though Mick Fitzgerald went close a few years back, it still stands today.'

The *Racing Post* presented Phil Tuck with a photographic collage of the feat.

The framed reminder hangs proudly above the staircase at Hill House. An amusing memory was GWR's contribution to the occasion. Maria Tuck's mother was at the meeting. After Easter Brig's defeat she expressed her disappointment: 'I am sorry he didn't win.'

The Boss replied curtly, 'Ooh, he cut his throat, y'know!'

Unfamiliar with such racing jargon, Phil's mother-in-law was aghast. 'Oh, I am sorry Gordon, I do hope he will be all right!'

Little Bay was a revelation to the new stable jockey. Phil reflects, 'I'd ridden him once before in public, in the Frogmore Chase at Ascot the previous December. Before that race I rang John Francome for advice. He asked me how many runners there were and when I answered seven, he replied at once, "Well, then, you sit eighth!"'

Francome's recommendation proved superflous on that occasion, as Little Bay fell at the sixth. The message was clear, though, and Phil endorses every word. 'He was some horse, really good,' he enthuses. 'The Boss rode him in much of his work at home and thought the world of him. You just had to drop him out and wait and wait and wait some more!'

Gordon could not have quibbled at Phil Tuck's handling of his favourite on his seasonal début at Uttoxeter. Little Bay, with 12st 7lb on his back, was held up patiently until making his challenge at the last. Despite the concession of 19lb to Jenny Pitman's Lochrun, he got the verdict by a head. Sharpened up by that pipe-opener, Little Bay then went south to Newbury for the North Street Handicap Chase on Hennessy Day, a trip which was to prove unpleasantly expensive if you were a bookmaker in Penrith. The price of 5–1 was mouthwatering for Little Bay supporters, though they probably had their hearts in their mouths as their hero hit the front between the final two fences.

A horrified Phil Tuck was powerless to halt the forward surge. He still shivers at the memory: 'I thought, Christ, the old man will go mad. I've come too far too soon. Going hot and cold all at the same moment, I never moved a muscle until we cleared the last and then I sat and sat. He didn't back off until we were about ten strides from the line. By then the race was in the bag and we passed the post almost at a walk.'

Happily for his jockey and for Little Bay's backers, the Greystoke star was five lengths ahead of Doubleton. The Boss gave his rider a quizzical look in the winner's circle but stayed silent!

The Castleford Chase at Wetherby's Christmas meeting was to become an annual treat for Little Bay. He was in vintage form for the 1986 contest, giving Phil Tuck an exhilarating ride. 'I've never been so fast in my life, yet never been going as well as we went down the back straight,' recalls Tuck. 'I couldn't believe how quick we were going, but Little Bay was still on the bridle. Good horses like Charcoal Wally were being treated like cannon fodder. I stalked the grey into the straight, but then got a nasty shock because he came down at the second last and once again I found myself in front too early. I sat quiet as a mouse till we were over the last, then I asked him to quicken. He ran for me until half-way to the line before trying to stop on me. But no matter, we had five lengths in hand from Badsworth Boy, who was only giving us five pounds. On his day Little Bay was a machine. The pity of it is that Cheltenham's demanding uphill finish too often found him out.'

As mentioned earlier, Gordon used to ride Little Bay out as often as he could and Phil recalls going up the gallops with him. He continues, 'I was in the middle, with John Hansen next to the wood and Little Bay with The Boss up on my outside. I remember him shouting out, "Keep hold of his head, son. Don't be going too fast. You've got to make him finish at the top, son." We were climbing the hill alongside the wood and all the time Gordon was peering across at me, looking across and checking. Then all of a sudden he yelled, "Go on m' son!" and within a flash he was four lengths clear and going away. Both John and I were scrubbing along without any chance of pegging him back. Eventually we reached the top and there was Little Bay, not even blowing, and The Boss laughing his head off. "If I was a few years younger I could ride you buggers to sleep," he wheezed. "I can still do it, y' know, though it helps a bit if you are on Little Bay!"'

Throughout his training career at Greystoke The Boss was fortunate enough to have a series of substantial owners who had upwards of half a dozen horses in training at any one time. Names like Philip Cussins, Caroline Berry, Jimmy McGhie, Pat Muldoon and Fiona Whitaker spring immediately to mind. From the mid-'80s onwards the Edinburgh Woollen Mill, the Langholm-based company with retail outlets in all the big cities in Britain, joined the list as major players.

Their first two horses were Wood Avon, whose three outings did nothing to boost sales; and the Little Buskins gelding Tartan Trader whom Neale Doughty partnered to win novice hurdles at Ayr and Perth in the spring of 1983. His success encouraged the company to expand their racing interests. David Stevenson, The Mill's managing director and chairman, commissioned GWR to buy two further horses. However this time they were to be unbroken jumping bred types, handpicked by the trainer. The Boss recommended a Deep Run gelding, later to be named Tartan Triumph, and a four-year-old by Crash Course, who was christened The Langholm Dyer. Phil Tuck rode the latter to victory over hurdles at Hexham in the spring of 1985. Steeplechasing was always going to be his game, though, and he carried the colours of the Edinburgh Woollen Mill with distinction for eight consecutive seasons before going on to further success between the flags.

David Stevenson's initiative to promote the firm's name to a wider audience by investing in a team of company-owned hurdlers and steeplechasers remains one of the success stories of corporate sponsorship in National Hunt racing. The team's achievements boosted the company's image and stimulated nationwide interest in their products. The Edinburgh Woollen Mill's colours were registered as beige, with brown hoops on the sleeves plus an orange cap – a combination reflecting the most popular colours used in the firm's woollen merchandise.

For similar reasons David Stevenson and his fellow directors opted to extend the use of the word 'Tartan' as a prefix to the names of their future purchases. Three exceptions to this rule have been those multiple winners Randolph Place, The Antartex and Whaat Fettle, but the 'Tartans' enjoyed plenty of success in their own right. Led by Tartan Trader and Tartan Triumph, they included Tartan Tailor, Tartan Trademark, Tartan Takeover, Tartan Tyrant and Tartan Tradewinds.

The last-named was still in action as a 12-year-old in the autumn of 1998, winning a handicap hurdle at Cartmel after trying his hand as a hunter-chaser the previous campaign. He was by Strong Gale and it was a persistent disappointment to The Boss that the Edinburgh Woollen Mill invested serious money into acquiring potential chasers by a wide range of top stallions without ever gaining the deserved reward of an outstanding performer. The great majority of the 'Tartans' proved admirable handicappers, but failed to make their mark at the highest level.

Tartan Tailor was the exception, but ironically his victory at the 1987 Cheltenham Festival was to come over hurdles. The son of Patch enjoyed a vintage campaign in 1986–87, winning four times, twice filling the runner-up berth and finishing fourth on his final outing in the Whitbread Best Scotch Novices' Hurdle at Aintree. His only defeat before Christmas came at the hands of Saffron Lord at Cheltenham's Mackeson meeting. No disgrace, this, as the winner played a prominent part in several of the season's top handicaps and contested the Champion Hurdle in March. Gordon had seen enough to realise that he was harbouring a Festival winner and Tartan Tailor was kept under wraps until Doncaster in early March.

Phil Tuck takes up the story: 'The Boss had left a bit to work on. Ibn Majed was favourite that day. He had run well in competitive hurdles in the autumn and had too much experience for The Tailor. We finished a good second and The Boss was well pleased.'

Tartan Tailor was entered for the Waterford Crystal Supreme Novices' Hurdle and the feeling at Greystoke was positive. Phil was looking forward to the ride: 'I knew this horse had a real chance, but at one moment I thought that I wasn't going to be fit enough to be in the saddle. I had a bad asthma attack on the drive down from Cumbria and used up an entire Intel inhaler by the time I had weighed out. Luckily everything went smoothly during the race. Tartan Tailor was always on the bridle. He gave me a great feel throughout, we took it up at the last and quickened clear. He was trained to the minute and did a great job. He wouldn't have blown out a candle in the winner's circle, which was more than could be said about his jockey! I could hardly breathe and was in such a poor way that I couldn't even go out to receive my trophy.'

Tartan Tailor failed to win in 1987–88, but showed his quality by finishing seventh in the Champion Hurdle and then doing all his best work close home when third to Pat's Jester in the Scottish variety at Ayr. Early in his chasing career Tartan Tailor threatened to become a leading contender for The Arkle, but though he won four times as a novice, he trailed in a well-beaten third behind Phoenix Gold in the valuable Nottinghamshire Novices' Chase, missed the Festival and never again shaped up to championship class. Nonetheless, he enjoyed jumping round Perth to the end, winning the Little Bay Chase at the Tayside course and bowing out there with an all-the-way success at the age of 12.

The two 'Tartans' who came closest to high-chasing honours were arguably Tartan Takeover and Tartan Tyrant. Takeover was a strapping stamp of staying chaser, powerful, rangy and so heavily framed that The Boss reported the reason he had been pulled up Ayr in December 1988, was 'sore shins' – caused by the horse ploughing through the soft going on top and coming into contact with the firm ground below the surface.

Unlike many of the chasers owned by the Edinburgh Woollen Mill, Tartan Takeover was neither bred in the purple nor expensive to buy. Tina Fort, his dam, had been a modest performer for Neville Crump. Perhaps because of his bulk he changed hands for only 1,400 guineas, but he won his point-to-point in the style of a useful prospect. Once The Boss had sorted out his jumping problems, his future looked assured.

Tartan Takeover had made several mistakes on his initial victory under rules at Carlisle as a six-year-old and early anxiety that his jumping technique would need plenty of attention was quickly confirmed. Clumsy errors prevented him from completing the course on his next three outings and The Boss prescribed a diet of rest and re-schooling. Back in action in the spring, Tartan Takeover was a reformed character. Ridden by stable amateur Philip Doyle, he came from off the pace to hit the front some 50 yards from the post and showed an impressive turn of foot to scoot six lengths clear of Zeta's Lad by the time he crossed the line. Brought back to two and a half miles for the final of the *Racing Post* Novices' Chase Series at Wetherby, he trounced Nick the Brief by 15 lengths and ended his season with a bloodless win at Ayr.

Tartan Takeover, partnered by Mark Dwyer, crowned his 1989–90 season by winning an admittedly substandard *Timeform* Chase at Haydock. Though still prone to the occasional monumental blunder, he was learning all the time. Almost too laid back for his own good, but splendidly tough and by no means devoid of acceleration, he seemed sure to play a leading role in top long-distance chases for several seasons. Indeed he attracted plenty of market support in the run-up to the 1990 William Hill Scottish National, despite being six pounds out of the handicap.

Gordon Richards also had Four Trix, sporting the Little Bay colours of the Catherwoods, in the line-up. The grey had done much of his winning over two and a half miles, but form students will not have forgotten that he had finished a four-and-a-half-length third to Roll A Joint in the 1989 Scottish National; and though he had been pulled up in the Mildmay of Flete the previous month, he had needed the race, having been off the course until February as a result of minor leg trouble sustained at Ayr the previous April. Four Trix was to be ridden by Derek Byrne and would be sent off at 25–1.

Playlord (Ron Barry) in the 1968 Totalisator Champion
Novices' Steeplechase, Cheltenham. © John Grant

Getting over carefully: Titus Oates (Ron Barry) in
the 1972 Swift Chase, Newcastle. © Kenneth Bright

LEFT: Ron Barry and Sea Pigeon (left), about to leave Superb Sam behind on their way to winning the 1975 Shoveller Novices' Hurdle, Newcastle.

BELOW: Man Alive (Neale Doughty) running his rivals ragged in the 1983 Kaltenberg Pils Chase, Aintree. He ran out in the lead at third last.

Hallo Dandy (Neale Doughty) in satisfied repose
after victory in the 1984 Grand National.

One Man (Richard Dunwoody) in splendid isolation
in the 1997 Comet Chase, Ascot.

ABOVE: The Grey Monk (Tony Dobbin) disputes the lead with Grange Break during the 1996 Hennessy Gold Cup, Newbury.

RIGHT: Noddy's Ryde (Neale Doughty) after winning the 1984 *Sporting Life* Weekender Chase, Aintree.

ABOVE: Special award by the Perth executive to Tony McCoy, marking his record-breaking achievements as Champion Jockey in 1997. GWR does the honours.
© Anne Grossick

LEFT: The Boss (left) with Oliver Sherwood, judging the 1996 Doncaster Bloodstock Spring Sales Championship.

Showing how it is done: The Boss at work aboard his favourite, One Man.
© Anne Grossick

The Boss (right) in his last summer watches The Grey Monk, with owner Alistair Duff in charge.
© *Cumberland News*

The Boss had jockey problems on the day. Neale Doughty had sustained a crashing fall from Jinxy Jack in the Scottish Champion Hurdle the previous afternoon. Mark Dwyer and Graham McCourt, successful on Tartan Takeover earlier in the season, were both unavailable. At the 11th hour Gordon booked Richard Rowe, who was up at Ayr riding for Josh Gifford. Richard had given Highfrith a fine ride in the Future Champions' Chase, but he was facing a difficult task on Tartan Takeover in the big race. The genial giant took a bit of knowing and that particular Scottish National was run at a flat-out gallop from the moment that the tapes rose.

Tartan Takeover was taken off his feet for the first two circuits and by the time he agreed to make a forward move he had given the leaders far too much rope. To his credit Tartan Takeover came within striking distance of bringing off the impossible. Three out, he had succeeded in getting into the shake-up, but he had used up valuable reserves of stamina too quickly in the process. He could not go with Four Trix as Derek Byrne struck for home and it wasn't until between the final two fences that he gained his second wind. Four Trix had not enjoyed the smoothest of runs, but had arrived full of running at the third last and was not stopping. He won by 15 lengths to follow in the hoofprints of Playlord, who had won the Scottish National for The Boss under 12 stone back in 1969.

David Stevenson was generous in defeat, no doubt hoping that Tartan Takeover would go on to win his share of lucrative handicaps the following season. He stood stoically in the runner-up berth while a strangely sheepish GWR skipped to and fro, doing his level best to congratulate the Catherwoods and commiserate with the Stevensons. Tartan Takeover scored first time out in 1989–90 at Kelso, only to collapse in his box at Greystoke and die from a massive heart attack shortly after returning from morning exercise a week later.

Mainly as a result of Tartan Takeover's victory in the *Timeform* Chase, the Edinburgh Woollen Mill had finished ninth in the owners' winning prize money list for 1989–90. Taking into account place money won as well, the firm would have risen to sixth in the table; and judged solely on the total of races won, it would have risen to fourth position. The Edinburgh Woollen Mill won 18 races that season. They have been tremendous supporters of National Hunt racing since 1982 and over the years have also been invaluable sponsors. Their name is still linked to the Future Champions' Chase at Ayr's Scottish National meeting, while in recent seasons they have provided funds for a prestigious two-and-a-half-mile chase at Carlisle's March fixture.

Tartan Tyrant, a full brother to Tartan Takeover, never realised his true potential. In 1992 this handsome individual met with defeat only once in seven outings between the flags for Alix Stevenson, David's wife. He was tapped for toe on the run-in at Witton Castle and caught close home by Glen Lochan, who went on to advertise the form by winning the Land Rover Final next time out. The year's point-to-pointing was to serve as an apprenticeship for his career under rules and with hindsight the warning issued by Iain

Mackenzie, in the 1993 edition of *Hunter Chasers and Point-to-Pointers*, was a model of accuracy. He drew attention to a recurrent fault in Tartan Tyrant's style of jumping, namely that he continually 'gets into the bottom of his fences and Gordon Richards will have to correct this fault if he is to hit the heights under rules'.

The Boss did his best, but Tartan Tyrant never fully managed to eradicate this weakness. If he completed the course he usually won. But in between these victories there were several expensive occasions when he either fell or parted company with his rider. As a novice chaser Tartan Tyrant won twice from four outings. In 1993–94 he picked up three handicaps but was pulled up in the Scottish National. The following season Tartan Tyrant gained two clear-cut wins at Haydock. He was travelling like a winner in a third visit to the Merseyside course, only to have a reversion to old habits and attempt to take liberties with the fence approaching the stands, and consequently paid the inevitable penalty. He also fell when 5–2 favourite for the Tote Eider Chase at Newcastle. In 1995–96 Paul Carberry gave him a memorably daring ride, forcing the pace in the Greenalls Grand National Trial and gaining a succession of breathtaking leaps which took the Richards' star into the final bend with what seemed an invincible advantage. Tartan Tyrant's stride shortened rapidly from two out, however, and he was overhauled close home by Lo Stregone. On the strength of that fine run, The Boss advised another attempt at the Scottish National. The plan misfired. Tartan Tyrant ran no sort of race and was pulled up. The gelding was still young enough to win more races, but he had to have soft ground to show his best form and for two consecutive seasons he fell victim to a nagging virus. He was never to race again. Like his brother, Tartan Tyrant developed a weak heart. He went back to Kevin Anderson at Lochmaben with a view to resuming his pointing career but died suddenly before making his reappearance.

GWR reckoned that Randolph Place would prove the champion which the Edinburgh Woollen Mill so richly deserved. Related to Arkle through My Cherry, his grandam, Randolph Place was bought for 15,000 guineas as an unbroken three-year-old at the Ballsbridge Tattersalls Derby Sales. After winning competitive bumpers by wide margins at Newbury and Chepstow, he graduated to hurdling and was far from disgraced in finishing a staying-on eighth in a maximum field for the 1987 Sun Alliance Novices' Hurdle.

Put over fences in the autumn of 1987, Randolph Place fell on his début at Kelso before setting up a sequence of five consecutive wins, culminating in a facile victory in the West of Scotland Pattern Novices' Chase in which he had started second favourite to the Lambourn star Private Views. That race was over two and a half miles, but The Boss was convinced that Randolph Place had the latent speed to be more effective at the minimum trip. Gordon had always regarded Cheltenham's Sun Alliance Novices' Chase as a gruelling contest from which some horses never recovered. It was his intention to saddle Randolph Place in the Arkle and to give him more racing experience at the distance he was entered in the Nottinghamshire Novices' Chase. The star misread the script. Randolph Place came down when still in contention at the fourth last. He then went to Cheltenham for the Arkle Chase and fell heavily at the final open ditch, five out. He was travelling well on the heels of the leading bunch at the time and to make matters worse he was cannoned-into by Romerhof as he tried to rise

Phil Tuck feels that the experience could have scarred him mentally for the remainder of his career. He explains: 'The Boss opted for the Arkle when it might have been better to keep him to two and a half miles. The Nottingham fall didn't do his confidence any good and after Cheltenham he seemed to lose his way. He went to Ayr for the Future Champions' Chase and fell again. He'd made a mistake at the sixth and I tried to make up his mind for him at the next, but he took no notice and ploughed straight into the birch.'

Randolph Place was placed in each of his three races in 1988–89. He won a handicap chase at Ayr the next season, after which The Boss switched him between chasing and hurdling, with the latter alternative proving the most successful. The 1990–91 campaign saw him win three competitive handicap hurdles and finish an excellent third to Danny Connors in the Coral Golden Hurdle Final at Cheltenham. By now Randolph Place had fallen between two stools. The handicapper had got his measure over hurdles but he could not be trusted over fences. His last 16 races under rules were over hurdles. He won 13 times for the Edinburgh Woollen Mill, seven hurdles and six chases. For a horse of his outstanding potential the latter total was a sorry tale. The final throw was to send him to Ian Stark. The famous three-day eventer, still based in the Borders, coaxed him back to winning form over the less exacting point-to-point fences.

To qualify him for the Christies Foxhunters, Ian Stark needed to win a couple of Opens. The first should have been landed on his point-to-point début at the Jedforest. Randolph Place was a length ahead of his rivals with the race seemingly under control, when he slipped up on the home turn. At the Badsworth the partnership had to be content with a close second to the experienced Many A Slip, but consecutive victories at Bogside made him eligible for Cheltenham. Stark was hopeful. Randolph Place was less positive. Taken wide to obtain a clear view of the fences, he still treated them with suspicion and it came as no real surprise when he took the 15th by the roots and unseated his eminent rider. It was a sad but fitting end to a career which had promised so much but achieved comparatively little.

If Randolph Place flattered only to deceive, both The Langholm Dyer and Whaat Fettle were made of sterner stuff. They were superb jumpers, but a crucial lack of finishing kick restricted their outright successes to handicap company. The Langholm Dyer raced 64 times. He won ten steeplechases and once over hurdles. Much more remarkable was his tally of near misses. He actually reached the frame on 29 other occasions, including such competitive events as the Eider Chase, the Flowers Bitter Handicap at Cheltenham and the

Rowland Meyrick Chase at Wetherby. His most important win was the Allied Dunbar Chase at Cheltenham in 1986. After his retirement he was ridden in ladies' races 'between the flags' by the Stevensons' elder daughter, Karen, who drove him out with steely determination to come from a long way off the pace and win the 1992 Cotswold Ladies' Open by two lengths from Lean Ort.

Phil Tuck and Neale Doughty rode The Langholm Dyer for much of his professional career, but this honest performer would go equally well for a claimer. Liam O'Hara, whose father Johnny rode plenty of winners for John Barclay and Billy Atkinson before injury caused him to retire and concentrate on building up his saddlery business in Carlisle, established a successful rapport with the veteran chaser. He guided him into second place in the Eider Chase and won on him at Carlisle in the autumn of 1990.

I have a vivid recollection of that victory because The Boss was far from happy with the manner in which poor Liam had achieved his win. Liam was, and still is, a stylish but quiet, unobtrusive rider – too low-key for The Boss, who was always on at him to 'take hold of the horse, ask him to jump and get him away quickly'. At Carlisle Gordon had been incensed by the way in which Liam had allowed The Langholm Dyer to coast over the final open ditch, a decision that led to him forfeiting at least a couple of lengths in the air, landing flat-footed and losing the lead. In the event Liam rallied The Langholm Dyer to some purpose up the home straight and forced his head back in front a few strides from the post. The win did not appease The Boss. In his eyes Liam had given the old horse a much harder race than had been necessary. Gordon made sure the rider realised the error of his ways, wagging his finger aggressively and giving vent to his feelings with a vociferous tirade in the winner's circle.

A similar outburst greeted young Neil Leach after he had partnered Pinemartin to a narrow success at Catterick the following season. GWR had issued clear instructions to his jockey to ride a patient waiting race and not to hit the front until the final fence, as Pinemartin tended to stop in front and he did not want the horse to have a hard race. Such orders may look simple on paper but in practice they are less easy to adopt. It was a very small field and as Pinemartin's rivals fell away one by one, the unfortunate Neil Leach found himself left in the lead fully three fences from home. The only course of action was to seize the initiative and set sail for the judge. Clearing the penultimate fence, all was well. Pinemartin was in a clear lead and still nicely on the bridle. Not for long. With dramatic suddenness his stride began to shorten. He scrambled over the final obstacle and Leach was forced to use all the aids to keep his head in front where it mattered the most. Pinemartin hung on but not in the manner that The Boss had prescribed and the members of the press shrank back at the ferocity of the trainer's reaction. It was the rough side of his nature: some would think it an unattractive characteristic, but strangely enough the riders themselves took the invective in their stride. Used no doubt to taking such flak at regular intervals at home on the gallops, they expected little else if orders were not obeyed on the course!

No such problem ever arose with Whaat Fettle. In later years this game front runner went best for Michael Molony, now back in Ballydoyle riding work for Aidan O'Brien. Whaat Fettle ran some fine races at Wetherby, but above all else he was a Kelso specialist, winning no fewer than eight times at the Border course where his bold jumping and speed into the bends so often left rivals floundering in his wake.

Neale Doughty and Phil Tuck were the jockeys who enjoyed the greatest success on the horses owned by the Edinburgh Woollen Mill. David Stevenson says that it would be invidious to choose between them. He affirms, 'Any jockey riding for Gordon had to be a first-rate rider with the welfare of the horse their first priority. Both Neale and Phil were outstanding examples. Phil enjoyed a lot of success at a time when out horses were at the top of their form, but Neale was in the saddle when Tartan Trader gave The Mill its very first winner. We are most grateful to each of them. They were both fine jockeys.'

TWENTY-ONE

Some Random Reflections

Asked if he had got on well with The Boss when riding out, Phil Tuck took a deep breath, hesitated and then sounded a shade less than convincing.

'Yeah, I think so. We didn't have too many arguments, but he could be quite difficult. Sometimes it seemed that he had an attitude problem with you and I remember going through a patch when anything I did or said was wrong and I thought, that's it, I'll say nothing.

'We were coming back off the gallops and The Boss turned round and said, "Ooh son, that horse will be fit now, won't he?"

'"Aye," I mumbled. The Boss didn't think that I had heard him. So he said it again.

'"Aye," I repeated.

'"Ooh now, what's the matter son?" he asked. "You're not very talkative today."

'I swung round in the saddle and let fly: "No, and the way you talk to me, there's little wonder. A trainer and jockey should be a partnership. You talk to me as though I'm a piece of grout. If you can't bother to talk to me with a civil tongue in your head, then don't bother to talk to me at all!"

'He was so surprised that it took all the wind out of his sails. He never spoke for about six days. Then he was grand again!'

Phil goes on to tell how, not long after that, he was riding a three-year-old up the gallop: 'The Boss was on Tartan Tailor and it was my turn to come in for attention. He fixed me with those laser-blue eyes and growled, "When you go up the gallop on that horse, son, don't you just sit on him, you've got to get hold of him and pull him up together and make him work for you." He let the opening salvo sink in and then continued, "When I broke this horse in he knew nothing. Now I can go up that gallop and I can switch him h'on and switch him h'off. You've got to take hold of him, pull him up together and make him work for you!"

'I was a bit annoyed about this outburst because I felt that I had been in racing long enough to know how to ride a young horse. The Boss jogged off to take up his watching position half-way up the hill, so I said to Chris Dennis, who was working alongside me, "Whatever happens, Chris, I finish half a length in front of you."

'"No problem, Phil," he replied with a grin. We worked up the gallop and we worked quite nicely. As we reined in, Gordon came across and called out to Chris, "How did he go, son?"

'"Oh he went all right, Boss. I think he's a nice horse."

'"Of course he's a nice horse, son," interjected The Boss. "Do you fink I'd have bought him if he wasn't?"

'Then he turned to me and rasped, "What about him?"

'Tongue firmly in cheek, I answered, "He went all right, Boss, because I got hold of him, pulled him up together and made him work for me!"

'No more needed to be said.'

A fortnight later Gordon and Joanie Richards joined the Tucks for a pub meal at The White Horse, a well-known watering hole on the A66 near the village of Threlkeld. The pub's landlord at the time, Larry Slattery, had a leg in a horse at Greystoke. Phil remembers, 'We'd had a few drinks over the evening – enough to persuade me to tackle Gordon about his truculent attitude on the gallops.

'I said, "You shouldn't talk to me like that. We should be a partnership, a team. You shouldn't talk to people like that."

'I was warming to my task when Joanie interrupted: "But Phil," she said, "he does that to me. Gordon, you are a *schmock*!"

'"Ooh, what's that, Joanie?" he asked. "What's one of them, dear?"

'"It's Jewish for penis," she explained.

'"Ooh," he went on, turning to Maria, "I've got one of them. It's not much good to me!"

'The attempt to embarrass misfired. Maria smiled and answered as quick as a flash, "Well, Gordon. You want to get hold of it, pull it up together and make it work for you!"'

Phil, later a Jockey Club official, had no doubts about Gordon's ability as a trainer: 'He was brilliant. The art of training horses is placing them. The Boss was great in this respect. That's why good horses like Jim Thorpe, Rinus and Randolph Place could win five or six on the trot. There was nobody better than The Boss at choosing the right race for a horse and a lot of his success stemmed from his remarkable rapport with his horses and, of course, his fantastic eye for a horse in the first place. The Boss was able to find the right races for the members of his team because he had the knack of assessing a horse's potential simply by watching – watching in the stables, on the gallops and at the racecourse.

'Yes, he would ask the work riders and the jockeys for their opinions, but it would be Gordon and Gordon alone who made the decisions; and once made they would very rarely need to be changed. At the sales, or out in Ireland on a buying trip with Jack White, he knew exactly what he was looking for. When a man can buy a horse like One Man from a dispersal sale there can be no argument. Most trainers can get their horses fit, but Gordon's weren't just physically fit. They were sound mentally as well. He treated them as his own and his motto was "keep them sweet and happy, son!" It served him well right up to the end.'

Like so many of those who either rode for The Boss or worked for him in other capacities, Phil Tuck never regarded Gordon as a man blessed with a great sense of humour – but rather as someone who created his own humorous situations, often without realising what he had done. Phil cherished Gordon's habit of getting words marginally wrong or out of place. 'They were never far from the right usage, but enough to cause a good chuckle,' he recalls. 'He once noticed that Ron Barry had bought a new Ford Orion and said to me, "Ooh son, look at this. That Ron Barry's gone and got himself one of those Ford Onions!"

'In the same way, someone he disagreed with was always "a h'ingorant man" rather than "a h'ignorant man"!'

Winding up The Boss was an art at which Ron Barry had no equal, so it was appropriate that one of the lads' favourite ploys was always reserved for the pre-season sortie to the fells above Ullswater. Ron and Liz Barry live at Roehead, high above Pooley Bridge, and The Boss was fond of repeating the words that Ron had once used to describe his surroundings: 'Ooh, that Ron Barry used to say, "There's only one place higher than this, Boss, and that's Heaven!"'

It had become part of the folklore about this particular excursion. As soon as the string had climbed the long steep incline up to the level ground alongside the Barrys' house, and were all assembled within earshot, one of the lads appointed for the task would pipe up with the words, 'Gosh, Boss, it's pretty high up here.' The Boss would inevitably reply, 'Ooh there's only one place higher than this son . . .' and never understood just why it was that he could never get the punch line out before the whole audience would burst out in fits of giggles.

'He was a great man, though,' says Phil Tuck. 'I'm just sad that I didn't ride longer for him.'

David Stevenson, of the Edinburgh Woollen Mill, remembers Gordon with 'great affection and respect'. He continues: 'The company had horses at Greystoke for a very long while and throughout that time he was always charming and amusing. Win or lose, his idea was that he should do the work and we, as owners, should enjoy the experience. He and Joanie were happy for us to visit the horses at any time and he was tremendous value when he came to company race nights to give a talk or answer questions. I know he had the reputation for being a hard man to please, but his staff were a credit to him and very loyal. He was a real professional, a hands-on trainer who insisted on nothing but the best.'

David and Alix Stevenson met The Boss on several occasions while he was 'enjoying' his holidays abroad. David adds that early on, Gordon was reluctant to take a holiday: 'Once out of the equine environment he was a little akin to a fish out of water, but as he grew more used to the idea he began to open up. He played a bit of golf and relaxed in the sun. When all is said and done, though, he lived for his horses. His whole life revolved about them and he would always try to steer the conversation back to horses if he got half the chance.'

The Stevensons agree that although The Boss may not have been blessed with a rollicking sense of humour, just being in his company was a source of much amusement. David explains: 'He was a catalyst for laughter and for creating comical situations, quite frequently remaining unaware of what he had said or done to cause such hilarity.'

David treasures one such occasion that illustrated Gordon's typical response to a 'non-racing' query: 'I had rung up to ask him something about the horses. Knowing that he had just returned from holiday I asked him how things had gone.

'"Ooh David,' he answered. "Joanie and I had a lovely time. We've spent a fortnight in Portugal, y'know."

'As my family were going to Portugal on our own holiday within the week, I remarked, "How interesting, Gordon. We'll be going there on Saturday. Whereabouts did you stay?"

'There was silence for a moment. Then The Boss replied testily, "Ooh David, you'd have to ask Joanie about that. It was in Portugal, though. We've been there for two weeks, great place for a holiday!"'

Many hardened observers of the jumping game never understood how David Goulding and The Boss managed to put up with each other for so long. The laid-back, practical-joking Goulding seemed as far removed from the forceful, demanding Richards as chalk from cheese. A meeting of opposites, perhaps?

Not really. David was working for Arthur Stephenson in the early '70s but he was on good terms with Ron Barry; when RB suggested that he might like to earn a few bob by riding work for The Boss after racing one day at Catterick, David agreed. His stylish horsemanship appealed to Gordon and it wasn't long before David was invited to ride for Greystoke on a more permanent basis. The Boss was always attracted to the best and he had recognised David Goulding as 'a quality article'.

For his part, the rider respected The Boss as a fine trainer who knew his job and was a master at teaching novice chasers to jump and enjoy their racing. David has happy memories of his time at Greystoke. 'The crack was grand,' he says. 'I had some great times with Jonjo and the lads and got on well with the owners. But it was the horses that I shall never forget. Gordon had such horsepower that almost every time you went to the races you would be expecting to ride a winner. Just to get a leg up on some of them was a privilege and riding them over fences was like going hunting. They flowed over the jumps with such fluency; and of course Greystoke was a fantastic place for horses. They built up their stamina going up the hills and developed their muscles both in the back and the legs walking back down. As any fell walker will tell you, it is harder coming down than it is going up.'

David Goulding relates an amusing tale about his early relationship with The Cantabfella: 'I was cleaning up after riding morning work in the small wash room next to the stable office. I heard The Boss talking to Paul Rimmer, the owner of a tricky jumper called The Cantabfella.

'Gordon was asked whether he had decided which of his jockeys was going to ride his horse. I stopped to listen and Gordon replied, "not Ron Barry, nor Jonjo, because I don't want either of them to get hurt! I'm going to ask David Goulding to take the mount."

'This was hardly good news, but I kept my mouth shut and sure enough The Boss told me to take the ride. It was at Hexham and The Cantabfella started joint favourite, but the two-mile distance was too short for him and he was outpaced, fading into third place. The stewards had me in to explain why I hadn't been more positive on the horse. I pointed out that in my view the trip was too short for The Cantabfella. Then I grinned and retold the events of the morning's telephone conversation. I went on to say, "Ron Barry has a big gap where his front teeth had been. Jonjo had both his front teeth knocked out and I'd no intention of going the same way." The stewards recorded the first part of my explanation and two outings later – over three miles this time – I rode The Cantabfella to win at Sedgefield.'

Goulding also recalls a spontaneous joke which rebounded on himself: 'On Sundays Jonjo and I were expected to put in several hours' work picking up stones on the gallops. One Sunday I didn't turn up and the following morning The Boss demanded an explanation.

'"Oh, Boss, I replied, "I rode seven times on Saturday and needed the lie-in."

'Quick as a flash Gordon retorted, "There were only six races on the card at Catterick, son. You're telling porkies."

'"That's where you're wrong, Boss," I answered. "You see, my fiancée came over on Saturday night and she's a very exhausting ride!"'

The Boss snorted and rode off into the dawn. But he had the last laugh, as Dave adds: 'I didn't get another ride for about a fortnight. Then, when I arrived in the paddock for instructions, The Boss growled, "She's an easy ride, this mare. Shouldn't tire you out, son. And I expect to see you in the gallops on Sunday!"'

Jimmy O'Brien was the first of Gordon's head lads at Greystoke. He was forced to resign through ill health. Ron Lauder, his successor, left the stable at the beginning of the '70s. This left room for Colin Parker, who held the fort for seven years and only gave up the position because he had the chance to set up his own livery yard, the launching pad for his successful transition to the ranks of the professional licence holders.

Colin, a Cumbrian by birth, had ridden plenty of winners over the jumps and had previously been asked by The Boss to join his team at Greystoke as understudy to Ron Barry. He recalls, 'I was tied up at the time and had to refuse. But in 1971, when he offered me the job of head lad, I jumped at the chance and never regretted it for one moment.'

They say that you only get to know someone really well if you work closely with them 'during the small hours'. If there is any truth in this old chestnut then Colin must have understood The Boss better than most. In his seven-year stint Gordon and Colin used to rendezvous in the feed room shortly before dawn and, almost without exchanging a word, divide the breakfast rations between them and set out to check and feed the horses. Colin would go in one direction, The Boss in the other and when they bumped into each other they knew that the whole stable had been fed and watered.

Colin reflects, 'We did the same last thing at night because The Boss believed in feeding the horses four times: breakfast, lunch, tea and a late-night "filler". We didn't talk much on our rounds – unless of course either one of us came across an emergency – but we both noted small details like horses who hadn't eaten up overnight, or others who had given a cough or two, or who didn't seem to be their usual bright selves. We would generally store these bits of news until riding out with first lot so we could have a closer look.'

Colin was very happy at Greystoke. He explains: 'There was a great buzz and friendly feeling about the place. Everyone pulled together. Everyone knew their jobs but there was no standing on ceremony. The Boss would be down in the yard helping out with the lads and the same went for the jockeys. The likes of Ron Barry, Jonjo and Dave Goulding all joined in the crack and helped out wherever they were needed. The routine went like clockwork and the team spirit was infectious.'

Colin hardly ever left the stable. Apart from his annual fortnight's holiday, he remembers going to the races at Carlisle once. But otherwise it was full-time working in the yard feeding, organising the lads' work timetable, watching over the horses and, most importantly, breaking in the youngsters. It was an art at which he excelled, just as The Boss was the expert when it came to teaching them to jump.

'He never interfered with my side of the business,' says Colin, 'and I left the training to Gordon, though every now and again I might think that a horse was being worked just that bit too hard for his own good. Then, I'd quietly arrange that he had something convenient like "a pricked foot" which kept him on the easy list for a day or even two!'

What about GWR's renowned outbursts of rage and invective? Colin grins at the memory.

'Yes, The Boss did have a bit of a temper and that's putting it mildly. But everyone accepted that and they also knew that after he had blown his top that would be it – all said and done and no recriminations. I can only remember having two serious rows with him. Each time we shouted at each other for several minutes and in a way it cleared the air. We both liked to come straight to the point and get things out into the open. The Boss was the same with his jockeys. Win or lose, he would play merry hell if they had not followed his instructions. It might have seemed harsh at the time, but he was often proved right and the lads knew that he would stand up for them if they were in trouble. He was a demanding employer but a loyal one too.'

Malcolm Jefferson, the stable's travelling head lad throughout Colin Parker's time as head lad, viewed The Boss with mixed emotions. Malcolm's family farmed locally. He had always been keen on horses and joined the Richards stable in 1968 as a stable lad. He recalls, 'I came in for my fair share of hassle, but the horses I looked after won rather more races than The Boss anticipated, and by and large we got on pretty well. I was never one for making a fuss. Throughout the time that I was travelling the horses there were no real problems. I was happy to be working for such a successful stable.'

Difficulties arose, though, after Colin Parker's departure. Malcolm was appointed head lad and together with Sue, his wife, moved into recently renovated accommodation at the Old Rectory farm. This was also the time when Gordon and Joanie were about to be married. With Joanie unwilling to live in the flat above the stables, The Boss applied pressure on the Jeffersons to vacate the property at the farm. Sue Jefferson relates: 'When we refused to move, Gordon's attitude to Malcolm changed for the worse. He began criticising the way Malcolm was doing his job, finding fault with him all the time and making life so stressful that we had to leave.'

In fact the split did Malcolm a favour in the long run. He was given the chance to set up as a trainer in his own right at Norton. Some 20 years later he is firmly established as one of the North's most successful dual-purpose licence holders, with a series of big race wins to his credit from such familiar names as High Debate, Tancred Sand and Dato Star.

Malcolm adds, 'With hindsight the move to Yorkshire has worked out better than we could possibly have imagined, but at the time things were very different. I had spent over ten happy years at Greystoke and all of a sudden I was no longer wanted. It was hard and The Boss didn't stop there. After we had gone he tried to block my trainer's application. He took a long while to accept that I could do the job, but relations improved gradually and if he was in a good mood he would sometimes come over and congratulate us when we'd had a winner!'

Martin Todhunter, who took over as travelling head lad, found The Boss to be 'a wonderful employer. I travelled the horses for 16 years and during that time I never knew him to sack a lad. He would bawl anyone out from the stable jockey downwards, but if you worked hard and worked with him then you got your just deserts. And he would stick up for any of his staff if he felt they were being unfairly treated. Greystoke was a great place and I enjoyed every moment.'

Martin joined the team because The Boss was short of a rider to partner his point-to-pointer General Branca. He explains, 'I was lodging with David Goulding at the time and riding a few winners between the flags. The Boss had never heard of me but Arthur Eubank put in a good word and I got the mount at the Cumberland Farmers'. We won and followed up at Alnwick. Then I rode General Branca in a maiden hunter chase at Carlisle and completed the three-timer without The Boss even seeing me ride. The first time he watched me was at Perth and on the way back he asked me to come and work for him and to ride as the stable amateur. I always found him good fun to be around and after racing I would sometimes act as his chauffeur to dinners and such like.'

Martin recalls taking The Boss to a dinner organised by David Stevenson at Langholm: 'The Boss was the guest speaker and he was a shade twitchy about making his speech. I reckon that we must have stopped off at every pub between Greystoke and Langholm. He was weaving a bit when I dropped him off, but he had them in stitches after dinner and even managed to worm out of a real nasty corner when asked to explain why the Edinburgh Woollen Mill hadn't had a winner at the Cheltenham Festival.'

In his job as travelling head lad Martin experienced all the highs and lows in close company with The Boss. He was at Newbury when One Man took the Hennessy and he was also at Haldon when Noddy's Ryde had to be destroyed after falling at the last. He recalls, 'The Boss was as gutted as Neale [Doughty]. He could be a bad loser, too, but when he was at his lowest ebb he would still remember "his lads". He put his arm round Neale's shoulders and said they would go and find another horse as good as Noddy's Ryde.'

Martin echoes the feelings of many close to Gordon when he declares that Noddy's Ryde was potentially the best horse that The Boss ever trained. 'Just think!' he continues, 'even after that amazing battle with Bobsline in the Arkle, he bounced back to win in a canter at Aintree and break the course record at Ayr. They say he had nothing to beat at Devon, but Fifty Dollars More was no slouch and he was a fence clear when he slipped up after the last. He would have been something really special if he had had the chance to show it.'

Martin's decision to leave Greystoke and start training at Ulverston on his own account didn't exactly delight The Boss but it was accepted with good grace. 'He wished me all the best,' says Martin, 'and told me that my job would always be waiting for me if I decided to return. This was even more generous of him when you consider that I was taking two good horses, Chipped Out and Will's Telmar, away with me. He kept them fed and watered until the yard was ready and then he sent them down to Ulverston at his own expense. He was a great boss to work for and his bark was always worse than his bite!'

Neale Doughty's admiration for The Boss stems from his 14-year association with the Greystoke stable. It survived a traumatic two-year break in the mid-'80s and was undiminished by the rumblings of discontent which accompanied his final departure in 1994. On both occasions Neale was at pains to point out that he had not 'fallen out' with the trainer but was leaving for the greater good of the stable.

Neale remembers GWR as 'a great bloke to work for', a quality trainer both of jockeys as well as horses, and can recount numerous rib-tickling moments when Gordon's unwitting sense of humour would brighten many a long journey back from the races. 'He didn't need to tell a joke,' recalls Neale, 'but he was a past master at producing situation comedy.

'One time we drew up at traffic lights on the way back from Nottingham, when a van came alongside us with a couple of windsurfing boards strapped to its luggage rack.

'"Ooh look, Ron," exclaimed The Boss. "There's one of them scurf boards. They stand up on them and scurf. I said to my Joanie when we were on holiday, I'd like to try a bit of scurfing!" He never understood why the rest of the car rocked with merriment.

'Then there was the day that Ron, Tony Meaney and myself were with The Boss driving home from Kelso. It was shortly before Christmas and the garage where we stopped to pick up some petrol was bedecked with Christmas trees. Some of these were hanging from the board that was advertising the price of four-star petrol sold by the litre. As Tony went in to pay for the fuel The Boss piped up, "Ooh Ron, look at that notice. They're selling f***ing li-trees for Christmas now!"

'Waking up from a cat-nap and misunderstanding a chance remark was another source of Gordon's unpremeditated humour. Once on the return journey from Ayr with Ron and me in the back, Joanie was star-gazing down the A74. She swerved suddenly and pointed excitedly through the windscreen: "Look, Gordon, there's Venus!"

'Before The Boss could come to, Ron, who was not a good passenger, growled, "Never mind f***ing Venus. Keep your eyes on the road."

'At which point The Boss woke up with a start and said, "Ooh he's right y'know, Joanie. Stop f***ing Venus and keep your hands on the wheel!"'

Neale was quick to stress that GWR had been responsible for elevating Ron Barry, Jonjo O'Neill, Tony Dobbin and himself into the big league. He added, 'I used to feel ten feet tall when I went out to ride one of his. His horses were always so well prepared. It was often a case of just pointing them in the right direction and steering them home.'

Referring to their not-infrequent shouting matches, Doughty added, 'The trouble was that we both wanted the best for the horses and the stable, but neither of us was going to admit we were wrong. Of all the jockeys, his relationship with me was the stormiest – maybe that's why I survived as long as I did. Of course he loved his horses more than any of us. And though he would never admit it, he never recovered from the tragic loss of One Man.'

Tony Dobbin will never forget the moment that The Boss asked him to become his stable jockey. He points out that he had been offered a number of other tempting posts, but that the only job which he wanted was the chance to ride for The Boss at Greystoke. He adds: 'I jumped at the opportunity and I learned an awful lot from him in a short time. I was pretty immature, lacking in experience and foolhardy to the point of lunacy! The Boss taught me to calm down and think through a race. He was also a perfectionist and wouldn't accept anything but the best for his horses.'

Tony singles out Gordon's ability with novice chasers as his greatest quality as a trainer. 'The Boss never hurried his novices. He had taught them all to jump, from taking them over rows of little poles, to getting them to stand off and jump a series of mini-jumps, and finally to have them schooled to his highest standards before they were let loose on the racecourse. Once there he never over-faced them. The Grey Monk was a perfect example. He refused to put him in at the deep end, but ran him in a series of low profile races to give him both experience and confidence. He won six races off the trot without ever breaking sweat.'

Dedication to the job was another lesson that Tony learned from his employer. 'Right up to the end he was thinking only about the job. We had been galloping horses after racing at Carlisle. On the way home, Brian [Harding] and I called in to visit him at the Infirmary. He was pretty poorly, but the first thing that he asked was about the gallop at Carlisle and how the horses had travelled.'

Brian Harding found it hard to settle at Greystoke when he first arrived from Ireland. He admits that he and The Boss didn't see eye to eye for quite a while: 'He was always at me to school the horses exactly as he wanted,' recalls Brian. 'It was the perfectionist streak in him. If the job wasn't done to his liking then there would be a lot of shouting and it would be back down the hill and do it all over again. At the time you didn't appreciate what he was doing, but out on the track it soon became obvious. His novice chasers always knew their job before they got to the course.'

Brian's respect and gratitude to The Boss arose from adversity. It was after he had been laid off for a year, by the Jockey Club's medical department, that The Boss rallied to his side. 'He was brilliant,' reflects Brian. 'He went on to Channel 4 and gave them a real rollicking. He stood by me throughout that year, encouraging me to ride work, seeing to it that there was always enough to keep me busy; and then once I got my licence back, he gave me every chance to regain my confidence by putting me up on a series of good horses.'

Brian was no stranger to riding One Man. He had exercised the grey and schooled him quite regularly during the period that Richard Dunwoody was riding him on the course. He explains, 'The Boss felt that it would be unfair to ask Tony to ride One Man at home and then have to watch Richard receive all the plaudits. Even so, I was surprised and delighted to be asked to ride the grey at Cheltenham. That was typical of The Boss. He was loyal to his own and would stand by them to the end.'

Clerks of courses did not tend to feature prominently on Gordon's list of dinner guests; but an exception was Tim Riley, 'The Major', with whose family The Boss had become close friends since arriving at Greystoke. Tim was cruelly struck down with a blood clot on the brain when he was at the zenith of his powers. At the time he was Clerk at Carlisle, Hamilton, Kelso and Cartmel (for whose transition, from little more than 'a Bank Holiday gaff-track' into a cult symbol, Tim had been chiefly responsible). He has since made an amazing recovery. The Boss had a great deal of time for The Major and the feeling was mutual.

Tim remarks, 'When Gordon first came to Greystoke, northern national racing was dominated by the likes of Arthur Stephenson, Ken Oliver, the Easterbys and Neville Crump. He had been in Cumbria for less than five years before he was competing on level terms with these formidable names and for the last 20 years of his career he proved to be one of the greats himself. His record will never be forgotten, but quite apart from his feats as a trainer, he was a source of much valuable help and advice. If I was worried about the condition of the turf or the fences at any of the courses where I was operating, he would always find the time to come over, walk the course and make sound practical suggestions.

'He had once been Secretary of the Trainers' Federation, though in his later years he became far from happy with their work and labelled them "toothless wonders". I regularly used to consult him before going down to Portman Square for meetings of the Horserace Advisory Committee and he would furnish me with some pungent views on vital issues!'

Tim Riley dismisses any ideas that The Boss was a hard man to please. He adds, 'I always found him a gentleman to deal with. My two daughters, Nicola and Antonia, are better equipped to speak about that. Between them they rode out and worked for Gordon for a long time. They loved their years at Greystoke and had nothing but praise for The Boss. They said he used to bully them along, but provided that you were prepared to stand up for yourself he was tremendous fun and a very fair guv'nor.'

Tim and Tarn Riley would often attend parties with Gordon and Joanie and they recall a particularly effective example of GWR's amusing misuse of words. Tarn Riley continues: 'We were at a Hunt Ball and there was this fellow dressed up as a Texan cowboy. The Boss was describing him to us and the thing that impressed him the most was "the Stilton" he had on his head!'

The Boss employed the same farrier for the last 26 years of his career – not surprising, really, when one considers that Roger Hale was GWR's brother-in-law, married to his sister Carol who herself died of cancer several years before Gordon suffered the same fate. The couple used to come and stay at Greystoke in the early days. Roger took over the job of shoeing the Richards' horses after Gordon's regular farrier from nearby Penruddock had gone down with multiple sclerosis. He declares, 'Being Gordon's brother-in-law didn't mean I was paid any favours. I must have given in my notice at least three times, but I'm still here!'

Roger nominates 'complete dedication' as GWR's most important quality as a trainer. He says, 'Gordon lived for his horses. It may not be a very original comment but it is true. He would have been happy never to leave the stables, but mind, if you did manage to get him away for a drink at the local pub, it would be a hard job to get him back home.

'He was a hard taskmaster with his staff, but a sentimental so-and-so with the horses. He was usually a bit moist-eyed after one of his favourites had won and he could never bear to watch any of them "getting cut". He used to leave the job to the vet and walk away.'

Roger can truthfully say that in all his time at Greystoke he has never once caused a horse to have to miss a race because of a 'pricked foot'. He does remember one occasion, though, when The Boss used that corny excuse to an owner. He explains: 'I was shoeing Jessolle prior to her going down to Bangor for a bumper. She was a great one for kicking out at the walls of her box and she actually managed to bang her hock with a vicious cow-kick just after I had finished the job. The vet was called and diagnosed a bruised hock, but Gordon blamed the farrier!

'He just grinned when I objected and said, "Don't get yourself all hot and bothered, Roger. I know it wasn't really your fault." That was typical of The Boss. I never actually heard him say the word "sorry" in all my years at Greystoke. I think he regarded the word as a show of weakness and that was something to which he would never admit.'

Loyalty, though, was a quality that Roger acknowledges came high among Gordon's attributes. He concludes: 'The lads were always on about the way that he had stuck up for them and I remember him telling me how he had been put on the spot by the officials at the Jockey Club when he had gone to London to apply for his trainer's licence. One of the officials had asked him if he was a friend of Jack Pearson, who had trained out of The Rectory Farm and had previously been "warned off". When The Boss admitted that this was the case, the committee suggested that it would be a good idea to sever the friendship. Apparently Gordon refused point blank to agree to this request and for one moment he reckoned that his loyalty to Jack was going to cost him his career.'

Roger reflects that the same Jack Pearson could get up to all kinds of cunning ploys. He treasures one story that Gordon had retold. 'Jack had asked Gordon to go with him down to Kendal to ride a horse of his in a piece of fast work on the old racecourse there, with a couple of other fancied animals partnered by Mike Sissons and Bill Haigh. All the way down to Kendal Jack kept handing Gordon pieces of lead and telling him to hide them in his pockets. By the time the horses reached the start of the trial gallop, Gordon reckoned that he must have been carrying at least a dozen pounds overweight and it was no surprise to him when he finished a comfortable last of three. All the way back to Greystoke Jack Pearson never stopped giggling, but it wasn't until Gordon read the *Life* the next week that he realised the reason. The horse which he had ridden had landed a touch at Carlisle from, of course, the two who had beaten him so conclusively in that gallop at Kendal!'

TWENTY-TWO

The 'Old Firm' Reunited

The 1988–89 season began with the Richards team in good heart and Phil Tuck firmly established as stable jockey. He had ridden 59 winners in his initial campaign and followed this with a tally of 71 for 1987–88, of which 40 came over the major obstacles. These statistics reflected two perennial aspects of the Greystoke operation, namely that The Boss was really only interested in producing quality chasers, and that his stable jockeys had neither the opportunity nor the inclination to enter the market for outside rides. GWR had saddled 72 winners in 1987–88 and come the following August he was bullish about his chances for the new campaign. Towards the end of the month Phil drove him down to Leeds to attend the Yorkshire Racing Club's monthly get-together to which they both had been invited as the evening's celebrity guests.

After a few drinks to loosen the tongue, the chairman introduced them to the members and the bulk of the evening was spent in a question-and-answer session. The Boss was in affable mood, pulling few punches as usual, and the questions flowed. Finally Phil was asked if his sights were set on becoming Champion Jockey. He replied that he would love to be in the position to challenge for such an honour, but concluded, 'To be fair Peter Scudamore will take an awful lot of catching with the resources of the Pipe stable behind him.'

Whether the allusion to Martin Pipe touched a raw nerve with The Boss is a matter of speculation; but he broke in sharpishly, 'Ooh, there you are again son. You are only three behind and you have given up already. That's not much of a compliment to my horses. You need to have a more positve h'attitude.'

Phil recalls, 'I wasn't going to take that lying down. So, without warning The Boss, I relayed the whole of the Joanie and Maria "pull it together and make it work for you" story. The Boss had to sit and suffer because he knew I was driving him back to Greystoke – it was a lift with me, or an expensive hotel in Leeds.'

The Boss had a strong hand of handicap chasers with which to go to war. Clever Folly and Centre Attraction were in cracking form for the Mason family and Jim Thorpe kicked off with a 15-length success over the Arthur Stephenson-trained Slieve Felim in the Cattal Handicap Chase at Wetherby. Phil Tuck's mount had belied his backward condition to quicken away from his rivals in decisive fashion. The bookmakers were impressed and next time out Jim Thorpe started 3–1 favourite for the Mackeson despite a steadier of

11st 10lb. It was asking a great deal for a chaser only just out of the novice stage, but then Jim Thorpe was no ordinary novice. Phil Tuck described him as 'a cracking good horse' – the sort which really appealed to The Boss, who regarded him as 'a real professional, tough as nails and unlucky not to have won the Arkle'. It is a view shared by Richard Dunwoody.

However it has to be said that although Jim Thorpe was finishing best of all, he was still about four lengths down approaching the last fence. No doubt it was the necessity to get a 'big one' at the final obstacle that caused him to unseat his rider. Speculating is no good, of course. Suffice it to say that Jim Thorpe won six times as a novice, including heart-warming victories in the Dipper Chase at Newcastle, the Perrier Jouet Chase at Aintree and the Edinburgh Woollen Mill Future Champions' Chase at Ayr. This was the record of an eminently durable performer and the handicapper was probably quite justified in allotting him topweight for the Mackeson.

Considering that Jim Thorpe was set to give Cheltenham specialist Pegwell Bay eight pounds, he didn't do at all badly in finishing a 12-length fourth, surviving a blunder at the fourth to improve from off the pace turning down the hill to the third last without ever reaching a challenging position. The jumping errors, first evident during his precocious novice chase career, led to his ultimate downfall. Runner-up to Desert Orchid in the Tingle Creek at Sandown, Jim Thorpe was an even-money favourite to regain the winning touch in the Castleford Chase at Wetherby. His backers soon knew their fate. Mistakes at both the fifth and the seventh fences left him struggling; and though Mark Dwyer persuaded him to close up under pressure in the home straight it was but a token effort and he weakened into a modest third behind Midnight Count and Somerled. Those frustrating errors left their mark. Jim Thorpe developed a leg. He missed the rest of the season and did not reappear in 1989–90. Despite returning spasmodically in subsequent seasons, he was never the force that he had threatened to become.

By the time Jim Thorpe travelled south to Sandown for the 1988 Tingle Creek Chase, Phil Tuck was convalescing at home with a badly broken left arm, the result of an awkward fall from Demi-John at Hexham. The visibility had been murky on the Yarridge Heights from mid-morning and by 2.45 p.m. the fog was swirling so thickly that the last fence was barely in view from the bank above the winning post. (Note the word 'bank' – no stands at Hexham.) Tuck remembers that Gerry Scott, the starter, was in two minds about calling a halt to proceedings: 'The fog kept coming in and out. It was touch and go whether Gerry let us race, but just before official off-time the mists thinned and we were away. Not that we got very far. Demi-John hardly raised a hoof at the third. He crashed straight into the ditch. I knew that the arm was badly broken and it seemed ages before transport arrived to take me to Hexham Hospital. The Boss was playing merry hell with the officials but it wasn't their fault. Ten years ago there was no hard-core track laid round the inside of the course and I had come down right on the far-side.'

Surgeons at Hexham inserted a metal plate to hold the fracture together. He was released from hospital the following day and came under the care of Hugh Barber at the Cumberland Infirmary. Hugh, who lives on the outskirts of Carlisle, has been a godsend to jump jockeys over the past two decades. An orthopaedic consultant who specialises in the treatment of injured sportsmen, he is regarded almost as a medical guru by riders across the North. They know that he will get them back in action as early as humanly possible and they have implicit confidence in his pronouncements.

Hugh Barber warned his patient that he would need two months on the sidelines and almost to the day Phil Tuck was back riding out. He says, 'The arm was all right at first but after a couple of sessions it started to give me a lot of pain. I had what I thought was an abscess on the stitch line and it was hellish sore.'

Painful it may have been, but The Boss had horses engaged at Ayr on 10 February, including Tartan Tempest for the Edinburgh Woollen Mill. Tuck adds, 'I knew that I had to prove myself and wasn't going to allow a bit of pain to stop me taking the ride. Tartan Tempest was up there all the way and when I pressed the button he went clear and stayed on to win by four lengths.'

Next morning Phil went to Carlisle to have his arm re-examined and an X-ray revealed that one of the screws holding the plate in place had worked loose and the fracture had failed to knit. Phil Tuck had ridden a winner with a broken arm. He had to have the break reset and would not be back in action for a further two months.

Tuck's impatient determination to return to the saddle had been partially fired by events at Greystoke. Neale Doughty was back in harness, riding plenty of winners and attracting much favourable comment in the racing press. During the first few days after Phil Tuck's fall at Hexham, The Boss had made use of the stable's very capable understudies, John Hansen and Philip Doyle. Both rode winners and the pair of them would no doubt have risen to the task and filled the gap. GWR, though, was less than convinced. As a short-term measure he booked Mark Dwyer to partner Jim Thorpe in the Tingle Creek at Sandown while he sounded out Neale Doughty on a possible return to Greystoke.

Neale had missed the opening two months of the season, preferring to complete the refurbishment of a dilapidated property he had bought at a knockdown price the previous year. The renovation of ramshackle houses and their subsequent resale has been a profitable second string to Neale Doughty's bow ever since he first moved north to Cumbria – not just a little subsidiary DIY, but the whole gamut of bricklaying, roofing and redecoration. Neale had only resumed riding in November and it had not been long before he proved to have lost none of his former style and strength. At Catterick on 19 November he made a dream comeback with a 3,084–1 treble, a feat which earned him three bottles of Aberlour 10-year-old Single Malt Whisky (the prize awarded to the winner of the monthly competition for the Aberlour High Achievement Award).

Doughty's long-priced treble had comprised three winners each for a different trainer: Monastic Habit for Mick Easterby; Oriental Express for Frank Carr; and Dubalea for Swannie Haldane. His return to action had not gone unnoticed by The Boss and the weekend after Phil Tuck had broken his arm at Hexham, Gordon was on the telephone doing his level best to mend bridges with his former stable jockey.

Neale was not keen to be drawn. He explains: 'The Boss rang to try and bury the hatchet. He added that things had been said in the heat of the moment which he had later regretted and he asked me to come over to Greystoke to school a few horses with a view to standing in for Phil Tuck. I was reluctant to go and told him so. The last thing I wanted to do was to upset Phil and anyhow I wasn't at all sure that I wanted the job.'

It was Jinxy Jack who swung the balance. The ex-Irish gelding had won three competitive heats for Roger Fisher as a three-year-old and The Boss had gone to 100,000 guineas to buy him at the 1987 Doncaster November Sales. Phil Tuck had ridden him on his hurdling début at Carlisle, where he had blazed a winning trail from the start, but his hurdling had left a lot to be desired. Jinxy Jack had started favourite for his next outing at Aintree, but he pulled so hard that his saddle slipped and he fell at the fourth flight. He then did his level best to run away with Phil Tuck in each of his last two runs at Ayr, where he eventually finished second to Young Snugfit, and at Wetherby where he ran out at the third last flight.

Neale continued, 'The Boss told me that Jinxy Jack had adopted the same tactics at home and no one could get a grip on him up the gallops. He ended by inviting me to ride him in a gallop after racing at Catterick the following Wednesday. In the end I agreed and once I got hold of him at Catterick he gave me no problem. In fact we both enjoyed the experience and later I rode him to plenty of good wins. The Boss was delighted with the way I had got on with him and insisted that I come across to Greystoke to ride out. I hesitated, but in the end the pull of those quality horses was too strong. I said I would come back and ride for the duration that Phil was recovering from his broken arm.'

The ride that really announced the return of Neale Doughty to the Richards ranks came at Edinburgh on 12 December. He was partnering Clever Folly for Norman Mason and between the last two fences Gold Options, the favourite, was driven up to challenge by Mark Dwyer. Gold Options appeared to be winning the battle until Doughty asked his mount for a 'big one' at the final obstacle. Clever Folly responded. He stood right off, put in a prodigious leap and landed running. This request for one last effort at the final fence was a hallmark of Doughty's riding. Very occasionally his partner misread the message and put down, but more often than not Neale's fine eye for a stride and precise sense of timing enabled his mount to gain a vital length in the air and settle the issue there and then.

Neale did not monopolise the situation at Greystoke. The Boss saw to it that the supporting team of Hansen, O'Hara and Doyle received their share of good rides and Graham McCourt also drove north from Wantage to help out. Graham scored three times on Tartan Tailor and later was to establish a successful rapport with Better Times Ahead.

The 1988–89 season had begun with The Boss in buoyant mood. On paper he had a powerful string: an encouraging blend of consistent handicap chasers backed up by an influx of classy youngsters, a few of whom had the potential to become Cheltenham prospects. In practice the handicappers played their part with admirable frequency but the new blood proved disappointing. Randolph Place, never properly right throughout the campaign, only raced three times and finished second on each occasion. Jim Thorpe went lame before he could reveal his true stature, Border Rambler suffered the same fate. He was to miss the following season and then be sold to go point-to-pointing. Sadly Border Rambler had to be destroyed after being pulled up in a hunter chase at Perth.

On the plus side Carrick Hill Lad, an athletic son of Royal Fountain and bought by Alec Picken as a replacement for the ill-fated Current Gold, impressed both in outlook and performance. The Boss predicted a big future when he made the transition to fences. Highfrith was another likely chasing prospect. The mare, who was owned in partnership by Hugh Cavendish, Joanie Richards and Tarn Riley, won four novice hurdles on the northern circuit before travelling south to Newbury for the Hoechst Panacur EBF Mares Only Final. Ridden by Philip Doyle (her regular pilot), Highfrith led from early in the home straight until headed at the last flight by Oliver Sherwood's Northern Jinks, who quickened away to score by six lengths. The Boss was far from downcast and fences beckoned for this good looking mare.

Four Trix was more exposed. A winning hurdler for the Catherwoods when with John Cox in Ireland, the grey had won four times over fences for GWR during 1987–88, his initial season at Greystoke, and progressed to be placed in valuable contests at Ascot and Aintree before finishing third to Roll A Joint in the Scottish National – a race in which he would have given the winner plenty to think about had he not blundered badly at the third from home. His record suggested that a substantial prize was just round the corner.

Phil Tuck's left arm healed in time for Kelso in April. The Boss had lined up Casual Pass as a welcome-back winner in the claimer and Phil made every yard of the running to land the spoils by eight lengths. Even more appropriately, he lifted the sponsored hurdle on the temperamental Demi-John, whose fall at Hexham the previous November had been responsible for keeping him on the sidelines for over four months. Phil recalls Gordon saying to him in the morning, 'You don't want to ride this Demi-John, do you son?'

'I blooming well do,' was the jockey's instant rejoinder; 'he owes me one.' Happily for both horse and rider, they came through the field with a sustained challenge to hit the front close home and complete a 53–1 double. The Boss saddled a further two wins that spring afternoon at Kelso. Centre Attraction took the Clyde Bridge Challenge Cup in the hands of Liam O'Hara, while

Neale Doughty wrapped up the four-timer by partnering Hug to victory in the four-year-old hurdle. Phil Tuck ended the season with 23 winners and felt that he had proved enough on his return to continue in his post as first jockey for 1989–90.

Ten years on he agrees that he should have realised the writing was on the wall: 'Neale was back on the scene, though it was sort of said that we would share the rides. That summer I had a bit of a break. Then went into ride out. If I had thought that things wouldn't change then I was pretty shaken by my greeting from The Boss as I arrived at the yard.

'He fixed me with an aggressive stare, rolled his eyes and thundered, "What the hell are you doing here?"

'I replied as sharply as I could muster, "What do you think? I've come to ride out."

'I got the message after that,' continues Phil, 'and the parting of the ways came sooner rather than later. The Boss had a runner in each of the six races at Carlisle's Autumn meeting. I wasn't booked for any of them. In fact I was going to Carlisle to ride just one horse for John Goulding.'

By coincidence Tuck arrived at the Trainers and Jockeys entrance at the same time as GWR. He recalls The Boss turning to him and saying, 'Ooh, we'll have to have a chat, son. This is hurting me!'

Phil replied, 'It's not doing me much bloody good either, is it? Why not stop by after racing and have this chat tonight?'

'Ooh, son, I'm a busy man. I'm galloping horses after racing,' said Gordon.

This was the straw that broke the camel's back as far as Phil was concerned. He didn't even know that The Boss was working horses after racing. Though he was still meant to be one of the yard's top two jockeys, he had never even been asked to ride work. He pointed out that GWR's road back to Greystoke went virtually straight past his front door and that surely it was not asking too much of him to stop off and have this talk. So The Boss agreed to break his journey.

The meeting took place in the Tucks' American-type barn. It housed six horses, three of which had been sent to Calthwaite to be broken in. The Boss was pleased with what he saw.

'Ooh, these horses look well, son,' was his opening remark. But when it came to the vital issue of Phil Tuck's future at Greystoke, Gordon's refrain was: 'It's not me, it's my h'owners.' Phil maintains that if the pair of them had stood in the yard until midnight The Boss would still have been repeating the same message.

Phil was waiting for The Boss to say, 'I'm sorry, son, but I don't want you any more'. He was left wondering whether GWR was trying to sugar the pill or didn't have the bottle to say it straight out. He explains: 'We were going round and round in circles, so in the end I gave him the get out by saying, "Look, Boss, I'll tell you what I'll do. I will ring the press and tell them that we've parted amicably but that hopefully I'll ride the odd one for you in the future."'

A relieved trainer stuttered, 'That's it, son. That's it. You do that.' Then he nearly bowled Phil Tuck completely over by adding, 'Now then, what about these horses?'

The question finally caused the jockey to lose his cool. He growled, 'You've just said how fit they looked. Well then, f*** off and leave them here!' Gordon did, and in fact after that he sent up a lot more to break in. 'He gave me great support in that way; and I did ride him another winner before I retired,' reflects Phil.

With the position of stable jockey settled early in the campaign, albeit in a less than sympathetic manner, the 1989–90 season proved an outstanding success story. GWR occupied fourth place in the trainers' table, notching 78 winners and winning his owners £324,480 – a total which enabled him to finish ahead of Arthur Stephenson by the wafer-thin margin of £172. Much to Gordon's pleasure, some 75 per cent of his prize money tally was won by chasers and a substantial slice of that was gained by the trainer's remarkable skill at placing his horses.

There was no better example of this selective ability than that provided by Highfrith. Though arguably a shade below top class, she still won six of her first eight races, and later in the season ran a brave fourth in the Cathcart at the Cheltenham Festival less than six lengths adrift of Brown Windsor. The mare also finished third to Celtic Shot in the Edinburgh Woollen Mills Future Champions' Chase at Ayr. A courageous, bold jumping, free running sort, she was a credit to her trainer.

Clever Folly was another major hero. His partnership with Neale Doughty was one of the most exciting sights in the North and their victories in the Peterborough Chase at Huntingdon, and more importantly in the A.F. Budge Gold Cup at Cheltenham in December, gave southern supporters the opportunity to watch this determined duo at their best. Some of Clever Folly's jumping at Cheltenham sent a tingle down the spine.

Hugely popular though Clever Folly continued to be throughout his long career, he never possessed the class of Carrick Hill Lad who at one stage of the season threatened to arrive at Cheltenham with an unbroken run of six consecutive novice chase victories. The Boss gave him a typically low-key start to his chasing career and it wasn't until late January when he accounted for Aston Express in the West of Scotland Pattern Novices' Chase at Ayr that he was asked a serious question. The gelding's task was made easier by the early fall of Blazing Walker, but for a brief moment approaching the third last Greystoke's rising star stared defeat in the face as Antinous forged to the front. Neale Doughty, though, gave Carrick Hill Lad the chance to gain his second wind. Sensing that Antinous was tiring in front, he set his mount alight approaching the last fence, landed running and stayed on in splendid style to regain the ascendancy and score by eight lengths.

Cheltenham beckoned, but The Boss was no lover of the Sun Alliance Novices' Chase and would not commit himself – an eminently understandable decision as the trainer himself had a great deal on his mind. For about the first time in his non-stop life he was unwell. Serious kidney trouble had been diagnosed and The Boss was admitted to the Cumberland Infirmary for major surgery. The operation to remove the diseased organ was successful but the trauma necessitated a relatively lengthy period of convalescence. This was sure to make Gordon fret, cooped up in the Old Rectory so close to the action but under doctor's orders not to become involved.

The Boss was 'sentenced' to a break in the sun. Joanie's father had been a High Court Judge in the Caribbean and the family had inherited his villa on the exotic island of Anguilla. When an annual holiday in late January to mid-February was first mooted, GWR did not take kindly to the idea. The thought of leaving the stable with Cheltenham only six weeks away went right against the grain; but once he had tasted life in the Caribbean the doubts disappeared and there was no opposition on his part when Joanie prescribed a month beside the surf. As the '90s progressed The Boss became quite a familiar figure out in the West Indies. He and Joanie played host to a coterie of their leading owners, including the Stevensons and the Whitakers. On occasions, too, visits were made to John Moreton's Treasure Beach Hotel in Barbados where John Hales, owner of One Man, and his family are regular guests.

Unlike Martin Pipe, The Boss developed the habit of switching off from stable matters while he was on holiday. Swimming did not figure highly on his list of recreations, but he indulged in plenty of lying in the sun and proved a mean opponent on the golf course. The Boss was assisted in this uncharacteristically laid-back attitude by the knowledge that the team he had left at home in Greystoke was more than capable of holding the fort while he was away.

Nicky Richards was delighting in the greater share of responsibility that his father was beginning to delegate. Nicky was now officially assisting his father, frequently representing him on forays down south and demonstrating that he had inherited his father's noted 'eye for a horse' by completing a series of astute purchases at the sales. Alongside Nicky were Martin Todhunter, the yard's much respected travelling head lad, and Pat Kavanagh, whose lifetime in racing both as a jockey and a tack-room regular had brought invaluable stability to the stable in his role of head lad. They were supported by the professional hands-on approach of Neale Doughty, backed up by long-serving stable staff of the calibre of Roger Hale, the farrier, Ted Stanners and Larry Poland to name but three.

The Boss had left for Anguilla by the time Carrick Hill Lad made the trip to Ascot for the Old Road Securities Reynoldstown Chase. This long-established Cheltenham trial had always been on the agenda for Alex Picken's star novice but the Reynoldstown came only 11 days after Carrick Hill Lad's comfortable but keenly contested victory at Ayr. The 'stand-in' command at Greystoke were confident that the seven-year-old was spot-on for Ascot, having worked with all his accustomed sparkle on the gallops.

The decision to run was unanimous, but in the event the Carrick Hill Lad who lined up at Ascot was a lack-lustre replica of the horse who had carried all before him in his previous five outings. He started favourite, but missed out the first, and from that moment onwards was never seriously in the hunt behind Royal Athlete. To his credit he plugged on in determined fashion when a lesser horse would have surrendered and it was no surprise to learn that subsequent tests showed that his blood was wrong. Others in the stable were similarly affected and The Boss was firmly back in harness by the time Carrick Hill Lad went a long way towards redeeming his reputation at Ayr two months later. He was beaten by Royal Athlete in the Souters of Stirling Novices' Chase, but jumped with much of his previous exuberance before his long absence from the course found him out.

TWENTY-THREE

Personal Best for The Boss

After the disquieting worries about GWR's health, the team at Greystoke were determined to celebrate his recovery with a concerted effort for winners. The raw material was there and the sense of optimism was such that many of the stable staff were quick to take advantage of the bookies' generous odds against the Richards string breaking the century barrier for the first time since 1975–76. Neale Doughty, very much a motivating force behind the sustained drive for success, was an inspiration. Refreshingly free of injury, the Welshman was at his peak all season and his eventual tally of 96 winners would prove by far the best of his long career.

The Boss was in equally good form, seemingly in robust health and none too pleased at the doctor's suggestion that he should reduce the intake of beer and cigarettes. He might have lost a kidney but the routine was unchanged, the tongue was still razor sharp and the pursuit of excellence as demanding as ever.

The 1990–91 season began with a flood of winners and much excitement was generated by the continued dominance of Full Strength. John Moreton's Strong Gale gelding had shown little over hurdles, but since being switched to fences had proved invincible. He ended his first campaign over the bigger obstacles setting up a sequence of four straight wins at Market Rasen, Bangor, Perth and Hexham. Revelling in the autumn's fast ground, Full Strength stretched his victory roll to an extraordinary ten consecutive wins. His triumphal progress from Stratford to Perth was finally halted by Arthur Stephenson's highly rated Blazing Walker in the prestigious H&T Walker Gold Cup at Ascot. Full Strength had tried to lead from pillar to post, but he could not match his rival's finishing burst and went down by three lengths. However he lost no caste by this narrow defeat at the hands of this brilliant chasing prospect, who went on to record a stunning victory over Katabatic and Waterloo Boy in the Glenlivet Melling Chase at Liverpool and was selected by *Timeform* as second only to Desert Orchid in their ratings for the country's top chaser.

Not surprisingly The Boss sent Full Strength back to Ascot for the SGB Chase in December. Neale Doughty picks up the story: 'The ground was still riding on top, 10st 7lb was a tempting weight and we felt that the race would tell us a lot about Full Strength's potential. He was just lobbing along in front when he slipped going into the water jump and broke his back. It was all so totally unnecessary and I was shattered. He could have gone right to the top.'

Opinions about the retention of the water splash are mixed. Some trainers abhor its continued presence, believing that horses find it disconcerting to jump, and asserting that mistakes at the obstacle often lead to serious injury. Their anxieties are shared by the growing number of racecourse executives who have replaced it with a plain fence. My own view is that a water jump positioned out in the country on the far side of the course serves no worthwhile purpose. Situated directly in front of the stands the water splash does make spectacular viewing, but at what cost? If you were to ask John Moreton he would answer that question with understandable vehemence.

Both GWR and Neale Doughty had a soft spot for Jinxy Jack, though Mrs McKinney's powerful gelding was a moody individual who never lived up to expectations over fences. And despite winning 12 races over hurdles, he too often missed out on the major prizes. I was at Carlisle when Jinxy Jack made his hurdling début. He gave Phil Tuck the most uncomfortable of rides, pulling for his head and diving through the majority of his hurdles. He won but the omens were not encouraging.

Neale Doughty, though, established an understanding with the son of Random Shot from the first time he sat on him in that post-race gallop at Catterick which signalled his return to Greystoke. He succeeded in settling the horse and the pair of them would have won more than 18 races between them had Jinxy Jack not been prone to back problems, a factor that inhibited his potential as a chaser. The gelding found it hard to bend his back and would not respond when Neale asked him to stand off his fences. As he grew older and wiser, Jinxy Jack partially overcame this deficiency and kept to tighter tracks with less demanding fences like Stratford, Catterick and Perth. He won his fair share over the major obstacles. As a hurdler he was a much more formidable performer. He won the Morebattle Hurdle at Kelso four years on the trot, ran out an impressive winner of the 1993 Champion Hurdle Trial at Haydock, was far from disgraced in two attempts at the Champion Hurdle itself and twice started favourite for the Scottish Champion Hurdle – only to fall. Jinxy Jack should have won more quality events. There can be very little doubt on that score, but he was an imposing character who gave his owner, trainer and jockey a great deal of pleasure. No horse at Greystoke loved his early morning rolls in the sandpit more than Jinxy Jack and The Boss saw that he got plenty of them. Neale Doughty summed him up accurately: 'On a good day he was very good, but he was never the smoothest of movers, and sometimes riding Jinxy Jack was like sitting on a square-wheeled bike!'

Last o' the Bunch, in contrast, was a sharpish ride. Bought out of Ernie Weymes's yard for Gary Middlebrook (the inspiration behind the continued success of Crowther Homes) Last o' the Bunch became a bold jumping front runner, the type on which Neale Doughty was always seen to good advantage. In 1990–91 Last o' the Bunch reeled off five consecutive novice chases before going to Cheltenham for the Arkle, in which he started third favourite behind

Remittance Man and Uncle Ernie. Had he not fallen at the second last when under pressure and tiring, he would also have finished third in the race itself. Last o' the Bunch went on to win the 1992 *Timeform* Chase at Haydock. Before falling fatally at Wetherby's 1993 Christmas meeting he had amassed 15 career wins and remains the most successful chaser that the Middlebrooks have owned.

Gary Middlebrook was an owner whom The Boss allowed to slip out of his clutches. I use the words 'slip out' advisedly. Back in 1990 Gary was comparatively new to the National Hunt game. He was soon to expand his interests to the flat while continuing to have a select number of jumpers in training with Kim Bailey and Jimmy FitzGerald. In addition he has become a steward at several northern courses; and Crowther Homes have sponsored races at a variety of racecourses, notably Aintree, where their name has become regularly linked to the Becher Chase at the November meeting.

Gary is one of the modern generation of racehorse owners who like to be kept informed of the progress of his horses, both with regard to their efforts on the racecourse and on the gallops at home. He basically wanted to play an active role in the plans for his horses, but his enthusiastic interest was not over-popular with The Boss (who of course liked to do things 'his own way' – an attitude which brooked very little interference from the owners). Gary wanted more open-handedness, so when The Boss proved intractable the Middlebrooks opted to move on. That is exactly what Gary Middlebrook's business and racing interests have continued to do. In addition to his stewarding duties he has become a successful owner on the flat with the majority of his horses, including Etterby Park and Robin Lane under the care of Mark Johnston. He also breeds his own winners and would have proved an invaluable addition to the Richards' list of patrons.

Neale Doughty's house in Windermere is called 'Twin Oaks', underlining his admiration and appreciation for this relentless galloper who did not arrive at Greystoke until he was already ten years old, yet in three seasons with the Richards team won nine times from 16 outings – including no fewer than eight victories over the demanding drop fences at Haydock. Twin Oaks had been a leading novice chaser in the 1987–88 season when trained by David Murray Smith for John Moreton. Leg trouble restricted the gelding to two outings in the next two campaigns and Moreton transferred him to The Boss with no strings attached. Nicky Richards remembers the event. 'John told Father that he wasn't expecting miracles with Twin Oaks, but that he would like him to have a shot with the horse: see if he would stand up to a little light training on the hills and perhaps place him to win a small race before he went into retirement.'

It was the sort of challenge that The Boss relished. He started by using Twin Oaks as his hack while he supervised morning exercise. Impressed by the horse's 'feel' in his slow paces, and satisfied that his legs were 'as cold as steel', The Boss decided to get some fast work into him and gave him a series of spins up the all-weather. Neale remembers The Boss reporting that he had been 'flying'. He chuckles: 'The lads weren't going to let him get away with that. They reminded him that even the slowest horse seems to be flying when galloping past a line of trees, but The Boss wasn't joking. He kept pointing out that Twin Oaks had very little mileage on the clock and that he thought he was well up to winning a couple of decent staying chases.'

Twin Oaks reappeared at Uttoxeter in November 1990. He was described by the formbook compiler as 'a bit backward' and was tailed off behind Pegwell Bay after blundering at the 12th. 'I told The Boss to forget Uttoxeter,' said Doughty. 'The course was much too fast for him and the fences much too easy. He was always struggling to go the pace and needed a big galloping course to bring the best out of him.'

GWR continued to ride work him. Just over a week after Uttoxeter he declared Twin Oaks for the Lang Whang Hurdle at Ayr. Neale continues, 'The Boss had been pleased with his work since Uttoxeter and advised the lads to have a bit of the 33s on offer. He told me to go out and enjoy myself. I did exactly that, pushing him into the lead from the start and letting him bowl along in front. He was the type of misleading horse who didn't seem to be travelling at more than a swinging gallop and it was only when one looked back to see how the others were going that one realised how powerful that relentless long stride of his really was. In that Lang Whang Hurdle he blew up on the bottom turn, but he was such a long way clear of his rivals that I was able to ease him right down and still pass the post an effortless winner. I told The Boss that he was still a long way from being fit.'

Six days later Twin Oaks went to Haydock for the Tim Molony Memorial. He jumped like the proverbial stag and raced prominently throughout, leading from the seventh to the tenth and being close on the heels of Remedy The Malady when that horse came down six out. Boraceva, the 9–4 favourite, fell at the fourth from home and Twin Oaks lengthened his stride between the last two fences to win by a comfortable two and a half lengths from Outside Edge with Cool Ground a further two lengths back in third. Said Doughty, 'It was his third race within less than a month and he still needed it. I told The Boss that once he was fully fit he would be about the best horse in the yard.'

Back at Haydock for the four-mile Ronnie Johnston Memorial, Twin Oaks set out to make all the running. He again jumped splendidly and stayed on too resolutely for Outside Edge, with Mick's Star six lengths back in third. Early in January Twin Oaks reappeared in the Oldham Chase at the Merseyside course. He made a couple of mistakes, but had the legs of the opposition by the time the field reached the final half mile.

Twin Oaks held a decisive advantage over Aquilifer and Stay On Tracks. Neale's earlier assessment, that John Moreton's then ten-year-old could be about the best horse in the yard when fully fit, was beginning to bear fruit. The problem now facing The Boss was whether to take him to Cheltenham for the Gold Cup or concentrate on winning a third Grand National. Connections opted to shelve the decision until after Twin Oaks had run his next race. This should have been the Peter Marsh Chase later in January, but the meeting fell victim to the weather and shortly afterwards Twin Oaks went down with the virus which was going the rounds at Greystoke. In an attempt to attract bigger fields for their steeplechases the Haydock executive had advertised a £50,000 bonus. Points were awarded to all those taking part in the chases at Haydock during the 1990–91 season. The number of points given was calculated on a sliding scale with the maximum hand-out going to the winner. From the opening fixture at the Merseyside course the Richards chasers went flat out for the prize. Twin Oaks had already won three consecutive steeplechases at Haydock.

The Peter Marsh would have provided the ideal chance for him to win the bonus. With that race abandoned, Twin Oaks had to go for broke in the Greenalls Gold Cup. Always a most competitive event, the 1991 renewal attracted a field of 16. A significant part of the £50,000 was to go direct to the stable staff at the award-winning yard. In the case of Twin Oaks this was doubly appropriate. The Greenalls Gold Cup took place on 2 March and the build-up to this race coincided with the Boss's annual holiday in the West Indies. His absence gave the supporting team of Nicky Richards, Pat Kavanagh, Martin Todhunter and Neale Doughty the chance to shine. The virus had deprived them of any worthwhile success the previous February – a notorious month for sniffs and coughs in Cumbria for human and equine victims alike – and for a worrying fortnight the same old story looked like dogging their footsteps once more.

The Boss had left for Anguilla telling the team to use their own initiative. The question of Twin Oaks's fitness for the Greenalls Gold Cup was pre-eminent. Had The Boss been at home, there would have been no problem. He would have ridden the big race favourite during the immediate lead-up to Haydock and his in-built vibes for sensing the physical and mental well-being of his horses would have settled the issue. His deputies were on a hiding to nothing. Withdraw Twin Oaks and there would always be that lurking suspicion that their caution had cost the yard their sizeable slice of fifty grand. At the same time the 11-year-old had not raced since early January. If he was sent down to Haydock only three-parts fit and dropped out well beaten from the home turn, they would be the obvious scapegoats.

In the end the decision was made for them. Twin Oaks passed all the relevant tests. His blood was right. He scoped clear and one glance at Neale Doughty's relaxed smile as the pair of them returned from the final workout lifted all doubts. Twin Oaks was ready to win – and win he did in the most handsome of styles. The Haydock regulars had taken Twin Oaks to their heart. They had no misgivings and one glance in the paddock was enough for the professionals. Twin Oaks was 'up for it'.

Neale exuded confidence, allowing Twin Oaks to maintain a prominent pitch from the outset. Few chasers in recent memory have measured those solid Haydock fences with such authority as Twin Oaks. Neale asked him to stride clear from the 16th and, staying on with powerful zest, he turned what had threatened to be a most competitive heat into a procession. Aquilifer could only run on at the one pace. Bonanza Boy came late, but had given himself an impossible task, and the £50,000 bonus which had beckoned with such tantalising proximity since the turn of the year was safely in the bag.

After Haydock it had to be Cheltenham for the Tote Gold Cup. Twin Oaks seemed sure to improve for the race. He had earnt his place in the Gold Cup line-up. The Grand National could wait another year, and given plenty of rain in the Cotswolds, Twin Oaks would provide his supporters with an exciting run for their money. He would be accompanied to the post by Carrick Hill Lad. Successful by a wide margin from Birling Jack in Ayr's Joan Mackay chase, he oozed class with an emphatic six-length victory over Mick's Star in the Save and Prosper Chase at Chepstow on the first Saturday of December. This impressive performance under 12 stone appeared to boost his chances for a winning return trip to the same course for the Coral Welsh National later in the month. Nicky Richards, though, sounded a timely warning: 'The ground was plenty fast enough for him today,' he observed; 'it will have to rain if we are going to come back for the big one.'

It did rain and Carrick Hill Lad duly started the well-backed 2–1 favourite to give The Boss his first Welsh National. Unbeknown to punters the Greystoke stayer had caught a tartar in the shape of Cool Ground, who had slipped into this gruelling marathon on the ten-stone mark. Carrick Hill Lad led round the bottom turn, but the writing was on the wall when he put in a tired leap at the fourth from home and in receipt of 11 pounds there was no stopping Cool Ground, something of a pirate off bottom weight when one considers that he was to land the Gold Cup off the regulation 12 stone some 15 months later.

Carrick Hill Lad then made it a day to remember for the Greystoke camp by landing the odds in the *Timeform* Chase at Haydock half an hour before Twin Oaks carried off the Greenalls. Neale Doughty's loyalty to Twin Oaks ruled that Mark Dwyer came in for the ride on Carrick Hill Lad at Cheltenham. Down the years certain trainers have found the Festival a lucrative venue while others, equally competent, have found fortune consistently eluding them. Gordon Richards, sadly, came into the latter category. Too often his big race hopes perished before the gates at Prestbury Park had opened, and even if the stars made the post, the weather turned against them. Playlord must have gone close to winning the 1969 Gold Cup on good going. Instead the heavens opened and the ground became a mudbath. Twenty-two years later, when both Twin Oaks and Carrick Hill Lad were crying out for rain, the sun shone and the going rode fast.

Neale Doughty accepted the situation early on. Realising that Twin Oaks could not match the pace of the leaders, he took care of his toiling partner and sensibly pulled him up down the back straight for the final time. Carrick Hill

Lad could have proved too brave for his own long-term good. He gave Mark Dwyer an exhilarating ride, jumping soundly and keeping up a relentless gallop on ground much quicker than he liked. On the run to three out, he accelerated through the field to approach the obstacle on the heels of the leading quartet. Carrick Hill Lad actually jumped the fence in third, but pitched on landing and was immediately pulled up lame. Back home in Cumbria The Boss licked his wounds. Twin Oaks was roughed off for the season. Carrick Hill Lad returned very sore. Only time would tell if he would be able to race again in the autumn. GWR was confident that his unlucky chaser would have finished in the shake up. He reported, 'Mark [Dwyer] thought he was going well enough to hold his place. He was travelling strongly at the time he went lame and would have stayed the trip. If there had been any cut in the ground he would have given the winner plenty to think about.'

Despite his Gold Cup disappointments, The Boss had enjoyed a tremendous 1990–91 campaign. He had notched up 118 winners, easily his best ever. He had won over £400,000 in prize money. And he had had no fewer than 80 steeplechase winners, a strike rate of over 30 per cent. Ironically his 'chasing' touch was to fail him at Aintree. The Antartex could not quite peg back J.J. Henry in the John Hughes; Last o' the Bunch was a well beaten third in the Perrier Jouet Novices' Chase; Rinus fell at the 19th when in third place in the Grand National; and ironically it was a hurdler who was to salvage the trainer's pride. Montpelier Lad, bought for 30,000 guineas out of the yard of William Hastings-Bass (soon to become Lord Huntingdon), waltzed away with the Glenlivet Anniversary Hurdle, rewarding his trainer's confidence in his ability.

Montpelier Lad had been beaten into third place behind Bonanza and Sir Peter Levy in the Northern Champion Handicap Hurdle at Newcastle in March, but the Greystoke hurdler was set to give over 20 pounds to both the first two home and The Boss was adamant that he would prove the form all wrong. There was a tragic twist to Montpelier Lad's victory at Liverpool. David Little, his owner, had died five days before the meeting. It had been his ambition to see Montpelier Lad win a big race and it was an emotional moment when his brother Stanley greeted the gelding in the winner's circle.

Neale Doughty said: 'He was always travelling like a winner. I didn't want to hit the front too early, but he quickened up well on the run to the last flight and I wasn't going to disappoint him.' Doughty finished the season on the 96 winner mark. Commenting on his narrow failure to break the century barrier, he added, 'It was more a matter of weight than lack of outside rides which beat me. Several of our late-season winners were down at the bottom of the handicap and it would have been unfair to their owners if I had put up four or five pounds overweight.'

TWENTY-FOUR

Hard Graft and Hardy Handicappers
Harvest a Third Century

Back in the mid-'80s Joanie and Gordon made a bold decision. The Old Rectory came on the market. Greystoke must have been a prosperous 'living' during the late Georgian and Victorian eras. Judged by the comfortable affluence of the church and the roomy elegance of the Rectory, the incumbents must have been the envy of the diocese.

Tommy Robson had lived in the Old Rectory while he trained at Greystoke and The Boss could have bought the property for £9,000 when he moved from Northumberland. He decided to keep what money he had to invest in the horses, occupying instead the spacious flat on the first floor of the stable block. Twenty years later Joanie and he decided that the purchase of the Old Rectory would be a sensible plan both for business and personal reasons. The property itself was the final piece in the Rectory jigsaw. Lumped together with the land already owned by the adjacent farm which Gordon had bought in the early '70s, it formed one complete estate, stretching from the Greystoke to Penrith road across to the church. By buying the Old Rectory Gordon was making ample provision for the creation of his own stable campus should the occasion ever arise that he was asked to vacate his present yard on the Greystoke Castle estate. The house might seem to be palatial for just the two of them, but for the purpose of entertaining the owners or putting up the family it was ideal. Gordon soon discovered that the price was significantly more than £9,000 but the investment was sound.

The autumn of 1991 was spoilt by the plight of Carrick Hill Lad. The ligament trouble which he had sustained at Cheltenham had improved over the summer. The Boss had been optimistic that his Gold Cup hope would be ready to reappear in public around the turn of the year, in plenty of time to be match fit for Cheltenham. Alas, it was not to be. On veterinary advice Carrick Hill Lad was to be rested for the whole season.

Never one to dwell on misfortune, however painful or expensive it may have been, The Boss lined up Pat's Jester as his intended Gold Cup substitute. In 1987–88 the gelding had enjoyed a splendid season over hurdles with Dick Allan, winning the Ekbalco Hurdle at Newcastle, the Bula at Cheltenham and the Scottish Champion Hurdle at Ayr. Though well beaten in the Champion Hurdle, Pat's Jester was among the best handicap hurdlers in Britain. In the grip of the handicapper he had been unable to sustain the level of his performances in 1988–89 and was forced to miss the whole of the following season with the suspicion of 'a leg'.

Geoff Adam, his owner, was keen that he should make the transition to fences on his recovery. Fearing that Dick Allan did not have the class of chaser to test Pat's Jester on the gallops at Cornhill, he sent the gelding to Gordon prior to going novice chasing. The Boss trained him to win three of his four novice chases, culminating in a handsome victory over Cashew King in a qualifier for the Arlington Chase Series at Haydock. He returned to Greystoke just a touch sore; rather than risk aggravating his previous leg injury, Gordon put him away for the rest of the campaign.

Fully fit for 1991–92 Pat's Jester scored first time out in handicap company, winning the Tennents Special Handicap Chase at Ayr's November meeting. In early January Pat's Jester travelled down to Haydock once more. Starting at 7–1, the Greystoke chaser trounced a classy field – including Katabatic, Sabin Du Loir and Docklands Express – in the Newton Chase. The Gold Cup was now a real possibility. But the 'big-race' jinx, which was never to relax its grip on Gordon's bids for Cheltenham glory, struck again.

Greystoke's Achilles' Heel as a major training centre for top-class chasers is the climate from January through to March. Soft southerners shiver at the thought of biting winds, deep snowdrifts and prolonged spells of arctic weather cold enough to freeze the diesel in the tank of even the sturdiest 4x4 vehicle. Those who actually live in John Peel country know that this is a myth. For the greatest part of the winter it is warmer in Cumbria than it is in Kent, but sadly the first three months of the year too often produce weather which is habitually wet – rarely below freezing but always dank, the ideal scenario for the incubation of sniffs, sneezes and viruses of every strain. Gordon used to pray for a fortnight's sub-zero temperatures to kill off the infections but his prayers were seldom answered. With frustrating regularity his horses would fall sick around the turn of the year. Such was the case in 1991–92. The horses went wrong in mid-January, and though Pat's Jester passed all the routine tests it was obvious to Neale Doughty in the thick of the action, and The Boss watching in the stands, that their Cheltenham hopes were being dashed in front of their eyes.

Pat's Jester struggled to come to terms with the front running Star's Delight in the Grade 2 Cavalier Chase at Worcester on 26 February. Two and a half miles round the tight Severn-side course was sharp enough for Pat's Jester, but it was a lack-lustre performance and a couple of days after the defeat The Boss admitted that Pat's Jester was suffering from the same viral infection that had been affecting many of his stable companions. Pat's Jester ran once more that spring, finishing a tailed-off third behind Remittance Man in the Mumm Melling Chase at Aintree.

The stable's established stars retained their status. Jinxy Jack was winning over fences in the autumn before reverting to the smaller obstacles, winning the Morebattle at Kelso and finishing runner-up to Granville Again in the Scottish Champion Hurdle. Last o'the Bunch won the *Timeform* Chase at Haydock – a venue which also saw Twin Oaks gaining a further two course wins and occupying a creditable third to Cool Ground and Kildimo in the Greenalls Gold Cup. Twin Oaks went on to finish fifth to Party Politics in the Grand National, when he was far from happy on the firmish ground.

Clever Folly was in outstanding form, picking up seven victories. The Boss was also quietly pleased with the promise shown by the newcomers Gallateen and Whispering Steel.

Then 1992–93 heralded the arrival of Robert Ogden among the ranks of Greystoke owners. His partnership with fellow Yorkshire business tycoon Jack Hanson had been a lucrative one on the flat. He was now keen to go it alone over the jumps not least because Adam, his son, was keen to ride under rules as an amateur. Byzantium and Frickley were the pioneers for the now-familiar pink-and-mauve checks, with Frickley rattling up five wins during his first season. He scored twice at Ayr and Doncaster; and while his missing victory came at Hexham, it was his performances at Cheltenham and Aintree which underlined his potential. Frickley took sixth place behind Montelado in the Trafalgar House Supreme Novices' Hurdle at the Cheltenham Festival and finished fourth to Roll A Dollar in the Seagram Top Novices' Hurdle at the Grand National meeting. The seven-year-old's bold showing fired the owner's appetite for the jumping game and in the ensuing five seasons the Ogden team played an important role in maintaining Greystoke's reputation in the premier league of British National Hunt stables.

The Richards horses avoided the curse of the virus and by the late spring of 1993 The Boss was celebrating the third 'century' of his training career. The full tally was 104 and a notable feature of the season was the number of doubles, trebles and even four-timers that the yard totted up at its favourite courses. The Boss sent out no less than 15 doubles, while his two four-timers were both achieved at Ayr. Neale Doughty rode an 80–1 accumulator at the New Year fixture, but earlier at the October meeting the winners had been shared by Michael Molony, Peter Niven and a first-ever double for Neil Leach. Neil was described by The Boss as a lad 'with lovely hands' but he never managed the major breakthrough which is so vital if a promising claimer is to make the grade as a fully fledged jockey. Neil swapped his riding licence for a local milk round later in the '90s but he continued to ride out; and with the departure of Ted Stanners to become private trainer to George Ward, he has returned full-time to Greystoke as travelling head lad.

Back in 1992 Neil Leach had ridden the stable's first winner of the season, Palm House at Bangor on the last day of July. Palm House was to chalk up two further 'firsts' that autumn. Adrian Maguire, making a very rare appearance for the Richards stable, booted him home at Sedgefield; and Robert Tyrer's gelding also gave young Brian Harding his initial winner in this country. Brian had arrived at Greystoke on the recommendation of Kevin Prendergast and was to develop into one of the most talented riders on the northern circuit.

As the season progressed the winners continued to roll in at regular intervals. Twin Oaks might have been approaching retirement but John Moreton was enjoying plenty of pleasure and profit from the exciting displays of Wind Force, his speedy front-running two-miler who scored four times in the autumn. Rested in mid-season to avoid the mud, he returned with renewed zest in the spring. He won at Ayr before going on to delight his sporting owner by giving a spectacular display of fast bold jumping to scorch home by 15 lengths from Guiburn's Nephew in the Tote Seventh Race Handicap Chase at Aintree.

In 1993 Better Times Ahead was seven years old, already being clobbered by the hurdles handicapper but proving his versatility by picking up three novice chases. *Timeform* noted that he lacked fluency over fences. Racegoers at Cartmel last August will testify that the gallant roan still misses out the odd fence, but can there be a greater living testimony to Gordon Richards's skill as a trainer of jumpers than this marvellously tough son of Scallywag, who is still as fit and keen as ever? The current victory roll is 20 and who is to say that he won't reach 25 before eventually retiring to his owner's paddocks near Garstang?

After Martin Todhunter had moved to Ulverston and was installed as a public trainer in premises once used by Roger Fisher, Ted Briggs caused a few feathers to fly at the Old Rectory by ringing up Gordon to tell him that Better Times Ahead would be sent to Martin (as he felt that his horse might benefit from a change of scenery) and that he might boost Martin's supply of winners. The sentiments were fine, but nobody had told Better Times Ahead who took a dim view of the move and refused to co-operate. Martin tried everything he knew to breathe renewed vigour into Better Times Ahead but the old hand was having none of it. Eventually he got his own way and was boxed back to Greystoke. After a suitable period of personal rehabilitation he condescended to win an amateur riders' hurdle at Kelso. Far from resting on his laurels, he has subsequently re-established himself as one of the most popular characters on the northern jumping scene.

Gallateen had been well bought out of Ben Hanbury's yard for 21,000 guineas at the 1991 July Newmarket Sales. The consistent grey added four more handicap successes to his novice hurdle wins of the previous season, including a clear-cut win over Olympian in the Oddbins Hurdle at Aintree – a much deserved reward for owner Ron Madden, who was to put a lot of money into buying horses to run in his striking blue-and-yellow chevrons with only a limited return.

The 1992–93 season had its downside. Carrick Hill Lad collapsed and died on the gallops and Twin Oaks bowed out in the 1993 Greenalls Gold Cup, pulled up lame before the 19th. He had won eight races round Haydock, the last of which had been the Tommy Whittle Chase the previous December. On the same card his potential successor, Whispering Steel, had justified favouritism in the Tony Dickinson Memorial Novices' Chase. It was his third consecutive victory and he returned to Haydock in January to record a fourth effortless win in the Arlington Premier Chase Series Qualifier. The Boss had hinted to me before the 1992–93 season had begun that he regarded the son of Furry Glen as potentially a Gold Cup horse.

By the time Whispering Steel lined up for the West of Scotland Pattern Chase at Ayr later in the month, his reputation had spread to a far wider audience. Neale Doughty relished the chance to ride bold, leaping front runners of this calibre and after Whispering Steel had accounted for the well-thought-of Candy Tuft by an eased-down three lengths, he was delighted to hear The Boss talking in terms of the Sun Alliance Novices' Chase. When it came to Cheltenham, however, GWR was not going to risk his growing star on the firm ground and Whispering Steel was roughed off without a further race.

Twin Oaks has thrived in retirement. Rising 20, he has been the guest of the Fenwicke-Clennel family for the last few years, enjoying the occasional day's hunting and making several public appearances with other charismatic stars of the past. The Boss ended the 1992–93 season as top northern trainer and a creditable fourth in the national trainers' list; but it was the opinion of many informed observers that the Greystoke trainer faced the threat of suspension for contravening the non-triers rule at Carlisle in February. That old penchant for running two horses in the same race was once again the root cause of the trouble. The EBF Novices' Hurdle Qualifier saw Neale Doughty riding Ron Madden's 9–2 chance Pakenham; while Michael Moloney took the mount on Ninfa, the stable's second string, who was owned by the triumvirate of Hugh Cavendish, Tarn Riley and Joanie Richards, and was sent off at 8–1.

Pakenham, off the course since running a fair fifth to Highland Poacher in a similar race at Haydock in November, was habitually ridden close to the leaders. Ninfa, whom Phil Tuck described as 'a difficult madam to break in', had been partnered by Moloney on each of her last two outings in which she had improved her position on the heels of the leaders three out – only to run on at one pace. On this occasion Ninfa was held up towards the rear of the 15-strong field while Doughty had Pakenham in the van throughout. Pakenham led from the fourth flight until two out, where he was joined by Caithness Prince (ironically trained by The Boss's former head lad Colin Parker). As the leaders duelled head to head into the final flight, Ninfa had made stealthy progress in the home straight to get within hailing distance of the two principal protagonists. Once on the run in, Caithness Prince would not be denied, holding on in the gamest possible style to pass the post a bare half-length clear of Pakenham with Ninfa finishing best of all just a length adrift in third.

Alan Amies, representing *Raceform*, and Steve Boggett of *Sporting Life*, the two official racereaders on duty that afternoon at Carlisle, both echoed the general view of the press room that Ninfa should have won. They felt that in the first place Ninfa had been given too much to do from the home turn and to compound the felony Michael Moloney had made no more than a token effort to close down the leaders from the last flight. In defence of the jockey, though, it should be pointed out here that his ability to ride a powerful finish had been inhibited by a recent shoulder injury.

The stewards did not hold an enquiry into the incident, but the tape of the race was forwarded to the Disciplinary Committee of the Jockey Club at Portman Square. On studying the video the committee decided to hold a retrospective enquiry. An infuriated Gordon Richards maintained there was no case to answer, but he was clearly rattled by the decision of the Jockey Club stewards to hold an enquiry. At Ayr the following weekend an ugly scene was narrowly averted when the then Garry Owen of the *Daily Record* had the effrontery to suggest that one of his Saturday winners had been ridden with a lot more dash than Ninfa had been at Carlisle!

In the run-up to the hearing in London, speculation was rife that both trainer and jockey would be found guilty of not allowing Ninfa either to run on her merits or to obtain her best possible placing. Indeed, matters looked grim for The Boss and Michael Moloney until salvation arrived in the guise of a legal technicality. The case was about to be heard before the Disciplinary Committee when the solicitor representing the Jockey Club was accused of failing to hand on an important letter concerning the case to the legal team acting for The Boss and Michael Moloney. The complaint was upheld and the enquiry was adjourned *sine die*. Journalists waiting outside to hear the verdict were then treated to a diatribe by The Boss suggesting a conspiracy on the part of the stewards to blacken his name. This would have made enthralling and lengthy reading in the next day's papers if Moloney had not been able to prise The Boss away and push him headlong into a waiting taxi on the grounds that he had said enough and anyway they were about to miss the last train back to Penrith . . .

Ninfa herself went on to race with notable success over fences. She won six times, including the EBF Tattersalls (Ireland) Mares Novices' Chase Final at Uttoxeter and competitive handicap chases at Newcastle and Ayr. Ninfa was named after a famous Italian garden once owned by Joanie Richards's uncle, Hubert Howard. She retired to the paddocks at the end of the 1995–96 season.

GWR's notoriety for 'educating' his horses on the race-track without receiving censure from the authorities in Portman Square was a source of some irritation to hawk-eyed Jockey Club officials. But it has to be restated that apart from the Ninfa incident at Carlisle, and a skirmish with the Ayr stewards over the running of Rionore in a handicap hurdle back in the spring of 1980, the Master of Greystoke had a clean if not completely unsullied disciplinary record. He was, though, a comparatively regular visitor to the local stewards' room to account for the running of his horses.

There were also occasions when the aggrieved racegoers, generally talking through their pockets, claimed that he was allowed too much leniency. The background to the running of The Grey Monk at Carlisle's Easter meeting in April 1995 comes quickly to mind. It was an open secret that this lovely grey by Roselier was held in the highest esteem at Greystoke. He ran in the tartan colours of Alistair Duff, at the time a director of Carlisle racecourse, though The Boss did retain a minor holding in the gelding. The Grey Monk had sustained a hairline fracture of the cannon bone the previous autumn and that Easter weekend a combination of sunshine and a blustery wind was drying out the ground by the hour. Alistair Duff was keen to run, as members of his family had driven up from the South especially to watch The Grey Monk in action. He also knew that The Boss would be becoming progressively anxious about the going and that if he had his way he would probably withdraw the grey from his intended engagement. A game of pretend hide-and-seek then took place throughout the afternoon. By declaration time for the final race The Boss had been unable to nail down his owner. Consequently The Grey Monk was still in the line-up.

The Boss, though, had found the time to acquaint Brian Harding with the situation and the rider had been left in no doubt about the part he was expected to play. Under pain of death, or at the very least the threat of instant dismissal, was Brian to give The Grey Monk a hard race. If the horse was happy in himself and striding out fluently on the sound surface, all well and good – he could go ahead and win his race. But if the jockey was in any way to suspect that his mount was 'feeling the ground' then he was to sit still and nurse him home.

The Grey Monk was sent off the 4–5 favourite, but he hit the third flight quite hard and, handled with kid gloves by his pilot, could only run on at one pace up the home straight. He finished third. Before the end of April The Grey Monk had reappeared to hack up at Hexham by a distance of 20 lengths. No questions were officially asked because the winner was running over a longer distance on his favourite rain-softened ground!

However Hexham was the venue for the one occasion when Phil Tuck, in his role as stewards' secretary, found himself officiating at an enquiry concerning the running of one of GWR's horses. Phil recalls: 'I felt sufficiently confident in my professional capacity to officiate, even though it was my former guv'nor who was being quizzed.' The enquiry concerned the placing of a horse called Raining Stairs. It was only his second outing in public and he had finished a staying on sixth in the Federation Brewery Medallion Lager Novices' Hurdle, 20 lengths adrift of Menshaar with no less a horse than Young Kenny back in second.

Phil Tuck continues: 'From the pictures it looked as though Brian Harding wasn't all that busy and the stewards felt it would be good for relations with the race-going public if Gordon was called in to explain things. I remember him getting himself worked up into quite a state, insisting that the horse had a breathing problem and that he had told his jockey to see that he got home in one piece if he heard him beginning to make a noise. Brian Harding then reported that Raining Stairs had started to gurgle at the bottom of the hill. The vet also gave evidence that the gelding had finished "in a distressed condition". So that was that, but The Boss was still steaming as he left the room!'

Later that evening both The Boss and Phil Tuck were taking part in a racing quiz night organised by Richard Hale at the Clickham Arms near Greystoke. Any differences of opinion were quickly sorted over a couple of pints though, as Phil records, 'The Boss had entered the bar with a fighting look in those steely blue eyes and it had been very much down to me to defuse the situation by forcing him to accept a pint and call it quits.'

Shortly before the end of the 1992–93 season The Boss made his final purchase from Arthur Stephenson's fortress at Crawleas. The incomparable trainer himself had died five months earlier. He and The Boss had been friends and sparring partners for well over 30 years. Indeed Sea View, the chaser whose fall at Perth was to end GWR's riding career, was originally trained by Arthur Stephenson; and 'careful' though he was reputed to be with his money, WA made the generous gesture of paying the injured Richards his riding retainer right up to Christmas. Gordon bought a number of horses from the Bishop Auckland trainer while he was alive and enjoyed recalling that the artful Stephenson, though scrupulously fair, occasionally forgot to impart one vital piece of information about his sales.

The first horse that Gordon bought from WA had passed through the sales only a few days earlier. GWR had liked the look of him and put it to the Crawleas trainer that he might be prepared to take a small profit on the deal. Business was discussed over a cup of tea, a beverage that Stephenson would drink in some quantity. Gordon announced that he would like to put a saddle on the horse and ride him round the yard for a couple of circuits just to check his action. WA pointed out that the horse was stabled down the road with a local farmer who would be happy to agree to his request. The only snag was that the farmer purported not to have a saddle in the house, so WA persuaded the prospective purchaser to do the test bareback. The horse behaved just as Gordon had hoped and the deal was completed. A couple of days later The Boss decided to saddle up his new arrival and ride him away. Alas, each time he vaulted into the saddle, the horse instantly bucked him off. He was as quiet as a mouse bareback, but a bucking bronco whenever he was tacked up, and nothing that Gordon tried would change his mind!

Later on Gordon was to buy Titus Oates and Canadius out of the Stephenson yard. Both would prove splendid bargains, but even here the 'wicked' WA was to enjoy a chuckle or two at GWR's expense. You may recall that Titus Oates refused point blank to be schooled over fences; while Canadius would not travel a yard unless his close colleague, the fearsome nanny goat, was at his side. In the latter case WA even attempted to put a price on the goat's head!

The Boss was fond of recounting the greeting with which WA addressed him on the first occasion that the pair had met after Gordon had trained his 100th winner in 1975–76: 'Well, well, well, GW, give me your hand. All that knowledge you've taken from me. You're the King now!'

Stephenson had long been christened the 'King' of northern National Hunt racing. In many ways it was a title which could have been shared. For upwards of 20 seasons Richards and Stephenson had duelled for supremacy. There were, of course, other top training families in the North, notably the Easterbys and the Dickinsons. Yet somehow, down in Yorkshire as they both were, they were divorced from the private battles between the two kings of the territory once patrolled by the forces of the Roman frontier legions – WA lording it over Co. Durham (perhaps better known as 'the Land of the Prince Bishops') and GWR, monarch of all he surveyed from his fellside castle in the Cumbrian hills, where back in the mists of history the Celts took refuge from the marauding Angles.

Typically both sovereigns liked nothing better than to plunder prize money in the heart of 'enemy' territory. The Stephenson team regarded Newcastle as their citadel but raiders from Greystoke regularly carried off the booty. It was the same at Carlisle, considered by GWR as his private demesne but never quite secure against the stormtroopers from the Stephenson camp. The friendly rivalry and continuous stream of private banter between the two of them lit up many a dank November afternoon. Often their runners would dominate the betting and it was at such moments that The Boss least wanted to hear WA's opening salvo of 'go careful today now, GW, go careful' as they waited for their runners in the paddock.

'He really fancied one of his, if he talked like that,' refelected Gordon, stroking his chin gingerly at the recollection. In the early days Stephenson and Richards would meet Friday evenings at the Turkish baths in Newcastle. Later they met at the races to enjoy an ice-cream cornet together. Recalled Gordon: 'WA loved his ice cream; but the doctors stopped him eating it towards the end.'

The ice cream was a standing dish at flat-race meetings in the summer – more relaxed occasions, but not without a competitive edge as both trainers sent out plenty of winners on the level despite WA's deprecating approach to the summer game. 'His first words would always be the same,' explained The Boss. 'He would touch you on the sleeve and repeat, "You silly young man. This is a little boy's game; a collar-and-tie game."' The Boss was genuinely upset when he heard the news of Stephenson's death and paid this moving tribute to his colleague and mentor:

> Arthur was a great man who knew his job and when you talked to him it was a pleasure because you knew he was talking sense. He loved his horses and worked hard at the business. I've ridden for him, bought horses from him, got beaten by him, eaten ice cream with him and very occasionally managed to put one over him.

He was a big man in every sense of the word. A great gentleman who never stopped working and who put an awful lot of money and effort into racing. As a jockey I was a bit impetuous and he was always saying to me, 'Cool yourself down, laddie. Don't get so excited. They won't run away from you.' If you fell off, his stock remark was, 'You silly young fella. What did you do that for?'

He had a silvery tongue when it came to selling you a horse but the ones I got from him, the likes of Titus Oates and Canadius, were really good types. When it came to knowing his horses, you couldn't beat him. I'll miss him. He was a grand old man and what he missed in his last few years was his ice cream. He couldn't eat it any more because it was bad for his kidneys. In all the years we competed against each other as trainers we remained the greatest of friends.

GWR remembered being at Hexham when One Man made his début over hurdles. WA was there too. The Boss was on record as saying, 'One Man was Arthur's type of horse. Tom Costello had bought him for IR4,000 guineas as an unbroken three-year-old, then sold him on to WA who passed him on to Peter Piller, one of his big owners. Arthur had only just started educating him over hurdles when illness ended his enjoyment.'

At Hexham, only a couple of months before WA's death, both trainers were in attendance and One Man was making his first appearance in public in the two-mile Beacon Novices' Hurdle. Described as 'backward in condition', the son of Remainder Man made headway at the half-way stage but weakened from two out to finish eighth of fifteen. It was a satisfactory début and to the watching GWR the newcomer was a striking individual. He remarked to his colleague, 'By God, he's got big feet.' Later he remembered thinking, 'I like that grey. He has the right way of going and he looks a strong little horse, laid back but with a lovely swagger about him.'

WA, who was clearly just as keen, chuckled: 'Your eyes are working well, GW – I think he's got a big heart, too, and that is what you need at this game. Watch him when he goes over the black ones!'

It was a piece of advice that The Boss was not going to forget.

TWENTY-FIVE

One Man Arrives

The Boss had plenty to keep him busy during the last two months of the 1992–93 season, but at the back of his mind lurked the ambition to add One Man to the strength at Greystoke. The publication of the catalogue for the dispersal sale of Arthur Stephenson's jumpers brought matters to a head. An equine empire was to come under the hammer at Crawleas in early May and Gordon had ensured that several of his leading owners received the catalogue from the Doncaster Bloodstock Sales auctioneers.

John Hales – the driving force behind Golden Bear Products, the family's soft toy manufacturing and merchandising firm from Telford – was eager to scan the catalogue. Pat, his wife, and Lisa, his daughter, were both accomplished horsewomen, already familiar names at The Horse of the Year Show and other leading showing venues up and down the country. Just down the road from the Hales home in rural Shropshire is the family stud and though John himself was equally enthusiastic about the consuming interests of his wife and daughter, he was a comparative newcomer to the racing scene and a very recent addition to the owners' ranks.

He was later to admit that his introduction to the sport had occurred through accident rather than design. He explained: 'As a family we are in the habit of taking our annual holiday in Barbados and have been friendly with John Moreton for a long while. John invited us to watch Twin Oaks run at Haydock at the time when he was winning all those top races. I was hooked by the whole experience. I met Gordon and was impressed.'

The upshot of this chance visit to Haydock was a call to Greystoke indicating that John Hales was interested in becoming an owner and asking Gordon to find him a suitable horse. The Boss suggested that John Hales should invest in a three-year-old by Strong Gale, but warned him that it would be a couple of seasons before he could expect to see him race with any frequency. The deal was struck and the gelding appropriately christened: The Toyman.

Hales recalls, 'He was a lovely long-term prospect. But I was impatient to see my colours carried over fences and Gordon knew that I might be in the market for a horse to run at much shorter notice if a likely sort came on the market.' By happy coincidence his attention was drawn to lot no. 111.

John thought three ones was a good omen. 'It was a grey called One Man, who had shown promise in an Irish point-to-point and had won three races over hurdles. The catalogue suggested that he was bred to be a chaser and winning those races over hurdles made me think that he ought to have a bit of speed. I rang Gordon to get his opinion.

'The Boss replied at once, "Ah, One Man – he's got big feet."

'I asked him if that made any difference and whether he thought the horse was any good.

'"Nope, the feet won't stop him and yep, he could be good," was the reply.

'That made up my mind. The Boss said that he reckoned we might get him for around 30,000 guineas. That was about my ceiling and we arranged to meet at Crawleas.'

Pat Hales told Lisa to accompany her father to the sale with instructions to look after him and to make sure that he didn't do anything silly, such as spending too much money! Lot 111 was the very first horse they saw as they began their inspection of the assorted collection of boxes, barns and sheds that combined to provide accommodation for upwards of 120 horses assembled for that sale.

John Hales recalls, 'We turned the first corner and there he was, standing quietly in this rather gloomy sunken box. Perhaps it was the surroundings but somehow he looked a bit small and physically nothing to write home about. In fact that first meeting was a shade disappointing. But we had come very much with One Man in mind and we kept going back to inspect him. We must have looked at him closely at least three or four times during the afternoon. In the end, though, both Lisa and I took a liking to Spanish Fair, who'd won a point-to-point in Ireland and had scored over hurdles at Newcastle the previous October. He was attracting plenty of attention but we asked Gordon to bid for him on our behalf. He did his best. However, Mrs Bramall was determined to have him and she got her wish at 72,000 guineas.'

Spanish Fair was lot 99 and the slightly disconsolate foursome of The Boss, Neale Doughty, and Hales father and daughter waited in a silent huddle to the left of the auctioneer's podium while a further 11 lots went under the hammer. Then it was the turn of One Man. John Hales thought he looked more the part under the lights in the small circular ring that was laid out in the centre of WA's most roomy and expensive barn. He had a certain presence about him. Out there in the open he no longer looked small but well rounded, muscular and bouncy: a pocket battleship of a horse.

The Boss had estimated an asking price of 30–40,000 guineas but the bids were coming in thick and fast. Spanish Fair had gone for over 70,000 guineas and decision time was coming all too close for John Hales's comfort. He remembers: 'I was already in a daze, caught up by the adrenalin of the occasion, yet still just aware that if I was to have One Man I must forget all about ceilings and throw caution to the wind. I turned to Gordon and a quick glance was enough. He wanted this horse. The determined set of the jaw and the excited sparkle in those clear blue eyes betrayed no self-doubt. He believed in One Man. A brief pause in the bidding gave me the chance to say to him, "Gordon, you really like him, don't you?"

'"Like him, John? I love him. I guarantee that I can win you five or six chases with him next season."

'There was nothing more to say. I motioned to him to keep bidding.'

The hammer fell at 68,000 guineas. The Boss was all smiles. Neale Doughty clenched his fist and let out a whoop of joy. John Hales was numbed into silence. He can still recall the moment: 'I was in a total state of shock. I couldn't believe what I had done. There was no way that I could justify spending that sort of money. It had to be the stupidest thing that I had done in my life. I left Gordon to deal with the press, signed the papers and did my best to help Lisa with getting One Man wrapped up and ready for the journey back to Shropshire.'

Any crumbs of comfort gleaned from the confidence of the Greystoke camp that One Man would win a hatful of races in his first season over fences, and that it was money well spent, were quickly swept aside when the ramp was lowered. One Man was led down for inspection by Pat Hales under the unforgiving brilliance of the stud's arc lamps. The initial reaction was worse than anticipated.

'My God, what have you done?' cried the knowledgeable breeder of top show horses. 'You've spent all that money buying a horse with feet like that and you say that his eyesight may be impaired too. You must have taken leave of your senses!'

Neither did the unfortunate Lisa escape a tongue lashing. She was roundly accused of failing in her duty. 'I sent you there to stop your father from doing anything stupid and you let him spend a fortune on an animal like this. You are both as bad as each other!'

Clearly it was difficult to explain their actions in face of such criticism. However John Hales recounts with a certain relish how after One Man had won his fourth race off the reel he overheard his wife remarking to a friend, 'That's four in a row. I think we've bought a good one here!'

(More cynical professional observers held their fire, though one could not resist the reflection that '68,000 guineas represented an awful lot of teddy bears'! He need not have worried. Golden Bear Products had bigger fish to fry. In addition to cornering the market for a wide range of popular soft toys, the company enjoyed the monopoly for the sale of World Cup Willie, the England football team's official mascot; and a few years later the insatiable demand for Teletubby dolls made Golden Bear the envy of the toy-producing world.)

Meanwhile, 150 miles to the north, the finishing touches were being applied to the construction of the spacious American-type barn which was the centre-piece of GWR's new stable complex at the Rectory Farm. The purchase of the Old Rectory had paid off. Neville Howard determined to fund the upkeep of the Greystoke Castle Estate by utilising its ample facilities to lay on corporate hospitality with a difference. The entertainment, mainly aimed at company executives, provides a challenging blend of team games, archery, off-road driving and quad-bike racing. From the start Neville needed to regain possession of the stable complex. A new lease was negotiated, allowing Gordon the continued use of the gallops but requiring him to vacate the stables during the summer. The 1993–94 season was to see The Boss sending out winners from his own property for the first time in 26 years as a fully licensed trainer. Gordon called it centralisation rather than change.

Come August and One Man was dropped off at Greystoke after his two-month holiday in Shropshire. He had done himself well. Eating was a real pleasure to 'Solo' and he would grow as round as a barrel if he got half the chance, a condition that the Hales family were quick to spot and one which they did their best to counter by ensuring that the grey had plenty of roadwork before he went back into training.

The Boss was delighted to see him looking so well and so laid back. Before One Man had left Crawleas the previous May Nancy Stephenson, WA's widow, had come up to him and said how pleased Arthur would have been to know that the grey had gone to Greystoke. Gordon had been very chuffed by the compliment. When he went round the stables at evening feed-time he reflected that One Man had been a grand buy. Nicky recalls him saying, 'I have seen nicer horses than One Man, taller ones and ones with more quality. He may be too small for some people's liking but he is strong and wide with a lovely big loping stride. It is the way he does it. When you ride him he is straight into his stride, so comfortable, so easy, so smooth. It isn't an effort for him.'

WA had schooled One Man over poles but Neale Doughty was the first to take him over a fence. He was a dream, as GWR described to *Sporting Life*'s David Ashforth when he came to interview The Boss before the grey travelled south to Cheltenham for a second attempt at the Gold Cup.

Gordon added, 'After clearing the first fence Doughty exclaimed, "Ooh, beautiful!" After two fences Neale didn't need to tell me. He was ready to run and had taken to jumping fences like a duck to water. He was a natural jumper. He didn't have to put in a big effort. He did it easy as sure as night follows day, like Night Nurse used to do it over hurdles.'

Gordon's boast that he would win John Hales five or six races in his first season, and Neale Doughty's forecast that he could be a future Gold Cup winner, looked good for a long-priced double as the partnership rattled off the wins.

'Should be pretty straightforward,' was GWR's pre-race comment when One Man made his chasing début in the Plasticisers Charisma Novices' Chase at Ayr's November meeting. The grey went off at 1–3 favourite but he tested Neale's stickability to the limit by giving the third last a careless clout. Neale sat tight and One Man gained an effortless success. His jumping was foot-perfect in follow-up triumphs at Haydock, Wetherby and Haydock again, before The Boss had seen enough. He told John Hales that it was time to tackle the big boys in the South and One Man travelled to Ascot's February meeting for the prestigious Reynoldstown Novices' Chase (often rated a serious Cheltenham trial). Northern-trained horses frequently go off at backable prices at Ascot and 2–1 against the chances of Greystoke's rising star did not please the bookmakers back in Cumbria.

Neale Doughty had no worries. He always had One Man close to the leaders, took it up at the 12th and beat Mailcom and company in facile style. The five-timer was completed and next stop would be the Sun Alliance Chase at the Cheltenham Festival. By now all had been forgiven at Hales's house in Shropshire. The grey had already repaid half his purchase price and he had yet to plunder the big prize money events. John Hales was a proud man but it had not made any difference to his inability to watch One Man's races from the comfort of the grandstand. Poor John was fighting a losing battle with his nerves. He simply couldn't force himself to watch the action 'live' in case anything dreadful should befall his pride and joy. Throughout the 26 races that One Man carried the bright yellow-and-red-starred colours of Golden Bear Ltd, John Hales paced nervously in the shadows below the stands, listening with ashen face to the race commentary until One Man was safely over the final fence – at which point a happy and much relieved owner would reappear in public to welcome back his popular warrior.

Not for the last time at Cheltenham, Hales was to endure a frustrating five minutes marking time in the passageway between lawn and paddock area while One Man and Neale Doughty duelled with Monsieur le Cure. Solo had cruised clear of the John Edwards-trained stayer at Haydock back in November; but here in the cauldron of the Sun Alliance, battle was joined with contrasting ferocity. One Man, the 3–1 favourite, had his supporters purring with anticipation as he galloped powerfully into the lead crossing the 13th; but their hearts were in their mouths as he squandered his advantage away with an energy-sapping blunder at the next, the last open ditch. Turning downhill, the grey appeared to have shrugged off the error. Doughty ranged alongside Niven at the third last, but significantly he could not step up the pace in the manner of the potential champion that he purported to be. Within the space of half a furlong One Man went from cruising to struggling. Back in fourth place approaching the last, he met the obstacle like an exhausted horse, ploughed through the birch and trailed in a bedraggled ninth.

The post-mortem was carried out on the triangle of grass beneath the electronic scoreboard as the cheers rang out for Monsieur le Cure in the winner's circle. The Boss was bemused, rendered well-nigh speechless by the disaster. Even the loosest interpretation of the formbook ruled that wherever Monsieur le Cure finished, One Man had to be alongside. But in the Sun Alliance he had not been in the same parish. Neale's initial explanation that the grey had not been the same horse after his mistake at the 14th was later endorsed by the discovery that he had returned home with a twisted back. The chiropractor did his job and One Man went home for his holidays with both owner and trainer believing that the mystery of his sudden decline at Cheltenham had been safely solved.

One Man's shock eclipse in the Sun Alliance did nothing to salvage a below-par season for the Richards stable. Whispering Steel only appeared twice. He won first time out in the Tennents Special Case at Ayr's November meeting and on the strength of that promising display Michael Gillow's outstanding prospect had started 4–1 second favourite for the Hennessy Gold Cup at Newbury. Nothing was going better on the home turn, but once Neale Doughty asked him to go on and win his race, he produced disappointingly little and weakened into fifth place. The Greystoke horses had been troubled by a blood disorder, an infection that remained with the stable for much of the season. Tests taken from Whispering Steel after his fade out at Newbury indicated that he had been sickening for the virus when he dropped out under pressure in the Hennessy. Whispering Steel was not to run again for the remainder of the season.

General Pershing won the Rowland Meyrick Chase at Wetherby before becoming another victim of the malaise. At least Jinxy Jack managed to win the Little Bay Chase at Perth in the spring. But by that time The Boss had been assailed by a sequence of reverses.

Pat Kavanagh, the stable's invaluable head lad suffered a heart attack. Happily he was to make a good recovery but his consultant suggested he must take things easy and advised him to seek a less stressful position. It would have been folly to reject such a warning and Pat reluctantly gave up his job at Greystoke – first to join up with Norman Mason, who was setting up as a permit holder in Co. Durham, and later to move back to Cumbria to work for Martin Todhunter at Ulverston.

Pat's arrival at Greystoke had halted a worrying trend of instability. Colin Parker had held down the job of head lad throughout the '70s; but on his departure, first to establish a livery yard of his own, and then to take out a public training licence, the tenure of his post at Greystoke had changed hands with upsetting frequency. Pat Kavanagh had reversed the flow and his untoward departure left a gap which was hard to plug. Chris Brownless, the former Greystoke jockey, was his immediate replacement but not on a permanent basis. He was replaced by Danny Barry, who had also ridden with limited success for The Boss. Danny was both popular and efficient. So much so that in the spring of 1998 he was offered a similar post with Charlie Swan back in his native Ireland, a job he could not afford to turn down.

The death of Last o' the Bunch was an added disaster. Gary Middlebrook's consistent two-miler had won 15 races before falling fatally at Wetherby on the same day that General Pershing landed the Rowland Meyrick. Neale Doughty was in the saddle. The stable jockey's rapport with One Man had been invaluable, but there had been undercurrents of disquiet and uncertainty about future riding arrangements at Greystoke.

Neale takes up the story: 'The Boss and I had discussed the need to find a number-two jockey, who would be groomed to take my place in good time in the same way that I had inherited the job from Ron Barry. This was a long-term project and it had been mutually understood that I would continue to ride as stable jockey during this transition period. Tony Dobbin, the top conditional jockey, riding mainly for Maurice Barnes at nearby Little Salkeld, was a popular contender and as the season began to wind down it was becoming increasingly clear that certain parties wanted me out sooner rather than later.'

Towards the end of April Neale had a meeting with GWR at the Old Rectory to clear the air. Neale continues, 'The results had not been going well and The Boss said that Joanie had received several complaints from owners criticising the way I had ridden their horses. I told him straight that I wasn't taking the blame when we all knew that the horses weren't right. He then got steamed up that I was accusing him of not training his horses properly and Joanie waded in as well, saying that both Ron Madden, the owner of Gallateen, and Robert Ogden had rung in to complain about my riding of their horses. Tempers started to fray and I left the house determined to get to the bottom of the business.'

Neale was so incensed by what Joanie had said that he wrote personally to the owners involved asking them to enlarge on their complaints. He adds, 'I got several supportive replies, but one owner rang The Boss to say that he had received my letter and wondered what was going on.

'Of course The Boss raised the roof, claiming that I had no right to contact his owners in this way and Joanie put in her oar as well. She and I had not been on the best of terms for some while and I sensed that she couldn't wait to get Tony Dobbin appointed in my place.'

The upshot was that Neale reverted to a freelance role and Tony Dobbin became stable jockey for the 1994–95 season. Neale actually partnered Addington Boy for The Boss at Perth in August, but he retired from the saddle altogether after partnering American Hero to win at Kelso for Dick Allan the following spring. He recalls meeting up with GWR at Kelso. 'He asked me if I would ride General Pershing in a gallop after racing, as the horse was due to run in the National and none of his jockeys could get him to settle. In the end I agreed and there was no problem with the horse. He asked me to reconsider my retirement and take the ride on General Pershing at Aintree but I couldn't have done the weight without a lot of sweat so I turned down the offer. It was a nice gesture on his part, though, and I shall never forget the great times we had together. I spent 14 years at Greystoke and I don't regret one minute.'

TWENTY-SIX

Trouble at Home

Tony Dobbin never had second thoughts about accepting the offer to ride as stable jockey at Greystoke. Little more than a year had elapsed since he had taken a calculated gamble to forsake the security of Jonjo O'Neill's high-profile yard to strike out on his own. The decision had proved a winner. He had moved base less than 15 miles as the crow flies to join forces with Maurice Barnes at Little Salkeld. His arrival at Bank House coincided with the ex-jump jockey's best ever season and thanks to Maurice's understanding nature he had also been in the position to accept an increasing number of outside rides. This dual role provided the 21-year-old Ulsterman with the opportunity to consolidate his status as one of the most promising claimers on the northern circuit.

Tony did more than that. He led the conditional jockeys' table from early in the season and clinched the title with a tally of 45 winners. It was hard on the Barnes family, who had encouraged his progress so wholeheartedly, but the inevitable could not be avoided. Tony's exciting blend of natural flair, youthful drive and innate horsemanship had combined to advertise his talents well beyond the boundaries of Cumbria.

Before the end of the 1993–94 season Tony had received several tempting offers but the call from Greystoke was irresistible. The Boss had been keeping an eye on him for a while, principally with a view to inviting him to join the team as understudy to Neale Doughty (with the promise of taking over as stable jockey on Neale's retirement). The events of the previous spring had accelerated matters, so the vacancy at Greystoke was that of an immediate replacement rather than an understudy. The Boss booked Dobbin to partner The Demon Barber in a claimer at Haydock's early May meeting. The 12-year-old duly obliged and the jockey also passed his final test. Tony was offered the job, and though there were several loose ends to tie up, he was always going to accept.

Those regarding GWR as an irascible ogre, addicted to bawling out his jockeys and impossibly hard to please, wondered if Tony Dobbin had the mental toughness for the job. They need not have worried. As a raw teenager fresh from home in Co. Down, Tony may not have had the bottle to survive more than a fortnight with Neville Callaghan at Newmarket; but six years had passed since that false start and the leading conditional jockey of 1993–94 was a self-confident, extrovert young man, prepared to stand his ground and not disposed to be browbeaten or unnerved by a ration of verbal abuse. He knew what he was taking on and he was determined to meet the challenge head-on.

Firm ground in the autumn prevented the Greystoke horses from making their accustomed fast start and it wasn't until early November that the stable warmed to its work. Dobbin chalked up the first of many Greystoke doubles at Haydock, when his winners were the potential stars Addington Boy and Unguided Missile. Two days later Tony rode a four-timer at Hexham. A treble, including an impressive victory on Robert Ogden's lovely horse General Command, followed on the first day of Ayr's November meeting. Two more winners came on the Saturday, the highlight being his first ride in public on One Man, who was making his seasonal reappearance in the Tennents Special Handicap Chase. The grey had a simple task and achieved it without raising a sweat, making all and sauntering home five lengths clear of Mr Boston. The win left One Man spot-on for the Hennessy Gold Cup at Newbury in a fortnight's time.

The Boss hoped to have won the 1993 Hennessy with Whispering Steel, but that much-fancied contender had faded into fifth place after looking poised for success jumping the third last. Whispering Steel was not right for a long while and he was rested for the remainder of the season. He returned south to Michael Gillows's property and Gordon was far from happy to receive the news that Whispering Steel would not be coming back to Greystoke. The owner intended to have him trained closer to home by Kim Bailey at Lambourn.

One Man was bouncing with vigour on the gallops. The Boss took enormous pleasure in riding him out, often using him as his hack. Unless crucial business kept him elsewhere, he would act as his personal valet, supervising his daily roll and opening the gate so that 'Solo' could enjoy his regular stint in his paddock with Gordon's ageing pony.

The stable was bullish about One Man's Hennessy prospects. He was in prime form and, off only ten stone, would never be more favourably handicapped to lift a major prize. While Martin Todhunter brought his valuable cargo southwards in his capacious box, The Boss and Tony Dobbin reached Newbury early to walk the course. Tony was instructed to get the grey nicely settled on the heels of the leading group, but to hold him up to last the trip and produce him between the final two fences to ping the last and cruise home on the bridle. Sounds easy, doesn't it? But Tony was bubbling with confidence and wouldn't hear of defeat. Gordon had made all the right noises to John Hales, who decided to use the occasion to provide his loyal staff from Golden Bear the chance to savour a day at the races – with the extra bonus of a 'surefire' big race winner.

Their stakes were never in doubt. One Man travelled supremely well throughout the race, measuring his fences with that fluent accuracy and ease of effort which is the hallmark of a natural chaser. He was causing Tony Dobbin palpitations, not because the jockey lacked confidence in his mount, but in contrast because he realised that One Man was running over his rivals and he knew that he was fighting a losing battle to prevent him hitting the front far too quickly for The Boss's peace of mind. Dobbin's aching arms surrendered at the third from home where One Man threw such a prodigious leap that the horseman in Dobbin convinced him it was no longer advisable even to attempt restraining tactics. Outwardly riding with consummate confidence – but inwardly dreading the wrath to come if the apparent impossible did occur and One Man got overhauled on the run for home – Dobbin sat tight, found the perfect stride at the last and eased One Man right down close home to win by a couple of lengths from Lord Relic.

He had scored with such an air of invincibility that the question of stamina did not enter the equation. A radiant John Hales emerged from his bolthole to doff his trilby to the admiring crowd and pose for celebratory photographs alongside his happy hero. Bookmakers were not yet convinced that One Man was true Gold Cup material; but their pessimism was not shared by the punters and the initial quote of 14–1 for Cheltenham was swallowed up in a deluge of ante-post vouchers. The cry was, 'Remember Jodami. He got beaten in the Hennessy off a similar low weight before going on to Gold Cup glory that same season.'

The Boss did not commit himself in public and in private he counselled a 'softly, softly' approach. After Newbury he had pencilled in the Rowland Meyrick at Wetherby on Boxing Day; then, if the wheels were still in place a trip down south for the *Racing Post* Chase at Kempton. 'Only then,' he advised, 'would it be sensible to discuss Cheltenham plans.' Tony Dobbin had little time for Christmas celebrations. His mind was set on more tangible rewards at Wetherby on Boxing Day. The Supermaster Chase went according to plan. General Pershing boosted his Aintree hopes with a demolition job over Blazing Walker. The middle leg of the anticipated treble was to be One Man in the Rowland Meyrick and the three-timer would be wrapped up with victory from Unguided Missile in the Boroughbridge Novices' Chase.

One Man traded at 4–6 favourite in what was widely canvassed as a head-to-head battle with John Yeadon's Gold Cup hero Jodami, who was set to give away 24 pounds to the Greystoke star. Cogent, the third runner, was discounted by all save those intrepid backers who always support 'the outsider of three'. The racecourse commentator with the plummy schoolmaster's intonation did his level best to disguise any Cumbrian bias in his delivery as the race developed. One Man, doing an excellent job of pulling Tony Dobbin's arms out of their sockets, uneasily settled a couple of lengths adrift of the front-running Cogent. Jodami, labouring under his 12 stone, was detached in third. Heading down the back straight for the final time, Dobbin let out an inch of rein and the favourite quickened instantly – alas a shade too eagerly. He was on the point of swallowing up the gallant Cogent at the 14th, the last plain fence before the home turn, when he took off with joyous abandon, blundered on landing and unseated his helpless pilot.

Chris Bonner, on Cogent, must have thought it was Christmas all over again. With One Man eliminated, he was then gifted the race at the third last where Jodami, on whom Mark Dwyer had been hard at work throughout the last mile, put in a tired jump and failed to get his undercarriage down in time. He was remounted to pass the post in second place at about the same moment as a red-faced Dobbin was doing his chirpy best to explain away One Man's demise. 'Rider taken unawares' was the general consensus of the media, though many observed that Dobbin had been faced with an invidious task in trying to obey instructions to hold up his mount, and that he would have been better advised to seize the initiative and allow the grey to stride clear inside the final mile. Right or wrong, poor Tony had been caught in the classic catch-22 situation and the only salvation was that One Man had come to no harm in the incident. A slightly subdued stable jockey emerged from the weighing room half an hour later to ride a perfectly judged race on the progressive Unguided Missile, who proved far too smart for his market rival Too Good To Be True, and scored by the slightly ominous distance of 13 lengths. Few words were exchanged between jockey and trainer in the winner's circle.

If misplaced exuberance could have been the root cause of One Man's unexpected reverse at Wetherby, no credible explanation has ever been given for his bone-shaking fall in the *Racing Post* Chase. The Boss had him looking a picture and there was quiet confidence in the camp that the 2–1 favourite would redeem his reputation. Watching on a fuzzy television set in the traditional gloom of the Edinburgh (as it still was!) press room, northern spirits were rising as the ghostly shape of One Man could be seen mowing down the leaders on the approach to the 12th fence.

Then 'crash!' – the spectre kept straight on. He never seemed to break stride, but galloped on regardless. His momentum sent him crashing into the unyielding belly of the fence, upwards and over, scattering his rider to the winds, thudding with sickening speed and force into the ground and bringing down Amtrak Express as he rolled sideways towards the running rail. The silence in that Scottish press room was tangible as a dozen pair of eyes strained to decypher images from the mottled screen. The cheer that greeted his eventual scrambling recovery would have silenced the crowd in the members' bar.

Out in the country at Kempton the relief, though less noisy, was equally sincere. Tony Dobbin was dazed and disorientated – in his own words later in the day, 'plain sick, half because of the fall and half in dread that One Man was not going to rise'. Audrey Walker, Solo's stable lass, and Martin Todhunter had both run from the paddock area to the 12th fence before One Man had struggled to his feet. Like his jockey, the grey was confused and badly shaken, but he was able to make his way gingerly towards the racecourse stables where the distraught Hales family were fearing the worst.

'We couldn't believe that he was uninjured,' recalls John. 'But when he got back to the tarmac surface Audrey walked him round and he was sound. The vet gave him a careful look over and could find nothing wrong. He was back in his box at Greystoke by midnight.'

Meanwhile the debriefing was only just beginning. The Boss had studied the re-run and was of the opinion that the horse had suddenly lost concentration and failed to see the fence in time. Tony Dobbin confirmed that he had been happy with the way One Man was travelling through the race, but that when he asked him to stand off as the ditch approached he hardly raised a leg and plummeted full-tilt into the middle of the fence. He could give no explanation for what had caused the horse's behaviour.

The Boss was down at One Man's box a full hour before dawn, to check on the grey's condition and run his hands carefully down each of his legs. They were cool to the touch but One Man was bruised and jarred up. Initially Gordon had been thinking of a race at Ayr in April to regain his confidence, but as the days passed and One Man continued to suffer from the equine equivalent of post-traumatic stress, the unanimous decision was that the grey should be roughed off for the season in the belief that a long summer out at grass on the Hales' stud would heal both mind and body.

The Boss saddled 43 winners in 1994–95. It had been a difficult season from the start and to aggravate the situation Cumbria was waterlogged from January through to April. Hardly a day went by without the gallops being subjected to a deluge. The all-weather was under water and the turf gallops sodden. It was almost impossible to keep more than a handful of horses properly fit, but despite the atrocious weather there were redeeming features. Unguided Missile excelled. Had he not fallen four out in the Sun Alliance Chase at the Cheltenham Festival, he would have finished in the frame; and he went on to win the keenly contested Edinburgh Woollen Mill Future Champion Novices' Chase at Ayr.

The Grey Monk missed much of the season recovering from a hairline fracture of the cannon bone, sustained during his first race of the campaign at Wetherby. He recovered to win two novice hurdles at Hexham by wide margins. He was to go chasing in 1995–96. Gordon spent much of his brief summer break renovating the all-weather gallop, but misfortunes continued to dog the stable. Gallateen died of a badly twisted gut. Whispering Steel remained with Kim Bailey. The promising Joliver moved to Martin Pipe. Chipped Out and Wills Telmar joined Martin Todhunter, newly established at Ulverston, and General Pershing was transferred to David Nicholson. In mid-summer there was even speculation that One Man was also on the move. This unsubstantiated story was quickly scotched by the news that One Man had already returned to Greystoke and that Tony Dobbin would retain the mount. To counteract the gossip it was vital that both One Man and The Grey Monk should advertise their talent with a series of early victories when the 1995–96 season got properly under way.

By November The Boss had produced at least two potential Cheltenham prospects in Addington Boy and General Command. The latter, a handsome son of Strong Gale, was one of Robert Ogden's powerful team at Greystoke. He opened his account with a clear-cut 5–1 success for Richard Dunwoody in a competitive novice chase at Perth. Next time out at Newbury Paul Carberry, the owner's newly retained jockey, partnered him to an equally impressive win. The Boss forecast a very bright future for both horse and jockey. Addington Boy is the property of Walter Gott, chairman of a Merseyside food imports business carrying his name. He had shown ability over hurdles and it was no surprise when he scored by a long-looking 15 lengths on his chasing début at Sedgefield.

Addington Boy was beaten next time out but lost little credibility in the defeat. Pitted against the Wetherby specialist Cumbrian Challenge, he tried to make all the running, but a mistake three out sealed his fate. Though staying on well close home, the winner had flown. He got back on the winning trail at Kelso in November and maintained his improvement as the season progressed.

By this stage of the season The Boss was launching his star names on their schedules. Unguided Missile, with Richard Dunwoody up, had no trouble disposing of sole rival Scotton Banks in the final of the Steel Plate and Sections Young Chasers' Series at Cheltenham. The Grey Monk had won his first two novice chases in hugely impressive manner; and One Man had proved that the nightmare of Kempton had left no permanent scars by running away from the likes of Jodami and Cogent on his reappearance at Ayr in the Sean Graham Motherwell Limited Handicap Chase. Tony Dobbin rode the grey with typical confidence, ensuring that he obtained a clear view of his fences and that he had every opportunity to see a good stride. One Man responded with a series of fast, accurate leaps and it was noticeable that this time round Dobbin had no hesitation in sweeping aside Cogent as early as the tenth fence and making the best of his way home. Solo won unchallenged from Jodami.

The Boss was not getting carried away, but he had the look of a satisfied man and confirmed that One Man's next objective would be the Hennessy at Newbury. It was not to be. For starters, Tony Dobbin did his collar bone in at Catterick the following week. He was partnering Stop The Waller for Maurice Barnes when the gelding came down heavily at the seventh. Mark Dwyer was booked to substitute, but the heavens opened on the morning of the Hennessy. The ground was on the heavy side of soft and The Boss was not going to risk One Man in the mud. He was withdrawn on the morning of the race and rerouted to the Tommy Whittle Chase at Haydock in a fortnight's time. With Dobbin still on the sidelines, Mark Dwyer retained the ride. Despite the presence of both Monsieur le Cure and Garrison Savannah among his rivals, the bookies quoted the Greystoke superstar at 1–3 favourite. The odds may have been a trifle mean but the layers were right to take no risks. Mark Dwyer settled the grey close to the leaders, pushed him into the lead at the seventh and gradually asserted his class to go clear in the home straight and beat Monsieur le Cure by 11 lengths. The Boss ground his teeth at the memory of what the John Edwards-trained chaser had done to One Man at Cheltenham the previous March.

Marcus Armytage, reporting for the *Daily Telegraph*, rang Mark Dwyer on the Sunday morning rather than interrogate him in the heat of the moment at Haydock. He reasoned that 'jockeys' thoughts are usually more realistic and reliable after they have slept on them'. He found Dwyer still singing the praises of One Man: 'He's very, very good. It is a long while since I have had a feel like that on a three-mile chaser. He reminds me of my first Gold Cup winner, Forgive 'N' Forget. He travels in his races and then has speed at the end of them. He has loads of gears too. He was foot perfect at his fences and he shortened up at the last ditch when I asked him to.'

High commendation indeed from a top-flight jockey who was having his first taste of riding One Man. Mark did add that everything was in One Man's favour for Haydock but he could not vouch how he would fare on heavy ground. This warning was echoed by The Boss himself, commenting on the grey's immediate target, the King George at Kempton: 'This grey horse has yet to do it. We are still talking about potential rather than proven form. All I can say is that he delighted us at Haydock and he has had a buck and a squeal in his paddock this morning. Unless the ground is heavy, he will go to Kempton on Boxing Day and Tony Dobbin will be on board.' That last half-sentence is interesting. It was an off-the-cuff remark and shows that after the Tommy Whittle GWR genuinely expected his stable jockey to be back in the saddle for Kempton.

A week after Haydock the feature race was the Betterware Cup at Ascot. Gordon had Unguided Missile in the line-up with Richard Dunwoody booked to ride while Tony Dobbin, back in action for the first time since his fall at Catterick, had three booked rides at Haydock. Richard gave Unguided Missile a tremendous ride at Ascot. He survived mistakes at the 12th and another at the fourth from home, but it was the manner in which he plucked Unguided Missile off the ground after his mount had nose-dived through the final fence that caught the attention. Dunwoody gathered Unguided Missile together in a matter of seconds and drove him in pursuit of Rough Quest with such single-minded determination that the partnership regained the lead in the shadow of the post. This was a virtuoso performance which merited and received rave notices in the racing press.

Up north at Haydock, Tony Dobbin had three rides and scored on Greystoke's Spanish Light in the novice chase. He had further mounts at Edinburgh on the following Monday and was also in action at Hexham on the Wednesday. Though the weather was closing in, Dobbin would be riding out at Greystoke in the days running up to Christmas. To all intents and purposes he was match fit. Yet Richard Dunwoody was booked to partner One Man in the King George. John Hales to his credit, shoulders the responsibility for triggering the decision. Speaking on the video *One Man, the Horse of a Lifetime*, he argues that with Dunwoody available and Dobbin only just back from injury, it was both sensible and advisable to invite Richard to take the mount.

The Boss accepted his owner's wishes and even with the advantage of hindsight it is hard to see what else he could have done. Ian Carnaby, though, writing in his (then) weekly column in *Sporting Life*, took the opposing view He considered that Tony Dobbin had 'been treated in the shabbiest way imaginable'. While accepting that connections might have had a case to book Richard Dunwoody for One Man at Kempton, Ian then reminded his readers of the statement which was released on 19 December. 'Both Gordon and I look forward to seeing Dobbin ride our horse in his next race, which is likely to be in February.'

Ian concluded that the whole question of the stable jockey's replacement boiled down to 'loyalty . . . or the absence of it'. It was an opinion shared by plenty of observers, both neutral and committed. Some pointed out that for a trainer with the reputation for being fiercely loyal to his jockeys, Gordon was acting out of character in rubber stamping the Dunwoody substitution. I am not so sure about this.

The Boss was himself caught between the frying pan and the fire. There was no question that Richard Dunwoody was pre-eminent among jumping's big race jockeys. He was also available and willing to take the mount and clearly John Hales, who was paying the bills, had come down in favour of this solution. Gordon's belief in One Man's ability to be a Champion was unshakeable. He couldn't contemplate the thought of the grey being removed from the stable on a matter of principle and at the back of his mind was the well-being of his jockey. Yes, he could insist that a 'fit-again' Tony Dobbin should retain the ride on One Man, but even if the owner accepted this ultimatum, the pressure on Tony would be unrelenting. Were One Man to meet with either defeat or disaster then, right or wrong, the finger of suspicion would be pointed at the comparatively inexperienced Dobbin. It was an unenviable decision to take. However, bitterly disappointing though it was to Tony at the time, he accepted the setback with commendable stoicism and in the long run the whole affair did nothing to damage his career.

Snow and sub-zero temperatures caused Kempton's Boxing Day programme to be abandoned, but thanks to the authorities' new found flexibility the King George was rearranged for Sandown's early January meeting. The Greystoke gallops were frostbound, but The Boss had the grass verges harrowed sufficiently to allow One Man a daily blow out. In his pre-race TV interview The Boss expressed himself a shade anxious about the grey's race fitness; but experience suggested that One Man ran his best races when fresh and this proved the case at Sandown. He was magnificent, jumping for fun and cruising on the bit throughout the contest. Forging clear from the home turn he approached the final fence, ears pricked, with an unassailable advantage. He did show slight signs of tiredness on the run in, but in the circumstances this was understandable. He had after all put up a virtuoso performance and had been out in front since taking a definite lead at the third last.

John Hales had watched the King George in Barbados. The family holiday had been booked to begin shortly after the race's Boxing Day date and not even One Man could alter that. Introduced to the local betting-shop proprietor by John Moreton, the Hales family assembled in the bookie's back room at 10 a.m. Barbados time to watch the race. Originally they were on their own, but as soon as the news got out, they became surrounded by a crush of local One Man fans. John did not have room to get up and pace the length of the passage. Instead he had to sit, head down, and listen to the SIS commentary. He recalls John Moreton saying confidently, 'Oh he's won this, easy!' – and thinking that the race was over, he looked up to discover there was still a mile to go!

The Boss decided to go straight to Cheltenham. Or rather, the weather decided it for him. Even Cumbria was frostbound and on Gold Cup day a penetrating north wind drove intermittent flurries of stinging snow pellets down the slopes of Cleeve Hill and up the home straight.

The Boss was well pleased with the grey's condition. He had been to Newcastle for a racecourse gallop and made several trips to the fells above Ron Barry's house at the northern end of Ullswater. He would be going to Cheltenham a fresh horse. Gordon reckoned he would go close if he got the run of the race. John Hales later admitted that he 'really thought One Man would win'. This view was shared by both punters and layers alike.

One Man went off the 11–8 favourite. Turning out of the back straight for the final time, Richard Dunwoody had him travelling on a tight rein poised to go past Couldn't Be Better and Imperial Call. He wasn't fluent at the third last but his backers were still optimistic when he joined Imperial Call as the pair straightened out to approach the second last. Seconds later – or to be more exact, three strides later – Richard Dunwoody was rowing away faster than a desperate member of a sinking University boat race crew. One Man had gone from potential Gold Cup winner to beaten favourite in a matter of three paces.

In an impromptu press conference with The Boss and John Hales, held alongside an exhausted One Man on the lawn below the paddock, the knot of sympathetic media men probed. The grey's confused yet patient connections did their best to explain away the inexplicable. The owner muttered about the 'Cheltenham factor'. Asked whether lack of stamina could be the answer, The Boss did not refute the suggestion, but he was at a loss to explain the dramatic suddenness of his eclipse. 'Richard said he went from cruising to gasping for air in a matter of strides,' confirmed the bemused trainer. 'We will take him back home, give him time to recover and then get the vets to examine him with a fine-tooth comb.'

That examination revealed nothing. One Man reached Greystoke 'still very tired but physically sound'. The alternatives were 'failure to stay' or 'not right on the day'. The preferred explanation was the latter. John Hales reflected much later, 'We reasoned that if One Man didn't stay the distance then he would have weakened gradually, rather than stop to nothing as though he had hit a brick wall. We concluded that he just had not fired on the day and neither of us were prepared to admit that it was a case of "a hill too far".'

One Man was finished for the season. For The Boss it was a frustrating anticlimax but he had plenty other exciting memories about which to enthuse. In fact he was to spend much of his last two seasons scouring the programme book in the near-impossible task of discovering enough top prizes to be shared out fairly between the quartet of One Man, Addington Boy, Unguided Missile and The Grey Monk. In 1995–96 Gordon managed to keep them apart and their owners happy. This was to prove progressively more difficult as the four grew older together.

Tony Dobbin, jocked off One Man, at least had the compensation of partnering The Grey Monk and Addington Boy whenever he was fit enough to do so. Both these outstanding prospects won six times over fences, with Addington Boy ending the season with a notable treble. He destroyed his rivals in the Pertemps Great Yorkshire Chase at Doncaster, stepped up the pace in the home straight to win the Mumm Mildmay Novices' Chase at Aintree and displayed gritty determination on unfavourably sticky ground to complete his three-timer in the Edinburgh Woollen Mill Future Champion Novices' Chase at Ayr.

Unguided Missile proved equally tough. David Harrison's splendid handicapper ran seven times, won three substantial prizes at Cheltenham, Ascot and Wetherby and was never out of the frame in his other four outings – including a courageous second to well-handicapped Maamur in the Ritz Club National Hunt Chase at the Festival.

The Grey Monk threatened to be the potential jewel in the Greystoke crown. Asked to identify Gordon's most outstanding quality as a trainer, many well-respected judges nominated his uncanny ability to place his top novice chasers to their most profitable advantage. The Grey Monk was unbeaten in all six of his races over fences. Critics carped that he was never given a serious test, but as a confidence-building operation this was a masterly exercise. Bookmakers quoted The Grey Monk at the head of their price lists for the Sun Alliance Chase around the turn of the year, but The Boss had never been keen on this particular race and instead successfully aimed his potential champion at the Edinburgh Woollen Mill Novices' Chase at Carlisle's March meeting. Valuable races at Aintree and Ayr were mentioned but passed over. The benefit of this 'little fish' policy was expected to be revealed in 1996–97.

Off the course The Boss suffered a devastating blow to morale. His marriage to Joanie effectively ended early in 1996. Gordon had celebrated his 65th birthday at the beginning of the 1995–96 season. Yet he showed no sign of slackening the pace. On the contrary, with such high-profile horses as One Man, The Grey Monk, Addington Boy and Unguided Missile all capable of winning major prizes, GWR's work ethic was insatiable. He had lost little, if any, of his competitive muscle since turning 60 and his love for his horses and his enthusiasm for the jumping game burned as fiercely as ever. Given such determination to be actively involved with the daily training, and his insistence on watching his stars in action at the racecourse, it was inevitable that home life would suffer.

Just how much Gordon's inability to slow down, and his near obsession with spending every possible minute of the working day with his beloved horses, contributed to the break-up of his second marriage is a question very hard to assess. One Man's rise to prominence had certainly led to The Boss spending long hours away from the Old Rectory and Joanie had begun to turn to her cousin Neville Howard for company. What is not in doubt, though, is the fact that by January 1996 Joanie's interests lay elsewhere and the relationship had reached the point of no return. She agreed to remain at the Old Rectory until the end of the season. This meant that the 'office' could continue to operate as normal; and gave time for a computer-literate replacement to be found, to assume responsibility for the ever-increasing volume of administration and the specialised problems facing a top trainer's secretary – including the taxing tasks of coping with the persistent demands of the media.

Outwardly the marriage had been an ongoing success. The Boss had been romantically swept off his feet. Joanie was attractive, witty, interested in horses and, as a bonus, fully conversant with secretarial skills. GWR felt he was a lucky man and in his own way he never forgot this throughout his career. But he tended to take people (as opposed to horses) for granted; and as the years passed and he continued to do things 'his own way', he assumed that Joanie was content with her role of holding the fort at home while he devoted all his energies to the practical side of the business.

The trauma of major kidney surgery had brought a temporary halt, but restored to health, Gordon was soon back on the treadmill. He was not for turning and Joanie's cherished wish – that once past 65 he would ease off and agree to train just a dozen horses or so for their close friends – was never to be realised. Thoughts of even partial retirement had never been seriously entertained by The Boss. In May Joanie left the Old Rectory for a break in Anguilla.

There was to be no reconciliation. On her return home Joanie moved back across the village to the Greystoke Castle estate run by Neville Howard. The break-up left The Boss confused and angry. He felt that he had done nothing wrong. He still loved his wife and his appetite for professional success had lost none of its edge. Feeling at a loss, he buried himself even deeper in the welfare and achievements of his horses. However the separation had its compensations – in particular the return of Joey, his daughter, whose love and understanding were to mean so much to him in the dark days ahead.

Joey's arrival coincided with Joanie's last night at the Old Rectory. Fortunately it was the close season and by the time that the horses came back in for the start of the 1996–97 season the secretarial staff had been augmented by the return of Antonia Reid, daughter of Tim and Tarn Riley. Antonia was computer literate and conversant with the responsibilities required of a trainer's secretary. She had worked in that capacity for such familiar names as Peter Calver, Geoff Lewis and Willie Haggas. Furthermore Antonia – together with her sister, Nicola – had worked and ridden out at Greystoke on a regular basis before moving to Newmarket and Antonia was on friendly terms with many of the staff still working for The Boss.

TWENTY-SEVEN

Triumph and Tragedy

The 1996–97 season began with contrasting fortunes for GWR. His marital separation was a *fait accompli*. While Joanie had moved out of the Old Rectory, Robert Ogden was poised to make a welcome return to the strength. The influential Wetherby-based owner had opted to concentrate his interests for the previous season with Ferdy Murphy at Middleham, leaving only a token force at Greystoke. The experiment came to a sudden end in the late autumn and the majority of the Ogden jumpers came back into training with Gordon.

The Boss had also invested in a useful recruit for John Hales in the shape of Solomon's Dancer, who had shown decent winning form for Bill Haigh both on the flat and over hurdles. Gordon persuaded Hales that the gelding would make a successful chaser and his advice paid off when the chasing débutant opened his account with novice chase wins at Carlisle and Newcastle.

General Command was to prove a trailblazer for the Ogden camp. He had shown plenty of promise as a novice chaser the previous season; and proved that he had retained all his old ability by completing a handicap treble in the lead-up to Christmas, winning from the front at Wetherby, Carlisle and Haydock in the style of a top-class handicapper. Meanwhile One Man delighted the Hales family with an authoritative first-time-out success in the Charlie Hall Chase at Wetherby's November meeting. His jumping was faultless and he had quickened away from old rivals Barton Bank and Young Hustler with nonchalant ease between the last two fences. The Boss reckoned that he had needed the run and intimated that he would reappear in the Tommy Whittle Chase at Haydock before heading to Kempton on Boxing Day to defend his King George title.

Haydock was abandoned but One Man duly landed the odds at Kempton. He had taken the measure of the front running Mr Mulligan at the second last and was going clear when the latter fell at the final obstacle. The grey was not exactly running away on the run in and a number of leading racing journalists restated their opinion that One Man did not have the stamina to win a Gold Cup. Their sniping tactics angered The Boss, who hit back aggressively in subsequent interviews on the Racing Channel (to which programme he was becoming a regular contributor). Referring to the King George he snorted, 'Of course he was tired, it was a track record. We had planned to win the race in the home straight but Mr Mulligan was travelling so strongly going into the bottom bend that Richard had to ask him to quicken earlier than he wanted. He had every right to be a bit weary!'

Gordon now aimed to bury the 'One Man hates Cheltenham' theory by sending him to Prestbury Park for the Pillar Property Chase in January. He won, but not in a manner that pleased his persistent critics – doing the bare minimum required to hold Barton Bank on the line. The Boss, looking uncharacteristically drawn and thin around the face, was nevertheless in cracking form when chatting to Channel 4's John Francome after the Pillar, pointing out that One Man had beaten his Cheltenham hoodoo at the fourth time of asking and that he'd done it at a canter.

The crucial question came mid-way through the interview. John Francome asked The Boss whether, if he had to put his money down, he would give One Man a better chance of winning the Gold Cup or the Queen Mother. GWR was quickly into the attack. He replied, 'They wouldn't take him off the bridle in the Queen Mother. He likes a battle and you know, John, when you've got a lovely horse who can jump like him, you can be up there with the best and always gain a length when you need it.' He went on to stress that he would be asking Richard Dunwoody his opinion, and then John Hales, and then he would make a decision.

Back in the autumn, when interviewing The Boss for his 'Stable to Follow' feature in *Sporting Life*, I heard him intimate that One Man might go for the Queen Mother because he was convinced he had the speed to win over the shorter trip. The upshot of Gordon's remarks in his post-Pillar interview was that One Man was sent down to Ascot only 11 days later for the Comet Chase run over a trip of two miles, three furlongs. There had been much 'chewing of the cud' between trainer and owner about Solo's Cheltenham target. John Hales had always been for another shot at the Gold Cup, but he accepted that The Boss was in two minds and the solution had been to put the choice to the test on the racecourse. The Comet was the only available trial.

In the event Ascot proved a rod for everyone's back, not least that of One Man himself. The grey was beaten a length by Strong Promise. His defeat triggered fighting talk from his critics, led by Geoff Lester who wrote in *Sporting Life* that the Comet Chase had detected 'flaws in One Man as plain as rich tea biscuits . . . He is like a boxer who cannot take a punch.' Colourful stuff and Geoff was not alone in voicing this opinion. But was the Comet Chase a fair test? I very much doubt it. The race came too quickly after the Pillar for the grey to reveal his latent talent over two miles. Fair or not, the defeat ensured that his Cheltenham Festival target for 1997 would indeed be the Gold Cup.

The Boss had six weeks to freshen up One Man for Cheltenham. He personally directed the progress, frequently using the grey as his hack, and on at least a couple of occasions boxing him up to give him a change of scenery on the fells above Ullswater. Nicky confirms that as the Cheltenham Festival approached, all concerned with One Man were upbeat, reckoning that he was even better prepared for the supreme test than he had been in 1996. As a final pipe-opener The Boss took advantage of a kind invitation extended by the

Carlisle executive to work One Man on their course, only a few days before Cheltenham. This became a very public workout with John Francome present on behalf of Channel 4, Gordon Brown wielding the microphone for the Racing Channel and numerous members of the written press all armed with notebooks and lap-top computers. One Man did not turn a hair but his performance was competent, rather than spectacular. The warm-up might not have enthused the watching media, but Richard Dunwoody was more than satisfied and The Boss fielded all questions with the patience and good humour which had been a consistent factor in his dealings with the press ever since One Man had begun to hit the headlines.

While One Man's Cheltenham preparation had been conducted in the full glare of nationwide publicity, a smaller but by no means less committed band of Greystoke supporters believed that The Boss would saddle the winner of the 1997 Gold Cup all right – but with Addington Boy rather than One Man. Walter Gott's admirable chaser had been specifically aimed at the Blue Riband since the start of the season and indeed all three of his previous outings had been at Cheltenham over two and a half miles, a distance arguably short of his best. Addington Boy had been third in the Murphy's Gold Cup, in which he lost momentum by slipping on the home turn. He had won the Tripleprint Gold Cup in December and had experienced the misfortune to come up against the Cheltenham specialist Dublin Flyer on one of his invincible days in the Ladbroke Trophy at the January meeting. The likelihood of fast ground for Cheltenham would also improve the chances of Addington Boy, who was well backed at odds as low as 8–1. Tony Dobbin had established a close rapport with Greystoke's second string. However all hopes were dashed on the Sunday before Cheltenham, when he was relaxing in his paddock and received a vicious kick from a jealous colleague, an injury which took much longer than anticipated to heal.

One Man gave a faultless display of jumping in the 1997 Gold Cup. Taking the third from home, he was running away and turning for home, travelling with such confidence that even The Boss began to believe that he was going to win. Between the last two fences he closed to within three lengths of Mr Mulligan, seemingly going every bit as well as the leader. He had lasted about half a furlong further than in 1996. But not a yard more.

One Man was an exhausted and beaten horse even before he scrambled over the last fence and staggered up the final hill to pass the post a distant sixth. There would be no more Gold Cup attempts for One Man and no more Cheltenham Festivals for The Boss. In addition to the trauma of One Man, he had earlier been visibly shaken by the demise of General Command in the Astec Buzz National Hunt Chase. His unchallenged victory in the Pertemps Great Yorkshire Chase at Doncaster had raised hopes that he would provide Robert Ogden with a much deserved Cheltenham success. Come the day and The Boss had been in two minds to withdraw him because of the drying ground. Perhaps against his better judgement he allowed General Command to take his place in the line-up with Jamie Osborne in the saddle. The partnership was bowling along in front from as early as the fifth fence, a lead that was maintained until after three out, at which stage General Command broke down on the firm ground, leaving him to struggle home on courage alone. General Command limped up the hill to finish third to Flyers Nap. It was a Festival victory gone begging.

While GWR had always found only limited success at the Cheltenham Festival, Aintree had treated him kindly over the years and The Martell Cup acted as a tempting potential consolation prize for One Man. It was not to be. A burst blood vessel caused him to be pulled up and a campaign that had begun with such high hopes had ended in disarray. Overall, though, the season had been encouraging. The Boss finished third in the national trainers' list with 69 winners. He also had the satisfaction of seeing Robert Ogden top the owners' table with 17 winners, earning nearly £265,000 in winning prize money. General Command was his major money-spinner and there were invaluable contributions from the likes of Colonel In Chief, Edelweis du Moulin, Disco des Mottes and Frickley.

The Grey Monk was unlucky with the weather. The son of Roselier is twice the horse on a soft surface, but his competitive streak is such that he will give of his best whatever the state of the ground – too often to the detriment of his physical well-being. Alistair Duff's outstanding chaser opened his season with an exciting win at Ayr's November meeting, where he took full advantage of a light weight to outjump and outstay both Morceli and Jodami in the Sean Graham Chase. The Hennessy Gold Cup at Newbury appeared his for the taking and on the run to four out, the first in the home straight, The Grey Monk was running over the field. His jumping had been impeccable and he looked an assured winner until joined by Coome Hill on the run to the final fence. Tony Dobbin's mount went down fighting but could not regain the advantage, ultimately being beaten two lengths.

The Grey Monk was off the course until mid-February, when he crossed to Ireland to contest the Irish Hennessy at Leopardstown. Nothing was travelling better than the Greystoke challenger until he was 'half-lengthed' by Danoli six fences out and failed to get his landing gear down in time. Safety-first critics would not commit themselves such a long way out, but watching on the monitor, I formed the definite impression that The Grey Monk would have played a leading part in the finish if he had stood up. He showed no ill effects next time out in the Black Death Vodka Chase at Haydock, defying topweight of 12 stone to hand out a decisive beating to three useful handicappers in Terao, Major Bell and Uncle Ernie (all of whom went on to run with distinction at Cheltenham).

The Grey Monk was not risked in the Gold Cup because of the fast going. But he was rather surprisingly declared to run in the Irish Grand National at Fairyhouse, a race in which he was set to carry 12 stone on ground much firmer than reports had indicated. Alistair Duff was at Leopardstown, as was

Ted Stanners, the stable's travelling head lad. After much heart searching The Grey Monk stood his ground. Though never able to land a blow, the topweight ran on gamely from the home turn to finish third. He had a much harder race than intended.

No owner could want for a more consistent trier than Unguided Missile. Once again he did David Harrison proud, winning the Edward Hanmer at Haydock in November; the Perrier Jouet Handicap at Aintree; and the Sun Life of Canada Chase at Perth in April. In between times Unguided Missile chased home the lightly weighted Go Ballistic in the Betterware Cup at Ascot; was pipped by Jodami in the Peter Marsh at Haydock; and finished an honourable second to Coome Hill in the Jim Ford Chase at Wincanton. Unguided Missile earned his place in the line-up for the Gold Cup but fell at the first fence on the second circuit when still going strongly in mid-field. The tactics employed at Cheltenham were unusual. Unguided Missile liked to dominate and, held up in the Gold Cup, he seemed to be unsighted when coming down.

The Boss had been stunned by the break-up of his marriage to Joanie. The process of reaching an equable separation settlement was dragging on and to aggravate matters his daughter Joey was seriously injured in a car accident in September. In addition to superficial cuts and bruises she damaged her ribs, punctured a lung, sustained a multiple fracture of her left femur and dislocated her right ankle. Some six months were to pass before she was able to walk without the help of, first, crutches and then a stick.

Joey spent nearly a month in hospital and on her return home she found her father to be in good spirits. She reflects: 'He had always been a workaholic, and though he seemed to get tired more quickly than he used to do, I put this down to the greater pressures he was facing at the time. Ever since his kidney surgery he had been going into hospital for six-monthly tests and there was nothing in the results during 1996 to suggest that he was anything but a very fit man for his age.'

Around the turn of the year Border Television asked The Boss whether he would co-operate in the filming of a half-hour documentary on his life. The idea intrigued him and he entered into the spirit of the programme with enthusiastic gusto, cutting quite a dash with Helen Hutchinson, the programme's producer. The completed documentary was networked in the early summer and received favourable reviews.

On the course The Boss was always much in evidence whether grabbing the headlines at the major meetings or chasing smaller fry at Hexham or Perth. The competition between Robert Ogden and Peter Deal for the honour of being the season's top owner went right down to the wire and Gordon reversed his customary policy of roughing off the majority of his horses by mid-April to ensure that the Ogden ammunition was not exhausted before the title was attained. The trainer's keenness to win the bout could be reflected by the winning appearance of a high-profile horse like Edelweis du Moulin at Uttoxeter on 29 May!

Shortly before that victory The Boss had been in sparkling form at the end-of-season bash, held in a roomy marquee on the Old Rectory tennis court. Also in rude health at this party was Brian Harding, Greystoke's talented number-two jockey, who was subject at the time to a 12-month lay-off resulting from injuries received in a fall from Len Lungo's Show of Hands at Newcastle the previous December. Brian had sustained neck injuries, plus a suspected hairline fracture to the skull, and had been concussed for sufficient time after the accident to warrant the prescribed 21 days on the sidelines. What was not relayed to the press, or indeed to The Boss in his capacity as Harding's employer, was the observation by one of the Newcastle racecourse doctors that Brian had exhibited the symptoms of a minor 'fit spasm' during the immediate aftermath of his fall. Under Jockey Club Medical Rules riders proved to have revealed such symptoms are automatically stood down for a period of a year. Brian Harding, though, had been unaware that he was being examined for such a condition. He anticipated that he would be passed fit to ride as soon as he had served his three-week concussion period and doctors were satisfied that his other injuries had responded to treatment. He was told that a brain scan would be required, but had imagined that this was simply a routine test to check that the suspected hairline fracture of the skull had healed over. Imagine his state of confused distress when he was told for the first time that the scan had supported the report of the racecourse doctor and that his jockey's licence would be suspended for the period of a year dating from the time of his fall . . .

The Boss had been incensed at the apparent unnecessary length of the medical ban, and even more by the lack of previous communication between the Jockey Club's medical department and his young rider. He went on TV at Doncaster to make an impassioned appeal for common sense to be applied in this case, labelling the treatment handed out to Harding as scandalous and calling on Dr Michael Turner, the Club's medical consultant, to reverse the decision. His appeal fell upon deaf ears, although Dr Turner did personally get in touch with Brian Harding to explain the reasoning behind the 12-month ruling. Gordon played his part, too, by providing Brian with the opportunity to work in the yard and later to school many of his top jumpers. When the ban was lifted in December 1997, he also saw to it that Brian received plenty of decent rides so that his confidence was quickly restored with a succession of winners.

In June 1997 The Boss and Joey went on holiday to Portugal. Joey recalls, 'Norman Mason invited us to make use of his villa and we had a great time. The weather was perfect and the rest did Father the power of good. Back at home, apart from his annual bout of hay fever, he had no health problems and busied himself going to the sales and working here on the farm.' Gordon enjoyed himself at the summer sales, buying a large batch of unraced, well-bred stores. He realised that his star chasers were all growing old together and he was keen to introduce new blood in time for the transition period – an excellent idea in theory, but difficult to put into practice when the majority of his new arrivals went down with a viral infection before they had set foot on the racecourse.

One Man made his customary reappearance in the Charlie Hall at Wetherby in early November. He beat Barton Bank for the fifth time, but not without a struggle from the final fence. The Gold Cup had been removed from his agenda, with a third King George now his chief target – to be followed by a possible attempt at the Queen Mother Champion Chase. The Boss had already won the Peterborough Chase with Clever Folly. He now selected Huntingdon's Grade Two Chase as a dual-purpose trial for One Man. The race came at a suitable time for a King George warm-up and with both Martha's Son and Viking Flagship in the line-up, the Peterborough would also give The Boss a significant clue to assessing his Queen Mother chances. One Man duly obliged by a wide margin from Viking Flagship, but because Martha's Son pulled up lame after jumping the fourth fence the race was hardly satisfactory as a true Cheltenham trial. The Boss was pleased, nevertheless: 'We always thought he was pretty quick and he proved it today,' he commented.

Heavy rain, falling from before dawn until shortly before the race, ruined One Man's chances of a third King George. The grey was hating the ground and never jumped with his usual fluency. He was lying handy in fourth place when a blunder at the 15th stopped him in his tracks. Dunwoody had to call upon all his reserves of stamina to regain the lost ground. Although he rallied to hold every chance three out he weakened quickly between the last two fences and dropped out well beaten. The defeat confirmed Gordon's gut feeling that in top class company One Man did not stay the trip.

John Hales invited Gordon to join the family on their winter holiday to Barbados. It was a most generous gesture and one for which Joey was very grateful. She explains: 'I had been worried about Father's health for a while. He had been prescribed a steroid-based mixture to improve his breathing; and though it did help in that respect, the steroids tended to make him hyper-active and cause him to get tired. I hoped that the holiday would act as a rest-cure in every way.'

The subject of One Man's immediate future was a major talking point out in Barbados and the eventual decision to go for the Queen Mother was hastened by advice from Jack Berry, who was also enjoying his brief winter break in Barbados. Jack had no doubts that One Man would be fast enough for the race and his views were echoed by The Boss. It was agreed that One Man's next race would be the Comet Chase at Ascot in February. But before One Man reached Ascot Richard Dunwoody, his regular partner, announced that he would not be available to ride One Man in the Queen Mother as he was committed to partner Klairon Davis.

This decision was good news for Tony Dobbin, whose patience over the matter of Dunwoody's booking to ride One Man had been remarkable. The Boss told John Hales that as Richard would not be able to ride One Man at

Cheltenham, there was no point in him partnering the horse in the Comet and Sony Chase. The owner agreed and Tony Dobbin was back on board One Man for the first time since winning the Sean Graham Chase at Ayr back in November 1995. He gave the grey a lovely ride and for me the telling point about the way One Man performed at Ascot was the reaction he showed once Strong Promise began to hustle him four out. Tony asked him to lengthen and he put his head down, battled back with determination and had seen off his challenger before getting to the second last. I (poor, biased fool!) was still in the minority who now believed that One Man would win the Queen Mother Champion Chase. Even The Boss had eleventh-hour doubts; strange, really, as he had been quietly campaigning for the grey to contest the race for some 18 months. He was quoted as saying, 'Two miles will not be ideal. I would like to run him over two and a half, but Mr Hales wants him to go to Cheltenham and the Queen Mother is the only race for him.'

I reckon that he was just putting people away because whenever we spoke about the Champion Chase that old fighting spirit resurfaced. He clearly relished both the challenge and the opportunity to prove that his instincts had not let him down.

By March 1998, however, The Boss was gravely ill. Rumours about his condition had been sweeping the North for several months and informed reports were less than encouraging. On the now rare appearances before the cameras he was outwardly chirpy, but he had visibly lost a great deal of weight, and since the turn of the year Nicky had been representing the Greystoke stable on the course with increasing frequency.

The gossip was close to the truth. Joey reflects: 'We had noticed that Father didn't have the energy to keep going through the day as he had done in the past. His breathing wasn't too good either, but he had always suffered from asthma trouble and we put it down to a combination of growing older and his extra workload. It was only when he came back from his holiday in Barbados and still complained of feeling tired and "tight around the chest" that we realised he must go to the doctor for a thorough check.'

Joey smiles as she describes the preparations for this visit to the surgery. 'I didn't think that I should go with him,' she recalls. 'But I knew that he wouldn't make any fuss and that he would do his best to play down his symptoms, so I sent him with a list and told him to hand it over to the doctor when he went in! I was inclined to think that he might have developed diabetes, but that theory was quickly disproved and the results of the blood test taken at the surgery and the doctor's other findings indicated that things were a lot worse.'

The Boss received an immediate call to attend the Cumberland Infirmary in Carlisle for an appointment with Dr Dyson, one of the hospital's senior cancer consultants. This time Joey went with him and the consultant did not mince his words. Joey continues, 'Dr Dyson was quite blunt. He told Father that he was suffering from cancer of the lung and that he must undergo a concentrated course of radiotherapy in the hope of reducing the tumour and gaining at least partial remission. While Father was out of the room, Dr Dyson estimated that he had another 18 months to live at the outside. It was shattering news and I doubted if Father would be able to handle it. So I asked the doctor not to say anything more to him, other than that he must undergo treatment at once "for a growth on the lung". I don't think that Father really understood the seriousness of the situation until much nearer the end.'

The Boss received the prescribed doses of radiotherapy at the Cumberland Infirmary during the next two months. He was incapacitated for a couple of days after each visit to the hospital, but otherwise continued his daily routine as normally as possible: making the entries, dealing with the owners and, above all, supervising morning work and ensuring that One Man was fully tuned up for Cheltenham. Nicky was in charge out on the gallops and Brian Harding also played his part in the pre-race build-up.

Cheltenham coincided with GWR's final radiotherapy session. He would be watching the Festival on the TV in his study. Tony Dobbin was planning to stay down at Cheltenham, but cruelly he too found himself watching the Queen Mother in front of the box in Cumbria. Tony had secured an attractive outside ride in The Arkle on Direct Route. Howard Johnson's exciting two-miler was much fancied to finish in the shake up and was well placed until taking a nasty fall at the seventh. The horse was unharmed but Tony had the wretched luck to fracture his thumb. He was away from the course having X-rays, while Paul Carberry substituted on Unguided Missile in the William Hill National Hunt Chase, a race in which he had finished runner-up to Maamur the previous spring.

Unguided Missile had not been anywhere near his best in the run-up to Cheltenham. Like many of his stable companions, he had been troubled by a virus and he had also been experiencing signs of a foot problem. Only the evidence of his past strike rate at Cheltenham prevented him from starting at a much longer price than 10–1 and loyal supporters of this brave chaser were delighted – if slightly surprised – when, responding to Carberry's gentle but confident persuasion, he cast aside a couple of early misjudgements to go clear between the last two fences and gallop relentlessly up the final climb to beat Glitter Isle by seven lengths.

The victory compensated for the disappointment afforded by the enigmatic Edelweis du Moulin in the Guinness Arkle Trophy. Robert Ogden's magnificent-looking horse had compiled an unbeaten sequence of four wins over fences without so much as turning a hair. His career over hurdles had, however, been scarred by failure to produce his best form in the heat of battle. The critics who pointed out that Edelweis du Moulin had reached The Arkle without yet coming under pressure over fences were to be proved correct. Nothing was travelling better on the home turn, but once the more resolute and competitive contenders arrived to throw down the gauntlet approaching the last Edelweis du Moulin shirked the issue. He refused to quicken and passed the post a comfortable fourth!

By the end of play on Tuesday Tony Dobbin's fate had been settled. He would not be riding again at the 1998 Festival. His absence required a replacement jockey for One Man's appearance in the Queen Mother Champion Chase. If The Boss could have been called in question for deserting Tony Dobbin at the time of One Man's first King George, his loyalty at this difficult chapter of his life was beyond reproach. He overcame any temptation to book the services of Paul Carberry and immediately phoned Brian Harding to take the ride. Brian had been in action at Sedgefield on the Tuesday; but he had done plenty of schooling on One Man at home and The Boss was adamant that he should have the chance to prove himself on the world stage.

It was the right choice. Brian and One Man performed with the easy fluency of Michael Schumacher and his Ferrari. They fitted hand and glove from the moment that the tapes rose. The plan had always been for One Man to lie up close to the leaders, utilising his slick jumping and putting his pacier rivals under early pressure to counter their reserves of latent acceleration. If the racing media had their doubts about One Man's abilty to burn off National Hunt's premier two-mile chasers, the public retained greater faith in the charismatic grey. The price of 7–2 was skinny, but it looked mighty generous as Brian Harding and One Man put distance between them and their hard-driven pursuers on the turn in. For a hesitant moment the massed gallery in the stands held their breath. Twice before, the unforgiving hill had snuffed out the fire in the grey's flaming nostrils within the space of five short strides. The memory evaporated within an instant. As One Man grabbed hold of the bit, flew the last and thrust towards the line, a crescendo of unfettered acclamation was uncorked. In the winner's circle a jubilant John Hales was incandescent with joy and admiration for his beloved Solo. At home in Skelton even poor Tony Dobbin 'could scarce forbear to cheer'. Meanwhile the scenes of exhilarated disbelief in the Richards' study at Greystoke, though perhaps less hectic than those in the winner's circle at Cheltenham, shared the same intoxicating mixture of rapturous, tear-filled emotion.

The victory acted as a tremendous morale booster to The Boss and helped compensate for the disappointment of Edelweis du Moulin, and the misfortune of Addington Boy who was badly hampered and pulled up six out in the Gold Cup while still in touch with the leading group. Addington Boy had taken time to recover from that gratuitous kicking in his paddock before the 1997 Gold Cup.

In the meantime The Grey Monk was fast gaining the reputation for being among the unluckiest of the top staying chasers in training – not that such a label will be of any comfort to those punters who allegedly took part in a massive ante-post Gold Cup gamble on the Greystoke chaser as a result of a strong recommendation from one of the popular telephone tipping lines. The Grey Monk's odds were cut from 20–1 down to 7s in a quarter of an hour's hectic betting, after which the bookies were said to have liabilities of at least £1 million on the Richards-trained grey. Peter Niven punched out The Grey

Monk to a comfortable win over Rough Quest in the Tommy Whittle Chase at Haydock before the gelding succumbed to the virus which went the rounds of the stable throughout the season. Post-racing gallops at Kelso and then Carlisle were inconclusive but The Boss was not satisfied that his condition was forward enough to warrant a run in the Gold Cup. The Grey Monk did reappear to finish a creditable third in the Martell Cup at Aintree and ended the season with a laboured success in the Grade Two chase sponsored by Faucets at Cheltenham's April meeting, an effort which led Gordon to remark: 'If he can win round Cheltenham when he is only half fit, he must be some horse!'

His radiotherapy treatment finished, The Boss enjoyed a brief period of remission. Nicky drove him to Aintree to watch One Man compete in the Mumm Melling Chase. He was touched to be clapped by racegoers lining the paddock rails.

Brian Harding retained the ride after his Cheltenham triumph and One Man went keenly to the post. Watching the race on the television monitor in the Sedgefield press room, I formed the impression that he was more on his toes than he had been at Cheltenham, but his jumping improved as the race developed. Harding had him travelling strongly in the lead as the partnership straightened up to the ninth, the first in the back straight; but only yards from the obstacle he veered slightly right, failed to get enough height and ploughed right through the fence, falling heavily. Brian was unharmed but One Man broke his right tibia. The fracture was described by the very experienced Jockey Club vet as 'unmendable'.

There are times when disaster is so gross that one has to be thankful that distance divorces one from the extreme agony of practical reality. That was the situation in which I found myself that grey April afternoon. Those of us covering the comparatively mundane events at Sedgefield said a silent prayer and got on with the job. At Aintree The Boss, on his first day back at the course, had no such escape. The enormity of the occasion was not lost on him. It was Noddy's Ryde revisited. He knew that the vets had no alternative save to put One Man out of his agony, but the logistics of the whole sorry affair were fraught with problems – not least the whereabouts of John Hales. The owner had followed his usual custom of listening to the race commentary hidden from view and separate from his trainer.

One Man was brought home to Shropshire and laid to rest on the lawn below the box he had occupied at the Hales family stud where he had spent his summer holidays. His owner was inconsolable and it was several days before he could steel himself to contact Greystoke. One Man's death was a body blow to The Boss. As a battle-hardened professional, he had seen it all before, but 'the grey horse' had been special and the horrendous nature of his passing could not have come at a worse time.

Distressing though the experience had been, The Boss was still able to dispense comfort to a devastated Brian Harding. The jockey had returned from Aintree, still in a state of shock. He recalls, 'I knew that I must go and see The Boss but was not sure what sort of reception I would get. I needn't have worried. He could not have been more supportive, stressing that I had nothing to blame myself for and that he would just have to go out and find another one good enough to take his place. I could see he was very upset, but he was determined to put my mind at rest and I shall always remember his understanding at what was a dreadful time for all of us.'

Ayr's Scottish National meeting produced mixed results. Colonel In Chief brought off a handsome success for Robert Ogden in the Hill House Quarry Handicap Chase. The progressive Paperising profited from the fall of Careysville to land the Scotsman Novices' Handicap Chase; but most important of the three, Edelweis du Moulin, could only finish second in the Edinburgh Woollen Mill Future Champions' Chase. He was beaten by Eirespray from the stable of Sue and Harvey Smith and would have been third if Bengers Moor had not come down at the last. Edelweis du Moulin finished sore and he was to be on the sidelines for a long while before appearing in public again.

Relations between The Boss and Robert Ogden had not always been smooth, but the pair had a healthy respect for each other. To put matters in perspective GWR had succeeded where no one else has yet managed even to approach. He had saddled sufficient winners to ensure that Robert Ogden ended the 1996–97 season as leading owner. Virus troubles had prevented him from repeating the effort in 1997–98 but Gordon had still managed to send out a number of good winners in the familiar pink-and-mauve checks. The 1998–99 season got underway without an Ogden-owned horse in training at Greystoke. The Boss, no doubt in company with the owner's other trainers, had received a letter outlining certain criteria which should be followed. It included the request that Mr Ogden's racing manager be informed when any of the owner's horses were due to be schooled. As one can imagine, this message was not well received. The Boss was renowned for his slogan 'I'll do it my way' and nothing was going to change that principle, even if it meant sacrificing one of the most influential owners in the yard.

The Boss approached the summer of 1998 in a positive frame of mind. He felt less tired and was looking forward to taking a short holiday in Cyprus with Joey before making plans for the autumn. Joey confirms that he was excellent company during his break in the Mediterranean sun. In fact he felt so refreshed that on the morning after his return to the Old Rectory, he was up at the crack of dawn and came back in for breakfast with a guilty smile on his face. 'I knew at once what he had been doing,' she added. 'Against all orders he had been riding out.'

Joey was quite correct. The Boss had been unable to resist the challenge to get the leg up on his old friend Better Times Ahead and supervise morning exercise. It was to be the very last time that he led the string through the village of Greystoke into the grounds of the castle and up the famous hill where all the heroes of the past 30 years had been put through their paces. And what more appropriate horse than Better Times Ahead to perform the privilege! Now a veteran of 12 years old, he had been Gordon's last winner of the 1997–98 season, holding off the youthful Karestino to score by a neck at his favourite Cartmel. In August he was to open his autumn campaign with yet another hard fought success at the Lakeland course.

A month later, with Ron Barry in the saddle, it was Better Times Ahead who led The Boss to his final resting place on that simple grassy mound from where his spirit will for ever guide the fortunes of the string he inspired with such love and dedication for so long. Then, as if determined to provide his own personal salute, it was Better Times Ahead who supplied Nicky Richards with his first-ever winner by leading from the front to record a memorable victory at Carlisle, the course where The Boss shared so many triumphs with his closest friends.

Time had been running out for The Boss. Those few precious months that the radiotherapy had won back for him were ebbing away. The lungs which had once been filled with the bracing breezes of the Cumbrian fells were slowly, but steadily, being corroded with fluid. The Infirmary visits to clear the tubes became more frequent, but to Gordon the horses still demanded pride of place. No longer able to ride with them, he drove alongside them, checking and cajoling before struggling with painful deliberation to open the gate at the bottom of the gallops and stand proudly by, as the line of hand-picked talent jostled for attention and snorted with impatience while filing head-to-tail down the lane into the rising sun.

Nicky Richards had been in practical charge of training the horses since mid-summer. He explains: 'Father knew then that he was dying and he tried his hardest to pass on his secrets before he went. We talked more closely in those last few weeks than we had ever done in the past. He was still filling me in with little hints and suggestions only days before he died.'

At Cartmel, on August Bank Holiday, Tartan Tradewinds won over hurdles for the first time since 1993. He will go down in history as the last winner ever to have been trained by Gordon W. Richards. It was fitting that the final score should be achieved by a 12-year-old, carrying the beige jacket and orange cap of David Stevenson's Ashleybank Investments. The winner was beginning his seventh consecutive season at Greystoke and the owner had been a loyal supporter for much longer.

The Boss was 68 on 7 September 1998. The family descended on the Old Rectory to celebrate the occasion and Gordon bravely joined in the fun. The next morning he was scouring the programme book to find suitable races for the small knot of early-season performers ready to run. The opportunities were hard to find and the ground was firming up. Down at the farm the boxes were once again full. Serious work about to begin, Gordon sat on a convenient bale of straw and watched. Local owners like Alistair Duff and Tarn Riley called to discuss prospects. Ron Barry stung The Boss to momentary action by jokingly suggesting that he was taking it easy in the sun!

The Boss enjoyed the crack but hadn't a great deal of energy for much further banter. Later in the month Tony Dobbin and Brian Harding visited him in the Cumberland Infirmary where he was receiving emergency treatment. They found him very weak but desperate to hear how the horses had been working. Back home on the Sunday John Hales telephoned. Before he could explain that he was ringing to find out how his trainer was feeling, Gordon had launched into a detailed report on the condition of his horses. That evening he was fighting for breath and becoming increasingly confused. The Boss returned to hospital. Under heavy sedation he quietly slipped away. He died peacefully on 29 September.

The Boss was not given to moralising about life in general or training in particular, but during Border Television's filmed documentary of his life he allowed himself a few moments of reflection. Describing his work as a trainer, he summarised his outlook: 'It's a lovely life training horses, but it needs lots and lots of work. It's been a struggle. I've had my coat off all my life. I've got stuck in as much as three or four men would, but then I've been doing it for myself!'

On the subject of getting the best out of his staff he continued, 'They all call me Boss! I call them by their first names. I like them and I work with them. As in any business we have our ups and downs and our little tiffs. I have to pull them up if they start getting a bit strong or stroppy or they're not doing things right. We do have our differences, but not that often, because if we did then I'd have to get rid of them. I have a happy staff and I like them to be happy with me!'

The Boss had a similar attitude towards his jockeys: 'I have to stand up for my boys. If anything goes wrong then I have to carry the can, so I expect them to do as they're told. If they abuse one of my horses I am the first to get very, very cross. The boys have lots of respect for me. I think that they know that I am usually right!'

Finally on the art of training, at which he excelled, The Boss had several words of advice and self-belief. 'Training horses is a tough, competitive sport. You've got to be up to it. You've got to be fit, super-fit, or you won't survive. You've got to be modern in your outlook as well. I try to keep up with all the modern trends, but then if gold blocks would make them go faster I would feed them with gold blocks. I shouldn't really say it, but I do have an h'eye for an 'orse and I have an eye for a bullock and a sheep in the same way. We know one another. I can talk to them and they can answer me back. We understand one another.

'If I ever do have to give up training, which I've no intention of doing at the moment, I'd have to have horses around me. I like farming too. I like cattle and sheep, everything that goes on in the country life. I love it all.'

The Boss was one of the finest jumping trainers of the late twentieth century. He was also a countryman at heart. On reflection I am pretty sure he had the best of both worlds!

Statistics

FULL NAME	Gordon Richards
BORN	Bath, 7 September 1930
DIED	Carlisle, 29 September 1998
FATHER	Thomas Richards (master haulier-turned-trainer)
APPRENTICED	Jack Waugh, Didcot; Ivor Anthony, Wroughton
RIDING CAREER	1944–59, runner-up in 1957 Scottish Grand National on Merry Windsor
STABLES	1964–67, Town Farm, Beadnell, Northumberland; 1967–93, Castle Stables, Greystoke, Cumbria; 1993–98, The Rectory Stables, Greystoke, Cumbria
FIRST WIN AS A TRAINER	Playlord (Jumbo Wilkinson) over hurdles at Bogside, 10 April 1965
FIRST BIG WIN	Playlord (1969 Great Yorks Chase)
GRAND NATIONAL WINNERS	Lucius (1978), Hallo Dandy (1984)
FIRST CHELTENHAM FESTIVAL WIN	Current Gold (1981 National Hunt Handicap Chase)
OTHER CHELTENHAM FESTIVAL WINNERS	Lord Greystoke (1981 Cathcart Chase), Tartan Tailor (1987 Supreme Novices' Hurdle), One Man (1998 Queen Mother Champion Chase), Unguided Missile (1998 William Hill National Hunt Handicap Chase)
OTHER BIG WINNERS	Playlord (1969 Great Yorks Chase, Scottish Grand National), Titus Oates (1969 Massey-Ferguson Gold Cup, King George VI Chase; 1971 Whitbread Gold Cup), Sea Pigeon (1975 Cheltenham Trial Hurdle), Man Alive (1979 Mackeson Gold Cup), Noddy's Ryde (1984 Future Champions' Chase), Clever Folly (1989 A.F. Budge Gold Cup), Four Trix (1990 Scottish National), One Man (1994 Hennessy Cognac Gold Cup; 1996 King George VI Chase [Jan], King George VI Chase [Dec]; 1998 Comet and Sony Chase), Addington Boy (1996 Tripleprint Gold Cup), General Command (1997 Great Yorks Chase)
LEADING TRAINER	1975–76 (105 races won)
MOST WINS IN A SEASON	1990–91 (118)
WINNERS OVER JUMPS (TOTAL TALLY)	1,911
FIVE WINS ON ONE CARD	Carlisle, 1 October 1979
BIGGEST FLAT WINS	Le Coq d'Or (1972 Ayrshire Handicap), Rundontwalk (1976 Tote Sprint Trophy, Ascot)
MAIN JOCKEYS	Ron Barry (1967–75), Jonjo O'Neill (1975–77), David Goulding (1977–78), Ron Barry (1978–81), Neale Doughty (1982–86), Phil Tuck (1986–88), Neale Doughty (1989–94), Tony Dobbin (1994–98)